From Romance to Reality

From Romance to Reality

Edited

by

Peggy O'Hara

Published by
HIGHWAY BOOK SHOP
Cobalt, Ontario P0J 1C0

Canadian Cataloguing in Publication Data

Main entry under title:
From romance to reality

ISBN 0-88954-285-6

1. Wives—Canada. 2. World War, 1939-1945—Women.
3. World War, 1939-1945—Personal narratives, English.
4. World War, 1939-1945—Great Britain—Social
aspects. 5. Women—Great Britain—Social conditions.
6. Canada—Emmigration and immigration. I. O'Hara,
Peggy, 1922-

HQ759.F76   306.8'7'0971   C83-098155-1

Contents

Preface

During two world wars, thousands of Canadian servicemen married British and European girls. Although the majority came from the British Isles, they all became known as "war brides," a name detested by many and hardly appropriate for those who arrived in Canada with one or more children. Nevertheless, they were unique.

My home was Sutton Surrey, England. It was here on a visit several years ago that the idea to write this book began to take shape. So much had changed in this town, yet traces of the past remained. Three-storied houses that had once been home to hundreds of Canadian soldiers during the Second World War, now stood silent and empty, their chimneys broken and the bricks strewn amongst the rubble that once were beautiful gardens.

As I looked at them, the echo of soldiers' voices seemed to come through the dirty, broken windows. My memory was cast back to the time when thousands of Canadian men, many of them boys, were on their way to help our homeland and among them the Royal Montreal Regiment who, a few months after landing, settled down in these houses for almost sixteen months.

I thought of all the young girls like myself who were destined to marry a Canadian serviceman, and wondered if they, like me, ever thought at that time they would one day sail to Canada as a war bride.

I suddenly, very desperately, wanted to find the answers to this and many more questions. What were their feelings about the war? How did they meet their husbands? Did they like Canada? What kind of difficulties did they have adjusting to an entirely new culture and environment? What were their first impressions of their new home?

The war brides were more than ready to relate their experiences—experiences that brought laughter to my lips and tears to my eyes. Hardships were endured by many but the majority were determined to "stick it out." With a stiff upper lip, lots of courage mingled with a good sense of humour—that almost failed at times—they came through the difficult times and apprehensions with flying colours.

To the women who took the time and patience to write their stories, who dug deeply into nooks and crannies for old and precious photographs—to all other contributors who helped make this book possible, my deepest and sincerest thanks.

Peggy O'Hara

From Romance to Reality

And where we love is home,
Home that our feet may leave, but not
  our hearts,
The chain may lengthen, but it never parts.

Oliver Wendell Holmes 1809-1891

Sunday, September 3, 1939
A Day to Remember

The British people knew that war with Germany was inevitable. Nevertheless, when it came it still presented a shock. The older generation had already endured one world war and were apprehensive and uneasy at the consequences of a second. Every man, woman and child were to be affected in one way or another.

To the young it represented a stimulating adventure; a challenge to do something entirely different; perhaps join the armed services; work in an ammunition factory or patrol the streets for the Air Raid Precaution. No matter what the change, they were headed for paths unknown. And one of these paths led to Canada for more than 45,000 British and European girls. The exigencies of war changed all their lives, and for them, the future war brides, it started the Sunday when Prime Minister Neville Chamberlain announced solemnly over the radio . . . "a state of war exists . . . ."

I was in church that Sunday morning when the air-raid siren sounded. I could not wait to get out of there, but nobody moved. Instead, we all knelt and started praying. Finally, I was out and running home as if Hitler himself were in pursuit.

When I rushed into the house, mum was standing by the diningroom fireplace wringing her hands and saying to my dad, very distraughtly, "Oh Wal! Whatever will we do?"

They both looked at me as I burst into the room, and dad very calmly said, "You'd better sit down. You're as white as a sheet."

3

"B-but the siren. W-what . . . ?" I stammered.

Dad told me that while I was in church, war had been declared. I was sixteen years old and had absolutely no idea what war was about, and that damned siren had scared the living daylights out of me.

I remember the telephone rang and my girlfriend, whom I was with in church, was phoning to ask if we were all right, and if I would like to go to her house for Sunday tea. War and sirens were soon forgotten as we gabbed away, until mum, somewhat calmed down, announced dinner was ready.

I had just finished school and had started working for the Ministry of Labour in Holborn, London. In our department we had the task of sending out "calling up" papers to the young men of Britain. The work was quite interesting, especially if one came across the papers of a friend, which happened frequently.

Whenever I did, I always slipped a note inside to wish them good luck—probably would have been fired had I been found out. I stayed there until the building was blown to bits during the bombing. Through medical reasons the services would not accept me, so I found local office work and joined the Air Raid Precaution, part-time.

I cried when I heard war had been declared. The first person I thought of was my brother who was in the Middlesex Regiment, Cadet Corps. He volunteered for service the very next day. Mum took it hard, and it was terrible for all of us when he was killed June 24, 1943 while serving with the Black Watch.

At the beginning of the war, I worked in a linoleum factory. We were all laid off while it was changed into making torpedoes for our ships. I didn't go back there, but went to Hastings and worked at making field kitchens for the army.

4

When we heard that war had been declared, the first thing my mum did was turn to me and say, "Now don't you get any ideas in your head about marrying any foreigner!" That seemed to bother her more than the war itself. Didn't do any good though. I married one anyway.

Where was I that fateful Sunday morning? In the bath! Boy! Did I get out of there in a hurry when that siren went. I ran down the stairs, out the front door and down the garden path to the front gate before I realized that the only thing I had on was a bath towel. I don't even remember draping it around me. I shudder to think what may have happened if I hadn't because, coming down the road, of all people, was a policeman. I'll never forget the grin on that bobby's face, or the neighbours' laughter when they saw me. Was my face red!

When the siren went off that Sunday, we were just going to have dinner. We were all quite disturbed as we lived in London and thought surely we were going to be bombed right there and then. But of course, nothing happened, and didn't for a long time. But the Germans sure made up for lost time.

I first heard the news in the servants' hall of Cherkley Court in Leatherhead, Surrey. I was head kitchen maid to Lord Beaverbrook, and we were spending a few weeks at his summer residence (104 rooms)!

This particular Sunday, the Butler called us all together to hear Chamberlain's speech. We were all stunned and it seemed so incredulous that this terrible thing could happen on such a glorious, peaceful, English summer

My father, a London fireman, had served through the First World War and had taken the news quite calmly. Eventually our family, including grandfather, aunts,

5

uncles, cousins, etc. served in the services one way or another. Grandfather received an award from Queen Elizabeth for services rendered.

Everyone was talking at once in our house after we had heard the news that war had been declared. I had six brothers and five sisters, and we were all trying to be heard above the other. Two of my brothers were ready to "join up" that very instant, and one of my younger sisters said she was going with them. We all laughed at her then. How little we knew! She did go into the WRNS and so did I, and four of my brothers joined the Royal Navy.

Like a lot of people, we were in church when war was declared. The minister announced it from the pulpit. Dad had said in 1938 that he "knew" we were headed for another war. He immediately packed us all off to Penzance in Cornwall as he thought Farnborough and Aldershot, the area where we lived, would soon be bombed. I was still in school and, because the teaching staff were busy making black-out curtains, we had an extra ten days holiday. Whoopee! No bombs fell and back home to Farnborough we came. The day after we left Penzance, the Germans bombed the hell out of the submarine base there.

The day war broke out, I was getting ready to go out on my bicycle when the news came over the radio. Of course, for weeks the air had been heavy with war news. I didn't feel scared when I heard, and only felt so when London was bombed, as we lived quite near in Slough, Berkshire.

I'll never forget that Sunday. I was eighteen years old and engaged to be married. Our wedding had been planned for Sunday, December 24 . . . Christmas Eve. A candlelight ceremony, early evening, with me in the traditional white, carrying a single red rose. Oh! I was going to look so glamorous and sophisticated! My fiancé, much to my amazement at such a sudden decision, enlisted in the army right away. He was stationed in some God-forsaken place in Scotland, and was due home three days before the wedding. He never arrived. Instead, our wedding was a funeral. Due to icy road conditions, the army truck that was taking him to the nearest railway station, skidded out of control and he was killed instantly.

Bexhill was a quiet seaside resort with no industries, but there were many private schools which were largely responsible for creating employment. I was employed as a housemaid at one of these schools until promoted to parlour maid. Our lives resembled those of the characters portrayed in the television series "Upstairs and Downstairs."

At the time of the Munich Agreement, I remember the Pacifists standing on street corners handing out peace pamphlets for the public to sign. When war was declared on September 3, it came as an anti-climax. This was it! My first reaction was to think of patriotic songs and fragments of poetry that we had learned in school in honour of Empire Day.

Next came the sobering thought that war would change our lives, and never would they be the same again. To some it would mean a dramatic change either for the better or worse. We little visualized how big these future changes would be.

Amongst the young there was a feeling of excitement, but for the older generation, sorrow and fear. They knew what we know now—that no one really ever wins.

After I graduated from the Royal Seamons Hospital in Greenwich, I joined the Nurses Co-operative Society in London. This Society assigned us to jobs in hospitals or in private homes if we preferred.

A nurse friend and I were looking after a partially paralysed solicitor in his country home in Ipswich, Suffolk. When war was declared the news made us feel terrible and affected our patient very deeply, so much so that his health became increasingly worse and he was eventually moved to a nursing home.

We had all been issued with gas masks prior to the outbreak of war, and I shall never forget my Aunt Bella coming down the stairs with her gas mask on when the siren sounded on that first day. My dad took one look at her and said, "Good God, Bella! You look like something from Mars." A few minutes after we all realized that my little sister was missing. The panic written on my mother's face is something I shall never forget. Mum ran down the road and I the other way. We finally found her. She was on her way home from a friend's house when the siren blew, and a neighbour had taken her in. When the three of us got back home, there was Aunt Bella still with her gas mask on. She sat with it on all through dinner, removing it only between mouthfuls of food!

I was only fourteen years old when the Second World War broke out. I remember that Sunday so well because it was my youngest sister's birthday. I didn't really understand at the time what a terrible impact it would have on our lives. But we learned to live with the terrible things that happened and the changes war made in our lives.

I must admit the news of war was very frightening to

8

me and yet, I was not surprised. Even at fifteen years of age, I felt it inevitable. My only brother was in the regular army at the time and stationed in India and was due to return home to England after seven years duty. Because of the outbreak of war he was forced to stay there until 1943. Then he came home on leave and was immediately sent to Europe which I felt was unfair.

Our reaction to the news of the war on Sunday, September 3, wasn't unexpected. I was peeling and pre-paring brussel sprouts for our Sunday dinner. My mother started quietly weeping into the potato peelings. She re-membered the Great War, and my brother was already in the Royal Marines somewhere in the Red Sea on the *H.M.S. Liverpool*. Her thoughts naturally went to him, her only son. My father said little but sat glued to the radio for news. We were sobered and certainly did not enjoy our Sunday roast and Yorkshire pudding.

Later that day I talked to girlfriends, all around my own age—sixteen. Some had romantic ideas of nursing the wounded. We weren't afraid then, being young and ignorant. I know this is hindsight, but looking back, even those innocent young boys and girls did incredibly well in some ghastly situations. I envied the girls in Britain who went into the forces and wished I had. I kept getting deferred because of a lung ailment I had when I was seventeen. I was already working on what was con-sidered work essential to the war effort, so the question of my being "called up" didn't seem to arise.

Two incidents remain very clear in my mind when I think of the Sunday war started. Firstly, my dear mum who loved all things created, sadly said, "Oh! The poor birds will all be killed," for we thought it was to be a war waged with gases.

Secondly, I remember going to the church to be issued

9

with gas masks and my elder sister panicking at the thought of putting her infant baby in the large masks issued for them. They had to be pumped by hand to ensure the infant didn't suffocate.

When the war started I was thirteen years old, and the one thing I remember most vividly was the beginning of the "black out." The street lights that were on every night, were suddenly turned off, and that was the start of it. It was such a weird feeling, almost as if the world was coming to an end. I suppose in one way it was, for the life we had known ended there.

I was still attending school in 1939, and a week after war started, I and a lot of other school children were evacuated from London to a small village in Kent which I hated. During this time there had been no bombing raids directed on London, so it wasn't long before I returned home. Consequently, I went through the whole bit—blitz, bombing and rocket raids.

I was sixteen when war became a reality in 1939. I reacted as I imagine most people did, with a fervent hope that the announcement would soon be followed by another—that negotiations had been worked out after all, and the dark cloud lifted, but all the while knowing it would not happen that way. There was no turning back, and we would have to face whatever awaited us.

I lived in Hornchurch, Essex, and with a Spitfire base a few miles away, and the railway to the coast nearby, our town was frequently chosen as a target by the Luftwaffe.

Even though we expected it, of course, the news of war was hard to take, especially for the older people who really suffered most in terms of worry, the struggle to exist and the damage to nerves and health in general. I think we all waited and longed for peace, and every setback we read, put us all in the dumps.

A lot of young people "enjoyed" the war, if that doesn't sound too unfeeling. Many led social lives that they never knew before, especially those in the forces. But, because of the times, young people, civilian or service personnel, travelled more frequently wherever they wished in the British Isles. There were more things to do, and the company of other young people, many of whom were destined to become lifelong friends.

Although we all wanted the war to end, we did not want this new way of life to end. After all, in pre-war days life for us was pretty hum-drum, and the war gave us a chance to see a little of what was on the other side of the fence.

From Romance to Reality

With the Canadians arriving in England en masse as early as December 1939, meetings with British girls were inevitable. The extrovert Canadian, not waiting for formal introduction, thought nothing of starting a conversation with the more reserved Britisher.

At first the girls were wary. They had heard stories from their elders about the Canadian's misconduct in Britain during World War I. But surely no more or less than the misdemeanors of any troops stationed in a strange land.

Despite their horror, the war years brought excitement and romance to the young girls of Britain. They met Canadian men in dance halls, pubs, through friends, in casual conversation on railway platforms and in NAAFI canteens. They dated and fell in love.

With the decisions to marry, came certain formalities. The procedure laid down by the Canadian military authorities had to be followed. The first step for the serviceman was to complete Form 1000/110, then to discover what his chances were of supporting a family after discharge, he had to declare his work and earnings before enlistment. Moreover, his Commanding Officer had to be satisfied that the man was not already married.

Blood tests and medical examinations were required of both parties. Some girls were interviewed by the CO or Chaplain and were asked such questions—"Do you have to get married?" . . . and "Are you aware that life in Canada is entirely different from your life here, and are you prepared to accept this?" Most girls were.

When all documents and certificates had been received, approved and signed, the wedding date could be determined. This in turn was given to the CO. A "permission granted" was then posted on regular daily orders telling the party concerned that he could marry on, or after, the given date. There were at least two months from the time of consent to the actual date.

Canada at this point seemed very remote, and most of the girls never thought they would ever leave their country. They did not choose Canada, but the men who came from there. Not until they said goodbye to beloved families, friends and homeland, did Canada become a reality. There was no turning back once the ship sailed, and that is when it really hit them.

Apprehension and fear travelled with them across the Atlantic and increased in volume as the train sped across Canada. They wondered what would be at the end of their journey. Would they be made welcome? Would they be accepted and liked? What would happen to them if they were not?

Many were not accepted. Even if husbands welcomed them, relatives were resentful and hostile. Some were terribly hurt and disappointed because husbands had told lies about their homes in Canada and life was not what they had been led to believe. Not wanted, they had no recourse but to seek help from the Canadian Red Cross and return to their homeland heartbroken and disillusioned.

This book contains many identified stories, written in the first person by girls who became war brides. They relate simply and sincerely what happened to them when they first arrived in Canada, and how the subsequent years have shaped their lives.

War Brides

They've chosen their partners, they're proud and glad
Of their Aussie, their Yank, or Canadian lad.
From parents and friends, from their land they'll depart,
What a great step for a very young heart.

Off to a country unknown and untried
To learn other methods and customs besides.
Even their husbands at first must be shared
With his people and friends, who have
waited and cared.

These brides must take courage and kindness along
For they can't rush back home when small things go
wrong.
They will speak for this land by behaviour and deed,
Must earn their acceptance and honour their breed.
Good luck and God bless them, these pioneer brides
And give them fine children, the best of both sides.

Author unknown

This poem was published in a British newspaper...1946

POST OFFICE

TELEGRAM

Charges to pay
s. _____ d. _____

RECEIVED

Prefix. **K11**

From

No. _____

To _____

Time handed in.   Office of Origin and Service instructions.   Words.

1.45 LONDON ZH 20 =

NEWLYWEDS 19 LIND RD SUTTON-SURREY =

NOW YOU HAVE REGISTERED FOR LIFE MAY YOUR

HAPPINESS NEVER BE RATIONED = JOHN AND PEGGY +

19 + ×

For **free** repetition of doubtful words telephone "TELEGRAMS ENQUIRY," or call, with this form at office of delivery. Other enquiries should be accompanied by this form, and, if possible, the envelope

B or C

Wt. 35576/P. 3431. 50,000 Pads. 12/42. 51-6853. J.D. & Co. Ltd.

ROYAL AIR FORCE STATION

LONG MARSTON

Farewell Dinner and Dance

ON

SUNDAY, 8th JULY, 1945

TO ALL RANKS AT LONG MARSTON.

NEVER in my life have I had the privilege of serving with such a first-class body of men and women. I shall never have that privilege to the same extent again.

Our work together has resulted in the creation of the finest O.T.U. in the country.

Our record is splendid : our results are amazing.

I thank you from the bottom of my heart and wish you well in the brighter days that lie ahead.

Good-bye and good luck.

G. V. LANE, D.F.C., A.F.C.,
Group Captain,
Commanding 24 *O.T.U.,*
Royal Air Force.

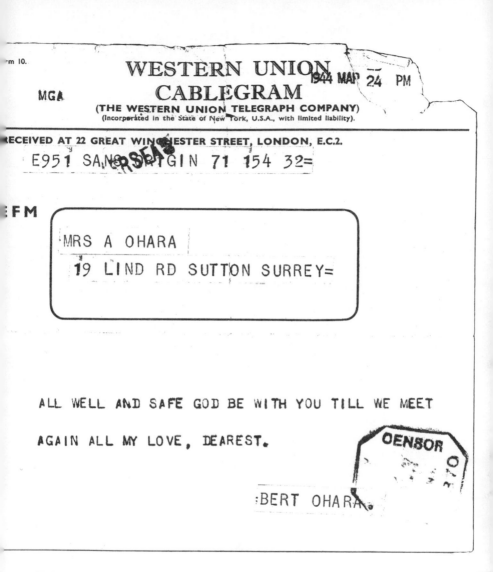

WESTERN UNION
CABLEGRAM

1944 MAR 24 PM

(THE WESTERN UNION TELEGRAPH COMPANY)
(Incorporated in the State of New York, U.S.A., with limited liability).

RECEIVED AT 22 GREAT WINCHESTER STREET, LONDON, E.C.2.

E951 SANS ORIGIN 71 154 32=

FM

MRS A OHARA

19 LIND RD SUTTON SURREY=

ALL WELL AND SAFE GOD BE WITH YOU TILL WE MEET

AGAIN ALL MY LOVE, DEAREST.

CENSOR

BERT OHARA

Telegram sent to Peggy O'Hara from husband, Bert, after arriving in Canada.

VISA (if required.)

CANADIAN
TRAVEL CERTIFICATE

N.º 372

Valid for single journey to Canada direct or via the United States of America.

Name of Holder :

....

MRS DOROTHY TRUMAN

Issued by authority of the High Commissioner for Canada at Canada House, London, S.W. 1.

on .... AUG 2 7 1944 ....

****

Jean and Bill Wacey
B.C.

Bill and I met at a camp dance in 1942. He was a sergeant in the Canadian army and had been sent to my hometown of Derby on a course. We dated that summer, but since he was engaged to a Canadian girl, neither of us took it too seriously. But in 1944 when he was spending his leave at my parents home, he proposed marriage saying he had asked to be released from his engagement, and his fiancée had very decently agreed.

So started the routine of having blood tests, medicals and being "screened" to be sure I met with all the requirements, and was a worthy bride-to-be of a Canadian serviceman—much to my mother's disgust. She thought any man would be lucky to get me!

19

Bill was stationed near Aldershot, and since troops had been forbidden to leave the area (it was just prior to D-Day) he borrowed some civvies and sneaked to Derby for the weekend. I nearly died with embarrassment when I saw his "get-up." A bottle-green corduroy suit and a fedora covering his almost shaved head—a pre D-Day requisite. He looked as if he had come right out of a George Raft gangster movie.

The British MPs patrolling the railway station gave him a "Who d'you think you're kidding?" look, but took pity on us and did not question him.

One evening in late July, Bill phoned and told me to take the early morning train for Aldershot and to bring the rings. What followed is hard to credit now.

To begin, we could not find anyone who would marry us. The staff at the Registrar's office said Bill had to be a resident for three consecutive weeks, but he had moved around quite a bit prior to going to France. Taxi-cabs were not allowed to go out of a certain radius during the war, but we were lucky to find a sympathetic driver who broke the law for us. From half-past two in the afternoon we chased from one district to the other; it was a real cliff-hanger! Everytime we reached a level crossing the gates swung shut and I chewed my finger nails down a bit more!

Finally, we were directed back to Aldershot only to find the staff had gone for the day and the office closed. To be legal in England, marriages have to be performed before 6 p.m. and by this time it was 5:30 p.m. Off we chased into the country and contacted the deputy lady Registrar who agreed to return with us after phoning the Chief Registrar who said he would meet us at the office. Returning once more to Aldershot, we asked our friendly cab driver and the char lady to stand as our witnesses. As the deputy started to read the wedding service a clock on a nearby building started to strike the hour of six, the

Registrar was bounding up the stairs two at a time. Bursting into the room, he took over just as the clock finished chiming. At times, Bill has jokingly said that we may not be legally married, but we would have a hard time proving that now. And I certainly would not change my wedding day for the traditional white wedding in church . . . mine was a lot more fun!

Bill and Jean Wacey

But this wasn't the end. Bill had forgotten which hotel he had booked us into, so we had to telephone them all until we found the right one. It was well past dining hours, but they gave us cabbage water masquerading as soup. We turned in early, both exhausted after such a hectic day. In the wee hours of the morning, Bill kissed me goodbye, and crept out. I didn't see him again until eleven months later when he came home from France on leave. When he left for Canada, I followed almost a year later on the good old *Aquitania*.

War brides from Derby, England, on board, courtesy of Jean Wacey

I enjoyed the voyage and remember our awe at seeing so much food, but before many days were over, only two of us turned up faithfully for every meal. The rest stayed in their bunks, seasick.

The wives without children were designated bunks in the bowels of the ship and quarters were small. One girl had a portable gramophone and only one record, the song

"Temptation." How we all resisted the temptation to chuck it overboard I'll never know, for she played it morning, noon and night.

We were not allowed to fraternize with the troops on board. One day when I was on deck, I was hissed at very persistently by a soldier. I kept shaking my head wishing he would go away. To keep him quiet I went to him and whispered, "What do you want?" Nothing sinister in mind. All the poor lad wanted was some duty-free fags which we could buy in the shop and he couldn't. I got them and met him later at a prearranged dark spot on deck. I didn't want to be one of those girls who were gossiped about. "She was caught in a life-boat, you know. Not allowed to land in Canada. Sent home in disgrace!" I wondered if some really did that. I wasn't about to find out!

The train journey to Toronto in the heat of a Canadian June, I found very trying. My memories coming through the eastern provinces were of women dressed in black going to church on Sunday. Invariably they wore their hair plaited and drawn up onto the top of the head. I asked someone if it was a day of national mourning.

An embarrassing thing happened to me on the train. We had been told that the toilets were situated at each end of the coaches. One night after I'd been in bed a few hours, I had to go to the lavatory. I padded down the corridor in my nightie, opened the door at the end and stepped inside, only to see to my great amazement about six officers seated around a table playing poker. All eyes turned toward me. Great consternation on my part. Rather lamely I said, "Oh! I beg your pardon. I was looking for the toilet." Feeling of course that they were all thinking, "Oh yeah! A likely tale!" One man kindly pointed to a smaller room off to the side and I said to myself, "No use turning back now. When in doubt, press on!'' I found out the next day that since we were in the last coach, the end compartment was reserved for the men and ''Off Limits'' to us.

I was made very welcome by my in-laws and they were very kind. The heat was almost unendurable and I thought I'd never be able to live through it. I never liked the taste of hot-dogs and thought our bread filled war-time sausages tasted better. And hamburger would never take the place of my mother's Lancashire Hot Pot, steak and kidney pie, and good old fish and chips. And I was homesick, oh! so very homesick and stayed so for about five years.

My husband had returned to civvy street in 1945, then in November 1946, decided to enter into the RCAF Permanent Force. He was posted to Trenton, Ontario for basic training. I went to Belleville and found a room with board. That winter, my first in Canada, was pretty awful, yet I don't remember feeling sorry for myself.

I discovered that my landlady, an English-born woman, had about forty pounds of butter in her fridge, and I understood how she acquired them when I left there. She had cut all my meat, butter and sugar coupons out of my ration book for several months ahead!

When Christmas came, Bill was in hospital with a very badly infected face. I hitch-hiked every day to see him as we had no car, and the bus schedule did not coincide with visiting hours. I could not afford a good warm winter coat and remember feeling darn cold standing at the Guard House in the snow and wind hoping that someone would take pity on me and offer me a ride back to town. My landlady would not give me meals on weekends and holidays, so I had my first Christmas dinner in one of the local greasy spoons, the cheapest I could find. The following March, Bill was posted to Barrie. Once again the hunt was on for somewhere to live. Not an easy task in those days.

During our stay in Barrie, Bill was posted back to Trenton on a course. While he was there, I had to enter hospital for an operation. I saw no point in worrying him, so sat down and wrote several post-dated letters and asked my landlady to mail them at three-day intervals. I took the bus into Barrie and walked to the hospital in a raging blizzard feeling like an orphan of the storm—Lillian Gish at her most poignant! The storm kept everyone home for a week, but after about ten days, Bill got leave and came to see me with out-of-season daffodils and a lecture to go with them.

After that first ghastly year, I more or less settled down. And now after thirty-odd years in Canada I have no regrets. I've happily lived in four provinces; seen a lot of Canada and the USA; made a wealth of good friends—what more could I ask for?

Bill retired from the forces in 1969, and we have lived on Vancouver Island ever since. When I look at an old photo of the Derby war brides taken in 1945, a few lines of verse come to mind.

"If there were dreams to sell, merry and sad to tell/And the crier rang his bell, what would you buy?" I think we all had a dream; certainly optimism and faith in the future. What did we buy? For most, a fair share of happiness and contentment—for a few perhaps heart-break and disillusionment.

****

Celia Phillips
London, England

One Saturday night in December 1940, I went to the local dance hall with my girlfriend. We hadn't attended many dances in the past, but had enjoyed them when we did. This night was to be a special one for me because, it was here that I met my future husband. From the minute I saw the tall good-looking soldier coming toward me, it was love at first sight for both of us.

Don was with the Canadian Black Watch and we spent as much time together as the army would allow. Eight months after we had met, Don asked me to marry him. He applied for permission and after the army requirements had been attended to, we married on March 7, 1942.

We were so happy that I could not believe it would last. It didn't. Don was killed in the Dieppe raid in August 1942 barely five months after our marriage. I thought my life had come to an end and wished it so. But I was going to have a baby and this alone gave me the will to live. My son was born in February 1943 and was a great joy to me and my mum and dad.

I had corresponded with Don's parents and sister who lived in Windsor, Ontario and shared with them the grief and heartbreak of Don's death. I sent them photos of little Donny all the time, and they kept expressing their dearest wish was to see their only grandchild who was then two years old. After much deliberation and not entirely against my parents wishes, I applied for transportation to Canada. Although I was an only child and the separation from my parents would be a terrible wrench, they understood how Don's parents must have felt.

We sailed for Canada aboard the *Ile de France* in March 1946. The voyage was uneventful, but I was full of mixed emotions. Other brides on board had their husbands waiting for them, and I wondered if I were doing the right thing. I cried a lot when I thought of my mum and dad, but it was a bit late for that. Saying goodbye had been awful, and I promised I would get back for a visit as soon as I could. It seemed then as if I was going to be torn between two sets of grandparents. I wanted dearly to be in England with my own family but, did I have the right to deny Don's parents their grandchild? I was in such a turmoil that I could hardly see straight.

Don's parents and his sister met me in Toronto. It was a tearful meeting and not one I would care to go through again. We drove to Windsor, and I thought we would never get there. After what was hours, we drove into the driveway of a nice looking brick house. I was very tired and Donny fretful and I was glad to bathe him and tuck him into his new bed.

Mother had made tea for us, and as conversation had been somewhat strained during the drive, I thought we could now relax and talk come easier. But they wanted to know all about Don which was only natural, and it was hard going over it all again.

It was obvious that he had been the "apple of his mum's eye" so to speak. And as the weeks passed, I began to realize that she didn't really want me, just her grandson. Don's father was a dear person, but never had much to say. I always felt that he would never stand a chance to say much anyway. My sister-in-law was only fifteen, and as we had nothing in common, I really had no one to talk to.

Mother suggested I find myself a job to help pass the time. Although I received an allowance, I thought it a good idea as I was lonely and hoped it would open the door to new friendships. What I didn't anticipate was her looking forward to having Donny all to herself.

I found a part-time job in a dress shop working Tuesdays, Thursdays, Saturdays and the odd Friday evening. I was able to meet people while also having time for Donny. At first I enjoyed it very much. After a few months I began to find my son hard to manage. He wouldn't do anything I asked, and when I scolded him he ran to his granny for support. At the time I was so timid that I didn't say anything.

Christmas 1946, our first in Canada and just before Donny's fourth birthday, things came to a climax. I had worked every day for three weeks prior to Christmas and was very tired and edgy. The situation at home had become increasingly worse. Although it had been mother's suggestion I work, she resented the fact that I wasn't able to help as much around the house. My sister-in-law did nothing to help, and I let her know it in no uncertain terms. A terrible scene followed and I finally admitted what had been at the back of my mind for a long time . . . that it had been a mistake to come here. It was a dreadful Christmas, and after it was over, I went to the local Red Cross and poured my heart out.

They were very helpful and sympathetic and advised me to write my parents of the situation that I had never mentioned in my letters.

Dad was able to pay our fares back, and through the Red Cross we got to Montreal where we sailed for home in March 1947, just a year after we had arrived.

It was wonderful to be home amongst my own family and friends. Mum and dad were horrified to hear about my life in so short a stay; disgusted and upset that because I was taking my mother-in-law's grandson away, she had called me an unfit mother, a tramp, and accused me of seeing men when she really knew I was working late.

Even to this day, I have always thought that had Don lived, my life in Canada would have been different. I had no chance to see anything of the country or find a real friend, so my memories of it are not good. This is sad because, I'm sure had the circumstances been different, I would have loved it.

****

Veronica and Tony Lamere
Quebec

I arrived in Canada in a thin English "utility" coat that I had used as a blanket on board ship, no hat or overshoes, on a bitterly cold night in March 1944. I had left a small peaceful Sussex village near Lewes with my two babies, one fourteen months, the other six weeks. My husband, Tony, a gunner with the Canadian artillery, was wounded and sent back to Canada nine months previously.

After fourteen days of travelling, I was utterly exhausted both mentally and physically. As if this wasn't enough, when we sighted land, a ship's officer informed me that in three months I'd be wishing I had never seen it. A cheering thought!

In spite of war-time secrecy, Tony had received my cable during the day telling him of our arrival. He had never seen his baby daughter as I barely realized I was pregnant when he left England, and our son at that time was only five months old.

When we arrived at a Montreal station, there was great excitement. A large party of my in-laws, newspaper reporters, men from a local radio station, and my dear husband were waiting to greet us. They were all shouting and talking at once. We eventually got through the crowd and were taken to a sister-in-law's home for an all night party. You can imagine I was ready for this! Everyone had gifts for me and the children; a huge meal was served; there was a lot of laughter, kissing, hugging and screaming in French. My two babies were terrified, tired and crying. I thought the night would never end as more and more people arrived . . . even the Parish priest.

We had travelled very roughly: nine women and their children with plank bunks for beds, in one small cabin meant for a ship's Officer. No baths or showers; chased off course by German U-boats with hardly a chance to

29

change our clothes. All I wanted was a good hot bath, clean clothes and a cup of tea. But the party went on and on. Then in came the fiddlers. The tables were pushed back, and on went the square dance. One may think I wasn't appreciative, but oh! I was. Everyone was so kind and I knew how lucky I was to have been so warmly welcomed. Some girls had not been met at the station and I wondered what would happen to them after the Red Cross took charge.

We were fortunate in finding a house and lived in Montreal for six years. By this time we had six children and decided a move to the south shore would be a better place for them to grow up than the bustling, busy city. We still live south of Montreal, and five of our eleven children are married, the others still at home.

They sent us to England for our 25th wedding anniversary and indeed it was a delightful surprise. England is still "home" to me even though I have had a truly marvellous life here, and love it. My husband is a wonderful person, and our children and grandchildren are a joy and pleasure.

We have been through hard times as there was very little work when all the servicemen were discharged, but somehow we always managed. Our married children live close by and we have marvellous get-togethers. Tony was one of nineteen children, all have large families, so I have many, many wonderful in-laws. As I had only one sister, I certainly made up for it. Everytime I wrote home to tell them another baby was on the way, my dad and sister were sure the snow and cold had driven me raving mad.

As a child I had polio which left me with a limp, so when called up for war service I was sent to work in a NAAFI canteen. This is where I met Tony. It's hard to believe that all this started over a "cuppa."

Tony and Veronica Lamere

****

In 1942 I became engaged to a young soldier who was serving with the Royal Montreal Regiment. Shortly after, he met with a very untimely death. I knew all his friends in the regiment, and a few months later while shopping, one stopped to say "Hello" and asked if he could take me out that evening. Although it was good to see Bert again, I refused. Too many memories, I suppose. About two weeks later he telephoned my home and asked if he could come and visit me. Not wanting to appear unfriendly, I agreed.

We had enjoyed some good times together in the past and I knew he missed his friend very much. Although I was not interested in Bert, the meeting did lead to others. Sometimes I was downright nasty to him and had I been in his place, I would have ditched me long ago but, he was very persistent.

Gradually I looked forward to his visits and in June 1943 he asked me to marry him. Medical and blood tests followed, (mother disgusted), permission granted, banns were read, and the date set for November 20, 1943.

My main problem was, what to wear. With clothing rationed one did not have much choice. I needed a new coat which would take eighteen of my precious coupons leaving hardly enough for a pair of shoes let alone anything else.

Lady Luck was with me. A co-worker in the office had been married in April. We were about the same size, so she offered me a complete bridal and bridesmaid ensemble. I was thrilled to bits. She and her husband even gave up their flat for us the weekend of our marriage. We have always felt eternally grateful to that couple for their thoughtfulness and generosity.

Bert did not give his best man very explicit details or

32

directions about the wedding. The night before, all the poor chap knew when he arrived in town was, a girl named Peggy was getting married at 3 p.m. the next day. There must have been a thousand Peggy's in Sutton. The weather, terribly foggy, delayed him from getting in earlier than 11 p.m. What an hour to start looking for me!

I don't recall how many churches there were in the area, but the poor devil walked to nearly all of them, apologizing to each minister for waking him up to ask if he was marrying Peggy at 3 p.m. on Saturday. Finally at 3 a.m. he found the right church and minister who, after being awakened at that ungodly hour—no pun intended—gave him my address. Needless to say we wondered who was banging on our door at 3:30 a.m. in the morning as I wasn't aware that he did not know where I lived and assumed he had other accommodations. Poor fellow! He was cold, hungry and awfully embarrassed about waking so many people.

We told him not to worry about it, but I'm sure the air was blue next morning when groom and best man met at my sister's home. But all went well, and the only unfavourable condition was the foggy weather. Even that had it's humorous side. Jokingly over the years, Bert and I have often said it was so foggy that neither of us saw what we had married.

In January 1944, the Canadian Wives Bureau sent me forms to fill out for my transportation to Canada. In February I was notified to report for a medical to determine if I was fit healthwise to undertake such a long journey. I shall always remember Dr. Jupp, the Canadian doctor who examined me. He was one of the kindliest gentleman I have ever met, putting me at ease right away. I did not know I was one month pregnant, so when asked I replied I was not.

The next month Bert left England for Canada. He had

Peg and Bert O'Hara

been in a very bad explosion which resulted in his medical discharge. I not only missed him as much as a wife can miss an occasional weekend husband, but was worried to the point of distraction knowing the Atlantic was swarming with German U-boats. I prayed for his safety and for those with him. Relief came in the form of a Western Union Cablegram about two weeks later. "All well and safe. God be with you till we meet again. All my love dearest." The tears flowed freely.

By now I knew I was expecting our first child and tried desperately to speed things up regarding my own transportation. Unfortunately at this point, the British Government imposed a ban on the country forbidding anyone to leave except VIPs. This news made me very despondent, but there was nothing to do but wait.

After four and one-half years of blackout, severe rationing, constant bombing attacks, the loss of hundreds of lives, we were to face the dreaded V 1 rocket—buzz bomb or flying bomb as they were commonly called. I and countless others could not, even in our wildest imagination sense anything more horrifying than these noisy guided missiles with their terrifying flame of fire at the rear, chugging across the English sky day and night, while we below waited for the dreaded engine to stop, knowing full well at that precise moment it would plunge to earth and explode. But there was something more horrifying—the V 2 rocket. These, unlike their predecessor, were silent. Only the terrible explosion was heard, and one never knew where or when.

It was during the V 1 attacks that my secret orders came telling me to report to the nearest London station on July 23, 1944. This was to be the first ship load of brides to leave after the ban had been lifted. Although everything was marked "secret," I did tell mum and dad that I was leaving from Gourock, Scotland on the troopship *Empress of Scotland*. I know they were worried sick. Not only was I six months pregnant and according to rules should not have been leaving at all, but the Atlantic was still full of U-boats.

It was a terrible wrench leaving my parents and sister

knowing they had to stay and face whatever other horror was in store for them. No goodbyes could be said to a brother fighting overseas and another sister stationed in Nottingham. The latter sailed for Australia a few years after the war ended, and we never have seen each other again. At Victoria station I hugged mum and dad and wondered as they must have whether we would ever see each other again. I never did see dad but, I'll always remember the sad look on his face as I waved for the last time.

All the brides and children were taken in buses to a hostel where we were given a hot meal. This was about 6 p.m. Had we known that no food whatsoever was to be given us during the long, tiresome journey to Gourock, we would have cleared the tables of the bread that was left. Around midnight, during a heavy air raid, we boarded a train. I really didn't think we'd make it and felt sure the damn train would be blown up at any minute. But we arrived in Gourock late the following afternoon. The journey was dreadful. Not only did we have to sit up all the way, but the children were crying from hunger, unable to understand why, and for that matter neither could any of us. When a young mother asked what appeared to be someone of importance if she could have some milk for her two-year-old, she was told curtly to wait. I befriended two girls, and the three of us helped those who were having a difficult time with their children. But how does one explain to a two or three-year-old that there was not anything to eat, or to the babies, no milk? No wonder we were glad to board the *Empress* where a beautiful dinner awaited us. I think the first things we noticed were the white bread and fresh fruit. I didn't know what kind of a sailor I was but if a shilling trip around the south coast was anything to go by, I was doomed!

There was an assortment of passengers on board: 202

war brides and children; 165 POWs—German officers including Major General H. Kreipe who had been captured at Crete; 109 POW escorts, and many Canadian servicemen returning home—a total of 979. We sailed just before midnight July 24, with a quarter moon silhouetting the outline of the liner as she headed for Canada.

Entering the diningroom for breakfast on our first morning at sea, we passed the German officers. I suppose they were just as curious about us as we were of them. We had never been face to face with the enemy and were all eyeing each other when one young officer looked me up and down, and as our eyes met, he winked! I was so self-conscious due to my obvious pregnancy that I showed contempt by giving back what I hoped, a real haughty English glare.

After that encounter, we caught glimpses of them on a roped-off section of the deck as they took the air morning and afternoon. The first time they were on deck, they were amazed that the ship sailed the high seas without escort and they were seen running from one side to the other in search of accompanying ships.

There was boat drill every day, our first in weather that was rough and foggy and a lot of us were sea-sick as the ship developed a more or less steady roll.

I shared a cabin with five other girls on "A" deck and next to us was a larger cabin occupied by some of the ship's Conducting Staff. They had a record player and we assumed one record—McNamara's Band. Even to this day when I hear that tune, I think of that voyage and the girls placing their hands over their ears and moaning, "Oh, surely not again!"

We were in the Gulf Stream on the 28th of July enjoying balmy weather when suddenly the ship gave a lurch to starboard and changed course. This was followed by wide sweeps to the left and right causing much consternation

37

among us. We wondered if German U-boats were diligently keeping vigil in the murky ocean depths. Rumour had it that they were, although they did not pursue their attack; perhaps they knew their own were on board. And weren't we lucky they were, otherwise we might have had to take to the life boats? Because of the change in course, we were back into the cold, foggy weather that remained with us until we tied up to pier 22 in Halifax harbour during the early hours of July 30.

We were allowed to bring ten pounds sterling out of the country. A great deal of it was spent in the shop on board. Not only did we have to buy a railway ticket to our destination, but pay for our meals as well. I remember the girl going to B.C. She was desperate as she had bought gifts for all her in-laws and did not have enough money to carry her through to Vancouver. I gave her what I could spare which wasn't too much, but it helped. I have yet to meet any war bride, other than those on this particular voyage, who had to pay her way from Halifax. There must have been a gross error somewhere down the line. I distinctly remember our travelling documents stating that all was paid from the time we left our home in England, until we reached our new home in Canada. Bert and I did report this to the Canadian Red Cross, and although quite concerned, they did not appear to know too much about it, and we did not pursue further.

The desolate scenery throughout the Maritime provinces depressed me and I thought, "Oh dear! what have I come to? Is this all it is?" We arrived in Montreal's Central station at 8 p.m., Tuesday, August 1. My husband, mother-in-law, and the parents of my former deceased fiancé, met me. More family and friends awaited at the house and I was presented with many gifts. It was a lovely evening; if anything, a bit confusing trying to sort people out.

38

I was extremely tired from the journey and did not feel too well. I had been very seasick, and when I think back now, I realize how lucky I was that I did not abort.

The next day, the Montreal tramways went out on strike and I was given a grand tour of the city in a taxicab. Rather extravagant admittedly, but far more comfortable than those awful street cars. Although food was rationed, it was plentiful compared to the rations we had received in England and I found grocery shopping a delight. I sent home lots of tea and sugar, and I pictured the joy on my mum's face at receiving them. I know she cut open the tea bags and poured the contents into her tea caddy not knowing what tea bags were, and I never thought to tell her.

Within a few weeks of my arrival, I was told a "shower" was to be given to me. In my state of pregnancy I wasn't looking forward to this at all. Nobody explained, and I suppose they assumed I knew, and I wasn't about to show my ignorance and ask. The big night eventually arrived. Alone in our bedroom and feeling quite shy about the whole thing, I said to Bert, "What do I take with me?" Rather curiously he said, "What do you mean, honey?" I could feel my face getting hotter and hotter as I mumbled, "Well. Do I take a bath towel?" He couldn't help laughing as he explained. Boy! Was I relieved!

I loved Montreal, and when the weather was good, I'd put the baby in his carriage and walk to close by Mount Royal and sit in the sun. The shops on Ste. Catherine Street fascinated me and it was a delight to buy clothes without worrying about coupons.

A few months after my arrival, Bert was hospitalized for six months. The home situation without him was not the happiest, and I tried hard to find another place to live. One lousy room would have done and I almost got one, literally. Pushing the carriage I walked downtown

Montreal and found this place that was advertised in the paper. Dump would be a better word. The room was an attic above the fourth floor of a very old, run-down house situated in Montreal's "red light" district—only I did not know it then. Had the landlady not been decent, I would have taken it. I was so desperate. But she wouldn't even let me in. No wonder! Looking at me and my son she gently but firmly said, "My dear child. This is no place for a young girl like you, especially with a baby." I begged her to let me see this room, but she was adamant, thank God!

If it were not for those kindhearted parents of my deceased fiancé, I do not know what would have happened to us. Shortly after, I arrived home one day to find we were locked out, and these dear people took us in. Two days after, Bert was allowed leave from the military hospital to settle things. I cried when I saw him hobbling on crutches. He arranged for our personal belongings and what furniture we owned to be removed and stored in our friend's basement. I had a box that contained photos of my family, two silver horseshoes that I had carried on my wedding day, the wedding cake decorations that my dear mum had searched for, for weeks, and all my travelling documents. None of these were with our personal things. Back Bert hobbled to get them, although he was positive they were not in the cupboard where they had lain for months. He was right! They were nowhere to be found. All this memorabilia had been destroyed. I was heartbroken.

Should I have been fortunate enough to have a daughter, I was keeping the lucky horseshoes for her to carry on her wedding day, and the cake decorations for her wedding cake. Now they were all gone.

A month later, Bert was released from hospital. It was late 1945 and he applied for a job with the Department of Veteran's Affairs and was accepted. He left for

Huntingdon, Quebec and I followed with the baby in the January.

During the time he was in hospital, I was, of course, very homesick and wanted desperately to return to England. Many letters I wrote mum and dad asking them to send the fare so that my son and I could return. I never mailed any of these letters because after I had put on paper my feelings and frustrations, I always felt better. So I tore them up, determined to stay where I was and make a success of marriage despite the resentment and jealousies of others. I'm glad I made this decision. We spent ten happy months in Huntingdon before we were transferred back to Montreal and were sorry to leave for we had made some very good friends.

One in particular comes to mind. She and I went shopping every Saturday morning, and I'll never forget the butcher we hounded every week asking for roasting chickens. The poor man had got to the point where he hardly spoke to us.

One morning as we opened his shop door, we saw him do a hasty retreat to the back of the store. Convinced he wasn't going to serve us, and uncertain whether to stay or leave, he suddenly appeared with two of the scrawniest looking chickens we had ever seen. Dangling from their necks, one in each hand, he thumped them onto the counter in front of us. The only words uttered were his. Abruptly he said, "1.50 each." We paid and left, never to ask for chicken again.

Back in Montreal we settled into a brand new war-time house. Our second child—yes, it was a daughter—was born in the spring of 1947. In July of that year, I heard on the radio that the *Empress of Scotland* was on her way up the St. Lawrence, her first voyage as a passenger ship since the war.

The river was within walking distance from our house, so my son and I walked down to watch her. She was painted battleship grey the last time I had seen her and now she was gleaming white. With her decks arrayed with bunting, flags proudly flying, and other ships saluting her, she sailed majestically . . . the flagship of the Canadian Pacific.

I felt very proud knowing I had sailed her just three years before. A lump formed in my throat, and tears came to my eyes as I watched. I have fond memories of her. After all, didn't she see me safely across a submarine infested ocean?

Happy as I was with my new home, the longing for my own family and dear England became more intense as the years passed. After nine years in Canada, the two children and I were at last to sail for a three-month visit. In my excitement at the thought of seeing my family and all things dear and familiar, except my dear dad who had passed away the year before, I didn't think of how Bert would feel at being parted from his wife and children for so long a time. I was elated when he suggested selling everything and making our home in England. Oh dear! What a dreadful mistake!

After the excitement of seeing everyone again and visiting places that had remained vividly in my memory, I knew without a doubt where I wanted to make my home . . . Canada.

Strangely, Bert was quite contented to settle in England although everything was still rationed and a great deal of items unavailable. But I had become a Canadian housewife in every sense and the buying of groceries every day got on my nerves, for I had become accustomed to shopping once every two weeks and having them delivered. I missed some of the material things I had taken for granted. We took our fridge with us, but it proved useless as there was never enough food to keep in it.

Everything appeared so much smaller after the

largeness of Canada, and I felt too confined. Most of all I missed the friends we had made. Nearly all my English friends had married and moved away and I had nothing in common with the few that were there. After nine years of separation, our lives had varied greatly. It wasn't so much that they or England had changed—I had. The one thing I did not miss was the Canadian winter. I hated snow and still do, more so as the years have passed.

After nine months we came back to Canada with two children and very little of anything else except hope for the future. We lived with another war bride and her husband until Bert was re-employed by the government. We moved back to Montreal where we both worked hard to re-establish a home where we stayed until our children were married. In 1971 when the forces base where Bert worked closed, we uprooted again for Ontario.

There are still things I miss about England and always will. My family mostly. I miss the sea; the quaint friendly villages and their pubs; the countryside and the beauty of an English spring. The experience going back to live cost a lot but was well worth it because I came back a wiser and happier person.

****

The main administration office of the Canadian Wives Bureau was in Sackville House, 40 Sackville Street, London, just west of Piccadilly Circus. On the third floor were our offices plus an "interview group" office. On the second floor was the office of Dr. Jupp where war brides reported for medicals before they left for Canada. The documentation office transferred its quarters from High Holborn to Regent Street.

When a Canadian serviceman married and claimed for

dependent allowance, the information was fed through our office at Sackville House. Once this was processed, we forwarded an application form to be completed by the wife for her transportation to Canada. These were sent to the documentation office. When the application was accepted, the wife was advised to report to Dr. Jupp for a medical. A wife who was more than five months pregnant was not allowed to travel. Other offices such as these were set up in other large cities throughout Great Britain.

Once this formality was completed, these papers were forwarded to another section of the Bureau where registration and travel documents were placed in a long brown envelope. These were numbered and given a certain type of priority such as pregnancy, number of children, or husbands already in Canada.

Wives were requested to forward their photograph which was placed on a Canadian Travel Certificate. The same procedure applied to a child over a certain age, otherwise he or she travelled on their mother's certificate.

When everything was completed and information received from the Admiralty that space was available on ships, a draft was made and those with the highest priority headed the list. Wives were then told to report to one of the London railway stations where further documentation was done as they arrived, such as ticketing by Cunard or whatever carrier was made available. Accommodation had been previously made at various hostels for wives and children until they boarded the train for the port of embarkation.

When the girls arrived at the port, we met and gave them their Canadian Travel Certificate along with other instructions, plus train ticket for their destination.

Some girls backed out at the last minute, but most of them eventually came to Canada. Many returned to their homeland never to return. Obviously, they could not burn that bridge behind them. Many husbands followed their wives to the old country and still reside there to this day. In the Brighton, Sussex area alone, there are over five hundred Canadian servicemen who settled after the war with their English brides.

Class distinction in England was very prominent in those days. I shall always remember the war bride who came aboard dressed to the nines and informed me that because she was the wife of a Captain she rated a cabin to herself. This was absolutely unheard of, and an impossibility. She got a bunk below the water-line like everyone else.

Many of the girls when boarding ship would mention where they were going in Canada. We would kid them and tell them all sorts of stories about how far out in the land of nowhere they would be living. So much of this was true although they did not believe us, but I'm sure they found out later we were right.

Of all the brides I have met and spoken to during the years, I have found most of them would like to return to their homeland to live out their last days. It would be ideal if they could have the best of two worlds, six months in Canada and the other six in their own country.

Contributed by Mr. Ed Davis who was with 1st Canadian Division in England 1939—Royal Canadian Army Service Corps. Later transferred to CMHQ attached to the Canadian Wives Bureau in Sackville House.

****

Dorothy and Gordon Newstead
Saskatchewan

When I volunteered for the Land Army during the war, twenty-six other girls and I took our training on a Government owned farm two miles from Bridgewater, England, where we resided in an old abbey. It was hard work. We rose at 5 a.m., walked two miles to the farm, milked the cows, cleaned the barns, then walked back for an 8 o'clock breakfast. The food was very good and I loved the outdoor life, but I was homesick. They moved me to another farm in Wales closer to my home. The work was twice as hard and the food terrible. I became ill, was medically discharged and sent home.

Shortly after my return, I witnessed a freak accident near our house that killed my mother. I was waiting for her to return from shopping when I heard this awful crashing sound and mum's voice screaming, "Oh my God! My leg!" I ran to the window and saw this car backing crazily off the sidewalk and my mother lying there.

I rushed out telling her I was coming to help, but the neighbours who had gathered, held me back. I could hear mum telling them, "Don't let Dorothy see me like this." I fought with them to get to her as the ambulance came and took her to hospital. I never saw her alive again. She died five hours later. The driver of the car was a Major in the Home Guard who was subjected to "black out" attacks. He had had one then, losing control of the car as it mounted the sidewalk pinning my dear mum against the wall.

When my married sister who lived with her family in Surrey, came for the funeral, she worried what the shock of mother's death might do to me and persuaded me to go back with her. This happened just before Christmas 1943.

A British regiment was camped behind where she lived and a Captain from it rented a room from her for himself and his wife. The regiment was holding a private dance in the local church hall and the Captain's wife, knowing I was single, invited me. With some misgivings at being amongst strangers, I went alone. There were two soldiers standing inside the entrance, one English, the other Canadian. The Englishman asked me if the dance was open to the public, so I explained it was with invitation only, so he left.

The Canadian soldier turned to me and said, "My name is Gordon, what's yours?" I told him and said I had been invited to the dance. He too was about to leave when the hall door opened and an officer said to me, "Aren't you and your boyfriend coming in?" Before I could explain, Gordon looked at me and said, "Why not?"

My sister had warned me about Canadians. The first to arrive in the area had done a lot of damage in the local pubs, so I was hesitant about him. He was so polite and quiet that I could not fit him into the mental image I had of Canadians.

We danced together nearly all evening, and just before the end we slipped away to walk home. Gordon asked me to go out the next evening, and I agreed. The Captain's wife arrived home ahead of me and told my sister that after inviting me to the dance so that I could meet some of the boys from the regiment, I arrived escorted by a CANADIAN, and to make matters worse I had danced with him ALL evening.

My sister was horrified. She waited up for me and after I had explained what had happened, she understood but insisted that Gordon call for me at the house. They all liked him, especially my two nephews because he supplied them with candies and gum.

In March 1944, Gordon asked me to marry him. We

47

Dorothy and Gordon Newstead with baby

visited the rest of the family in Wales and were married on May 26, 1944. Our first son was born in April 1945 and when he was fourteen months old, we sailed for Canada on the *Letitia* arriving in Halifax June 27, 1946.

I was four months pregnant, so the journey was very unpleasant for me. The children on board suffered with dysentery. This was bad enough, but when one is seasick as well, coping wasn't easy. I had four dozen terry cloth diapers when I boarded that ship and within a few days they were gone. I'm sorry to say that other mothers took them, and I had to ask the Red Cross for more.

The train ride across Canada was a nightmare. Washroom facilities were very inadequate and with the heat and dust we were dirty all the time. I had made up my mind that somehow or other I was going to be clean when we reached Regina. I went to the chef in the dining car and got two small galvanised tubs of hot water. Oh joy of joys! Four of us found a small baggage car, minus a door, and while two of us took sponge baths and washed our hair, the other two stood guard.

We arrived in Regina and were met by members of Gordon's family. My son Wayne and I stayed with my sister-in-law on her farm until Gordon came home.

Dorothy Newstead's farm in Saskatchewan

When he did come home, we decided to visit his younger brother who, after returning home from overseas,

49

had bought a farm in northern Saskatchewan. Plenty of bush up there! Deciding to stay, Gordon and three of his brothers built us a very cosy log cabin. After living in England with inside plumbing, electricity and other commodities that one takes for granted, I was now without these—only the barest of furniture; in the middle of nowhere; fourteen miles from the nearest town, Arborfield; no hospital, and expecting a baby at the end of November.

That winter of 1946/47 set in early and was very cold and severe. Once a week the train went to Arborfield and one morning at 4 a.m., Gordon put me on it and sent me to the nearest hospital in Tisdale, thirty miles away. Arriving there, I was told that unless in labour, they could not take me. I tried to explain how difficult it was to reach there from where I lived, but this was their rule and had to be abided. Now, I had to find my way back. I had very little money; in a strange town; didn't know a soul; and a baby due any time, no train for another WEEK!

The good Lord must have been watching over me, for a farmer from Arborfield was taking his son home from hospital and offered me a lift. I had no choice but to accept.

Again, someone up there was with me. A neighbour of my brother-in-law was in Arborfield that day and I was able to ride the other fourteen miles with him. While I was waiting for him to finish his business, I found out there was a retired doctor in town, also a French Canadian lady, the equivalent of a midwife who took into her home one maternity case at a time. I was able to make arrangements to go there and knew it would be soon as I was then overdue.

On Saturday night, November 30, forty-five degrees below zero, wrapped in a quilt, and in labour, I set out with Gordon on a fourteen-mile trip to Arborfield in an old unheated truck, armed with string and a pair of scissors, just in case. We made it, and after I was settled in the midwife's house, Gordon left to ride back in the rickety old truck. Our second son, Brent, was born 8 o'clock Sunday morning. That dear doctor stayed with me all night and only charged us five dollars.

Gordon, of course, did not know he had another son until he and his sister came on the Monday. On the way to see me, the housing fell out of the old truck. Had that happened on the Saturday night, we surely would have froze to death.

Doris, my sister-in-law, had one cow that supplied us all with milk. When put out to graze she had the habit of straying and forgetting to return home at milking time. One particular time she did not return all night, and of course we were all out of milk. I left my children with Doris and started out determined to find that cow. I didn't know the country too well, but did know that I could run into a bear anytime, so I was very careful. I found her in a small pasture about three miles away and managed to get her headed toward home. I was chasing her along this narrow trail and screaming at her to get a move on, when two Government Inspectors passed and looked at me as if I were crazy. I must have presented a comical picture.

Before I had left, I told Doris to have the milk pail ready because once I had the cow in the barn, she could milk her. When Doris saw us coming, she accidently dropped the pail with a clutter and the cow headed in the opposite direction with me right behind. That damn cow took me through creeks, bush and God knows what until she finally got away. I was so mad after going through all the trouble of finding her and bringing her home only to have her run away again . . . and still no milk!

When Gordon came back from cutting lumber in the bush, I told him my tale of woe. He set out to look for

51

her taking with him an old raincoat. When he saw her, he put the raincoat over his head, came out from behind a bush, and the cow, taking one look at him, headed for home as if the very devil were chasing her. We finally got our milk, and needless to say, she didn't stray too far after that.

To make the trip to the country store during the winter by horse and toboggan for groceries and the mail, was quite an ordeal. But Doris and I thought we could manage all right. Leaving Brent and her two youngest with her dad, we took two-year-old Wayne, her daughter Mae, aged three, and started off on a slow two and one-half mile trip through bush and narrow trails. Doris was driving with Mae sitting next to her, and Wayne and I were seated at the back. After the slow bumpy ride, we reached the store, picked up the mail and groceries, and headed back.

The trail cut through a farmyard, and as we passed under a high straw stack, a wolfhound jumped from it right on to the horse's back. Of course, he took off like a bat out of hell and went straight for a small bridge over a creek. The back of the toboggan broke, and I fell out. Picking myself up, I ran behind trying to catch up with the others.

Wayne, still on the toboggan, was screaming bloody murder, and I knew that once they hit the bridge both children would fall into the creek. When the horse took off, the whipple tree broke and Doris was hanging onto the reins yelling and cursing a blue streak. Just before the horse reached the bridge, he came to a dead stop. We gathered the mail and groceries that were scattered all along the trail, and Doris and Mae climbed back into the toboggan and we started again. This time though, even slower because no way would Wayne get back into it so I had to walk behind and carry him the rest of the way.

We were exhausted when we reached home. Gordon,

wondering what had happened to us, had started walking to meet us. After that experience we never ventured to the country store on a toboggan again.

When Brent was six months old, Gordon decided to move back to his hometown in southern Saskatchewan. He fixed the old truck, and one night off we went again. It took us until 6 p.m. the following night to cover 350 miles—an unending journey if ever there was! Wayne sat between us and slept most of the time, and I carried the baby on my lap all the way. I know what aching arms feel like. We stayed with relatives until Gordon bought and moved a house to the next town where he had to hold down two jobs to keep us going.

We moved back to the north again in 1953, leased some land which we had to buy from the Government after Gordon broke it in his spare time. I hauled our water from a well that Gordon dug himself, and in the winter I melted buckets and buckets of snow. It was a good thing my health was okay, as it really was tough going and took lots of willpower to survive.

Gordon and I had a wonderful life together even though it was hard. We finally sold the farm in 1973 and moved right into town; later that year Gordon passed away. My two sons live here, yet life does get lonely at times, but my grandchildren are a great joy.

I never discuss the hardships with my children now because they think they have it hard with running water, washing machines, dryers and every modern convenience imaginable. We had none of these things, and when I look back, I wonder how I ever survived it all. But I did, and so have a lot of the war brides who came from the large cities of England and knew nothing at all about farming and rural life in the forties.

****

I write not as a war bride, but as a Canadian Red Cross member. Our Corps began when the Red Cross Society decided there was a need for a group of uniformed volunteers during the war years. I joined the detachment in Fredericton N.B. and one of my duties was meeting the returning troops and the war brides.

Fredericton was the end of the line for a lot of the brides and they were met there by husbands or inlaws. One girl remains in my memory. She was going to Woodstock N.B. and for some reason was not met. One of our members put her up overnight, and the next morning we saw her onto the train. She was the only passenger and there were no facilities for meals, but the train crew assured us they would see that she was fed. I have often wondered how she made out on that day-long ride.

In 1945 I volunteered for overseas service and was sent to London, England. From May until October 1946, I worked in one of the hostels on South Street behind the Dorchester Hotel that accommodated brides before they boarded the train that took them to their port of sail.

During the ten months the hostel was open, we had about twelve thousand brides assembled there by the Canadian authorities. The usual length of stay was one night.

There was a smaller hostel close by for those who had to stay longer, usually European brides whose papers were more complicated. We did have one group of these brides who stayed for five days, and they were the only ones we really got to know. They were all in one large room, and one night we had to separate them because the Dutch girls wanted to sleep, and the French girls wanted to stay up all night and talk. I can remember them helping us with the dishes, and we in turn took them to the movies. A lot of these girls could not speak English, and we knew it wasn't going to be easy for those going to English provinces.

When the Victory parade was held in London in June 1946, we had a house full of brides who had to stay two nights because of the traffic situation. In the evening I took six of them out to see the sights and LOST one in the crowd! Not only did I worry about what had happened to her, but what would happen to me if she came to grief. When we got back to the hostel, the soldier who opened the door said, "You lost one of them, didn't you?" I was so relieved because I knew she had at least been in touch and hadn't come to any harm.

Some of our Red Cross girls were going home with a boat load of wives and children. A number of these children were in their care because, they had lost their mothers and were going to their father in Canada. These children had been brought up by doting grandparents and, poor little mites! this separation must have been a terrible ordeal for all concerned.

After the boat left Liverpool, it was rammed, and they all had to come back to London. It was reported that when the boat was ready to sail again, some of the brides didn't show up. Perhaps they took it as an omen to stay in England.

Some brides came complete with two families; one by a British father who had probably been killed in action, the second by a Canadian. The latter was usually a babe in arms and the former would include children up to sixteen years of age.

Then there were the grandparents—dependent mothers who were accompanying their daughters. The army found it easier to process the mothers along with their daughters as civilian travel was still very restricted.

I remember having trouble finding a place for a young lad of sixteen in a house full of women. The rooms in the hostel were large and filled with bunk beds and there were no private bathrooms. The problem was solved by having the boy sleep in the basement where the army staff had a bunk room should the need arise to stay overnight.

Those of us who served overseas in World War II and later in Korea, have a club that meets monthly in the major cities, and once a year for a reunion. Although we cannot grow in size, we are growing in interest as possible members have raised their families and now have the time to renew old friendships. The money we raise goes to the Canadian Red Cross Society to establish or replenish their loan cupboards.

Contributed by Miss Evelyn Clark—Canadian Red Cross member.

****

Kathleen and Ross Anderson
Ontario

I joined the ATS in 1942 and was attached to the War Office. A year later while stationed in Wembley, I met my future husband, Ross. He was stationed there as well and we ate in the same canteen. We were married in 1945, and in March 1946 I left England for Canada.

We were delayed for two or three days in Liverpool because there was a fire in the hold of the *Letitia*, the ship we were sailing on to Canada. Crossing the Irish Sea, many brides were seasick. I don't know whether it was hearing the band play, "Will Ye Know Come Back Again?" or the rough choppy sea—a combination of both perhaps.

Kathleen and Ross Anderson

The food was the main topic of conversation, and we enjoyed if after years of austerity. The *Letitia* travelled a southern route to avoid icebergs, and one day anchored to allow a steward to have his appendix removed. It took nine days to cross the Atlantic, and none of us were looking forward to another three to four days on a train.

It turned into a bit of a nightmare for me when I was told to alight at Belleville and I knew Ross was waiting in Toronto. I tried to explain this to the officer, but all he said was, "I'm sorry. But you can stay overnight at a Red Cross Hospital and catch the train to your destination tomorrow." I was just about in tears, and wondered what on earth to do. When we arrived in Belleville and I got off the train, very reluctantly, the first person I saw was my beloved. He had had the foresight to phone the Red Cross and they told him where I would be. I was so glad I was not one of those travelling to Vancouver, I don't think I could have stood that long ride. One lucky soul had no train journey at all; her husband met her in Halifax. . . . Envious sighs from us all. . . .

After the hustle and bustle of the War Office right in the midst of things, it was quite a contrast coming to this tiny village, nestled in the Haliburton Highlands of Ontario, surrounded by lakes and hills, with no paved roads, hydro, telephone or running water. More important to me was the fact that there was no pre-natal clinic. Surprisingly, there were no negative reactions from me. Spring was coming, also a baby, and I was with my husband. Everything was new and different.

My in-laws were marvellous and always have been. My mother-in-law drove me all over the countryside where I met so many nice people.

I was so fascinated with the abundance of food in the village grocery shops, and it wasn't long before food parcels were winging their way home. Like all war brides, I had no idea what a "shower" was. Ross and I were invited out one evening, and I noticed that we were sitting apart from everyone else, also I appeared to be the only woman smoking—apparently, this was something that wasn't done. Embarrassment! Beautiful gifts were handed to us along with an explanation of what it was all about. This was my introduction to a "shower."

I had never seen a wood stove and was petrified and positive I would burn the house down everytime I opened

58

the lid. And those dangerous stove pipes that at times turned red with heat, frightened me out of my wits. I wouldn't touch the oil lamps—I was sure they would explode, so during the winter months Ross lit them for me at noon. We carried all our water from a well and what a lovely washing machine I had. It was a gas one that jumped all over the kitchen floor. I sure got my exercise on wash days! The "privy" outside was our only "plumbing." Oh! Those cold winter mornings.

Two children were born to us during the first two years, both in a Red Cross Outpost Hospital. In 1948 I flew home with both boys and what a trip that turned into.

The first plane took us to Toronto, then another to Montreal where there was a twelve-hour delay. From there to Sydney, Nova Scotia, then another plane to Shannon, Ireland. A further delay there until finally, take-off for London. It was lovely to be in the family circle again, and I thought, "Oh I just can't leave here again and go back to Canada." But of course, I did.

We were quite isolated where we were living, and one needed to drive a car, so I decided to get my driver's license. When the examiner asked me how the brakes were, I answered, "Oooh! Well! You'll have to ask my husband." I got my license.

Many times I have been lonely, but who in their life hasn't been? But nostalgia is another thing which will remain with most of the war brides for always. One hears a song, especially if the vocalist is Vera Lynn, then memories of the war come flooding back; the Queen's Christmas message; phone calls to and from home; British magazines, and the tearful partings at the airport. But so much has made up for such moments: the joyful arrival of loved ones; their wonderful accents; and the pride in showing them our beautiful country we have chosen to live in; and the most important of all, our husbands and children that have made it all worthwhile to have been a "War Bride."

****

Irene and Bill Bracken
Ontario

I was born in London, England when my parents were managing the "Pembroke Arms" in the Earl's Court Road. Father died at the age of thirty-four when I was six. Mother later remarried and I was given three sisters and two brothers.

When war started I was employed as a bookkeeper with a firm situated in Shepherd's Bush. Later, I joined the Civil Defense and worked as a Red Cross nurse during the air raids in a mobile first-aid unit, a first-aid post in public air raid shelters. Later, I switched to hospital training at the West London Hospital in Hammersmith Road.

Invitations were sometimes put up on the nurses' notice board to attend tea dances sponsored by the Knights of Columbus centre near Bayswater Road in Kensington. They were held in a house that had been turned over as a place for servicemen to stay when on leave in London. This is where I met Bill. I had, at that time, made up my mind to remain single as I was not interested in marriage. But my mind was soon changed. We were married on March 11, 1944 in the church of Our Lady and St. Catherine which was later bombed to the ground.

Before marriage, I was amongst a group of nurses sent to Prewett Hospital near Basingstoke to prepare for the casualties expected from the Invasion of Europe. Bill was stationed in Aldershot at the time, so on alternate weekends we visited each other and did lots of rambling around the countryside on bicycles.

60

Irene and Bill Bracken

Later, Bill was sent to Holland and Germany with the
23rd Field Company, RCE, where he took part in
building Bailey Bridges, mine detecting, servicing
vehicles and even commandeering an old caravan to use as
a mobile shop.

At war's end, we were able to be together for quite
some time, until Bill received his orders to leave England
in October 1945. We were separated for ten months until

I was able to join him in August 1946 coming over on the *Queen Mary* and landing in Halifax on the 13th.

Bill met me in Toronto and we spent a few days with his parents. Then we left for Severn Falls in a car loaned to us by a friend. Bill had returned to the job he had when he was called up, which was an Ontario Hydro operator at the Big Chute power generating plant. There was no housing available except in a boarding house, so Bill bought an eleven-acre island down stream from the power house on the Severn River. There were a few summer cottages on the island, and he winterized the main one, and that was our first home.

Irene and Bill Bracken's home on Severn River, Ontario

The last few miles was a narrow, stony road through bush. At the end of it was a small-store-cum-post-office where he bought supplies, loaded them and luggage onto his boat, and started down the Severn River for a few miles. The scenery was beautiful.

The boat was once a steel life boat from a laker and converted for pleasure use. It was eighteen-feet long,

62

with an inboard motor, and had a built-on cabin. It was quite comfortable with a top speed of about ten miles per hour. But the engine was old, and we hadn't gone very far when it quit. We drifted around in the bay until Bill persuaded it to go again. By this time, the chief operator from the power plant was getting anxious as to our whereabouts and came up river looking for us. He escorted us to our destination—the Big Chute. There, I was invited into his home where his wife offered me tea which I gracefully declined, not without embarrassment, because I do not like it.

From there, we had to get our boat down to the lower level of the river by way of the marine railway. This was run by an Englishman who had been an officer in World War I, and a Scotsman who had been a sergeant, both strongly different characters. Just as we were going to the boat, Scotty came running over with news that a couple of rattle snakes had just been killed. The others around tried to silence him, obviously concerned about my reaction to this news, but I found it interesting and looked forward to this new life in the bush.

We got to our island, and home was a pleasant cottage with two bedrooms, large livingroom and a sun porch, all lined with tongue and groove B.C. fir. There was a room set aside for a bathroom, but nothing in it until Bill built in the bath, wash basin and toilet the following year. Until then, we used a "two-holer" outside, and a chemical toilet in the winter.

Bill worked three different shifts, and there was usually a seven day rest in between. He was paid once a month, and it took a whole day to go by boat to Midland to replenish supplies. When the freeze came, we had to be prepared and have supplies to last until the river thawed. It took me a while to get used to ordering large quantities of food.

The boat slip was under the living quarters, and Bill

63

Bill Bracken cutting boat out of ice on Severn River

had built a lovely large dock where we sat and sunned, after a swim in the lovely warm water.

That first year we entertained many visitors, and we soon found out that having a cottage on the Severn River made us a target for all sorts of people who thought they should visit us. We did what we could to make them welcome, but a low salary made it difficult to make ends meet and buy things necessary when beginning married life. The following spring, we planted a vegetable garden and the forest animals promptly ate the first shoots. We tried another location with better results.

The last of our guests that first year were a couple from Niagara Falls, the man an old friend of Bill's and his new wife. It was November, and after their first day, Mary looked around and said, "Irene, what is there to do around here?" Well! One just had to be content with the quiet life. No telephone, no radio, and of course no T.V. When Bill left for work with the boat, I was isolated with our one-year-old baby. Quite some change after being a part of a large family living in London, and working in a busy hospital.

So, the newlyweds decided to go hunting. Bill got the boat ready, and somehow Mary promptly fell off the dock into twelve feet of icy water dressed in winter clothing. As she rose to the surface, the men grabbed and pulled her out. We got her into the house, and I helped her towel down. The trouble was, she didn't bring enough clothes to change into, and I couldn't help her because I was 5'1" to her 5'10". Somehow we got her clothes dried as quickly as possible, and she was glad when it was time to go home. She never wanted to see the place again. But they did return the following summer when it was hot and the water warm.

As winter came, so came times of loneliness and a longing to see my family. But I was determined to look forward and not backward. A song I learned as a child came back to me over and over again, "Count your blessings, name them one by one, and it will surprise you what the Lord has done." And the blessings were many. My Bible was an inspiration, and there were quiet times of communion with my Lord Jesus.

The main Christmas celebration for this little Hydro colony was held at the log cabin school house. The children of the workers, about a dozen, had one teacher for the eight grades. These children entertained us, and Scotty dressed as Santa Claus and gave us gifts. There was a lovely Christmas tree, refreshments, and we all enjoyed ourselves immensely.

The second Christmas, the teacher asked if I would help out with the programme by acting as "Mrs. Wiggs of the Cabbage Patch." Since I weighed only one hundred pounds, it was obvious I needed to look more buxom. A cushion was used on my chest, a pillow for my behind, with an ample dress and apron over top. On the night of the play, my onstage appearance caused such an uproar amongst the audience, that I had to wait several minutes before commencing my lines. We really had fun entertaining ourselves, and at next to no cost, too.

When the snow and ice came, boating was out and skiing and skating in. I learned to ski with no more instruction than Bill telling me that it was easy. Just slide over the snow with the skiis, he said. Herring bone up hill and lean forward going down. All went well until late February, when I had a very nasty fall. My back was painful, but getting to a doctor would have involved great discomfort and difficulty. I took it easy the rest of the winter, and when we did get to the doctor's in May, X-rays showed there had been a bad break, but it had healed as well as it could have, even if there had been medical care.

The one thing I didn't find good in that next to perfect paradise, were the insects. With the warmth of spring, black flies came by the thousands, and hungrily attacked any exposed flesh for fresh blood. They stayed until the heat of mid-June cleared them away. Then came the hordes of mosquitoes who also welcomed my blood. Ants and roaches had designs on our food, therefore, everything had to be kept in tins and sealed containers. There was an endless variety of insects of all colours, shapes and sizes. Some useful, some destructive and some with stings like red hot needles.

Other island habitants made their share of noise; tree toads, crickets, ducks and loons, all had their trillings and croakings. The chipmunks loved teasing our cat and playing hide-go-seek. There was also a great variety of birds, and the cry of the whip-poor-will would sometimes carry on for ages during the night.

At first, I gave heed and avoided three-leaved plants which Bill informed me was poison ivy. He had previously entered hospital for a few days with a bad rash from this obnoxious weed. But what he pointed out looked much like strawberry leaves, and I found out later that that was exactly what they were and quite different from the other. At first I was a bit nervous about snakes, but found our local ones were harmless and ate insects and insect larvae, and anything that ate this had to be my friend. So when a family of water snakes took up residence under our dock, they were allowed to remain. And if they swam around when I did, it didn't bother me, although it startled some of our guests.

In those days the water was not polluted and fishing was good. We caught bass, pickerel and pike which were good eating and a great help for our meals and budget.

One of our neighbours ran a tourist camp further down the river off Gloucester Pool. He had a maple sugar bush, and in late winter and early spring, he collected the sap, and boiled it down in his special "sugar hut" and used the syrup to serve guests on their pancakes. He would invite everyone at "sugaring off" time, and we would gather round the sugar shack sampling the sticky delight.

Once a month the women would gather for a Women's Institute meeting. It was a small social event and kept our minds busy as we learned different skills. The men kept busy maintaining the boats, engines, and other equipment which had to be kept in good running order at all times. They helped each other build things like furniture, boats and trailers. There was also wood to be cut, and ice to be cut out of the bay to fill the ice house for the ice-boxes in our kitchens for the rest of the year.

Eventually a road was put through and that immediately opened the way for summer cottages, which were built by the hundreds and ended the quiet isolation. Modernization deleted the full staff from the power house which was made to operate by remote control.

We made several moves with the company, the last to

Niagara Falls where we stayed until Bill retired in December 1972.

I still have lots of relatives in England, although my mother and step-father are now dead. I could, I think, be quite happy living in England again, although after visiting, I am always ready to return to Canada and my own family.

We look back with fondness on those early island years. They are very special to us and left us with some very happy memories.

Five out of the seven years since Bill has been retired, we have gone south for the winter months. Our two children have done well with their lives and we have much to thank God for, as we are only pilgrims in this life, and we look ahead to what is next.

****

Frances and James Montgomery
Ontario

Born in Galway, Ireland, I came to Birmingham, England with my widowed mother when I was seven. When World War II started, I was seventeen and in training for private service. Wanting to do my part for the war effort, I tried to join the ATS then the WAAF but because of an eye defect I was turned down. I was accepted into the NAAFI canteen. And so began six years of hard work, long hours and working mainly in army and air-force camps throughout the midland area. It was at Long Marston RAF camp that I met my husband, James Montgomery, called "Monty" for short.

My mum and I were more like sisters than mother and daughter, and she had joined up as well and was stationed at the same camp. While attending a dance at the

68

sergeants' mess Christmas Eve, 1944, I was aware of someone watching me. I looked up into a pair of very blue eyes in a young and serious face of a tall brown-haired Canadian airman.

James Montgomery

Frances Montgomery

We exchanged shy smiles, and at that moment, everyone was joining hands for a dance. My mum took the airman by the hand and brought him into the circle next to me. When the dance ended he held tightly to my hand. We talked a bit, danced some more, then just past midnight mum once more joined in and said he could walk me back to the canteen. He was the only sober guy at the dance for he didn't drink.

This was the beginning of many dates. He was very quiet and my workmates often found him standing outside the canteen hoping to see me, for he was too shy to come in and ask for me. On our dates he always showed up with a box of Mars bars, and to this day they are still my favourite.

After three months of dating, Monty received word that he was to be posted to Topcliffe, Yorkshire, as a bombardier with 426 Thunderbird Squadron. One evening after a long walk we came back to camp and sat in the empty airmen's lounge before a blazing fire. Here, after several attempts, he asked me to marry him. It was about 2 a.m. and mum came looking for us scaring us half to death as she put her head through the open window and shouted, "What are you doing here at this hour?" I immediately burst into tears and said, "Monty has just asked me to marry him." To which mum replied, "Took him long enough to get the words out!"

We planned to be married in Stratford-on-Avon, but ran into problems because of different religious denominations. Monty said he would get the camp Padre in Yorkshire to perform the ceremony. He had a rough time rounding up his crew. They were on leave in London, but he finally located them and persuaded his navigator to be our best man.

In the meantime, Monty had transferred to Topcliffe, and this meant that mum and I had to travel to Yorkshire for the wedding. We did a lot of scrounging around and gathered enough clothing coupons to purchase a beautiful white silk wedding gown and white shoes. Then all food rations were pooled to get enough ingredients for the wedding cake because all camp personnel were determined I should have a reception when I got back.

Transferred again, Monty was now stationed at Dishforth. Mum and I sat on our suitcases all the way from Birmingham to Yorkshire, arriving at 7:30 a.m. in what appeared to be the wilds of Yorkshire. We found a small café, not yet open, and persuaded the not-too-happy owner to make us a cup of tea. We found the bus to take us to the aerodrome then walked miles lugging our suitcases until we located the guard house. They sent for

Monty and offered us some tea that was so strong it almost poisoned us.

My hero arrived only to inform us that the Padre would not marry us because he, Monty, was not yet twenty-one. This, and the fact that we hadn't had any breakfast, left me very weak and ready to faint, so Monty went looking for some food and came back with a terrible combination—a package of sweet biscuits and a can of cold chicken. How we have laughed about that over the years.

We now decided to try a civil ceremony to take place in Thirsk on June 12, 1945, two days later. James, as I now called him, wasn't allowed off camp until next day so mum and I went looking for a place to stay. We found a room over a café—not great, but the owner was very kind and the place clean.

James got a pass the next day, and that evening mum conveniently went to the pictures leaving us alone for a few hours on the eve of our wedding. We were sitting in the sitting room and as we embraced we kept hearing a soft giggle. We noticed a partition at the end of the room, and two little blonde heads peering over the top—were we embarrassed! At two minutes to midnight James left—old superstition about not seeing the bride after midnight until the ceremony. I went looking for a bouquet the next morning, and in my excitement, forgot to get a corsage for mum.

Because we were to be married in a registry office located above a harness shop, my lovely wedding gown wasn't quite "the thing," so I settled for a short blue dress and coat I had with me. Imagine my predicament when I unpacked my new shoes and found odd sizes, one size three, the other size four. Squeezing my foot into the three, I hobbled to the taxi which was taking us to Thirsk. The best man and mum were the only people at

71

the wedding and when the registrar asked James if he wanted the ten shilling ceremony or a more expensive one, my dear one said the ten shilling one would do!

This was to be the day my new husband was to take his first alcoholic drink . . . or so he thought. When he ordered them at the hotel, he was informed they only had ginger ale. So the bride and groom were toasted with "pop." At the luncheon afterward, poor James was so nervous he tipped all the salt from the shaker over his bangers and mash!

Two hours after our wedding, James left. He was being shipped home to Canada, and then to the Japanese war zone. It was pouring rain when we left the hotel, and I can still see him running down the road after the camp bus, his best man hanging out the back trying to catch his hand and pull him aboard. It was ten months before I saw him again. How many brides can say they slept with their mother on their wedding night? I can!

I received my papers to sail for Canada in April 1946. On the fourth day of that month, I left mum and all my relatives and friends in a flood of tears and boarded the train in Birmingham for London. I found myself in a carriage full of servicemen, trying to hold back the tears when a sailor pulled out his hanky and said, "Have a good cry girlie." When he found I was heading for Canada, he said I had a right to a good "blubber" going so far from home.

That night in a London hostel, all was quiet for a while, then one by one the sobs started and ended in wholesale wailing with all of us vowing to return home the next morning. Next day we had second thoughts and made up our minds to go through with the deal for better or worse. We boarded the *Aquitania* in Southampton to the music of the Salvation Army band as they played "Wish Me Luck as you Wave me Goodbye" and "Auld Lang Syne," causing more tears to flow.

On board there was lots of chatter and excitement; wonderful food, and after six years of rationing, it was like manna from heaven. Our five days on board gave us time for some deep thinking, also to make new friends.

It was sad to see some of the war brides left stranded with no one to meet them, but wonderful to watch husbands and wives meeting and seeing their joy at starting a new life.

I boarded the train out of Halifax bound for Kingston, Ontario. Many brides were heading for the west and we were all very excited. I remember peering out of the train window looking for Indian tents and Indians and feeling so very disappointed when I didn't see any. When we pulled into Montreal, my name was called to disembark. Doing so, I found that James had come to meet me and I walked right past him, not recognizing him in civilian clothes.

We spent a week in Montreal having the honeymoon we missed in England. What a delight to see stores full of so many good things.

We proceeded to Smiths Falls, Ontario—a lovely clean town in the Ottawa Valley. I felt at home right away after I got over the nervousness of meeting all my new relatives. My husband lived with his grandparents, his father having died many years ago. His mother lived in Kingston. I learned much later that she and James' sister waited hours on the Kingston platform meeting each train that brought war brides. There had been a misunderstanding about my place of arrival.

I now started calling my husband Jim, as did all his family. His grandfather was a dear man and I loved him right away. Gramma and Jim's aunt were very kind to me and we became great friends.

In no time I had become acquainted with half the population of Smiths Falls. Jim had started work with the railroad and was away from home quite a lot so I was glad of all my new friends. There were also quite a few war brides in town, so we formed a club. This continued until we started raising families, then we were too busy to carry it on.

My first winter in Canada was quite something. Never having seen so much snow it was a big thrill for me to set out after a bad storm, dressed in Gramp's boots and trousers and Gram's old beaver coat, to meet my friend Molly, a Scottish war bride. As we skipped over the drifts, the man on the snow plough called out that we should go home before we got buried in them. But we just laughed and continued on to town to buy a "novelty" drink called a milk shake.

It took time to learn the value of Canadian money, also the different name for some items. I had quite a time getting Jim undershirts. I asked for vests and was shown a variety of waist-coats before finally getting the right garment.

Four years passed, and I began to give up hope of ever having a family. But on Valentine's Day 1949, our first son, Peter, was born. Then in rapid succession the two girls and another son. We now had a millionaire's family but alas! not the millions to go with them. Although work was slow for Jim and money scarce, we managed to have a lot of fun with our little family. Jim's relatives and my mum who lives with us now, were very good to us. And so the years fled by and our children grew into fine adults and started families of their own. Only our oldest is single, as of now.

A few years ago, we all moved to Ottawa, with James working for Ontario Housing. Our daugher Chris will be leaving soon to live in the States as she married an American boy.

Life goes on and the tall brown-haired boy and the slim blonde girl have grown to be slightly plump, almost silvery-haired grandparents with darling little ones to love and spoil a little.

I have never returned to England. I hope to someday for a holiday. Canada is my country and I wouldn't want to change that.

****

Mid Atlantic

Canada's big and Canada's new, and Canada's far away,
Has Canada anything half as fun as Epsom on Derby day?

Canada's days are warm and dry and Canada's skies are clear,
Does Canada know what it's like to fish from
Southend Pier?

Canada works and Canada plays but always
Canada grows,
Can Canada show me anything as dear as an
English rose?

Canada's hearts are young and strong and I am one
of them now,
Does Canada know how the sparrows sing as they
follow an English plough?

Canada's plains are broad and long and Canada's
lakes are deep,
Does Canada know of the Sussex downs and the
bleat of English sheep?

Canada's coming closer now and we'll soon see
the Maple trees,

But part of my heart has been left behind in the wash
of the English seas.

Author unknown

****

Barbara and Ron Tonkin
Ontario

Lord Beaverbrook was Lord Privy Seal during the war,
and I worked several times in his Whitehall office. I was
a telephone operator with the Civil Service, transferred to
PBX Control as a relief operator for all government
exchanges. This led to work in all branches of the War
Office, Air Ministry, Admiralty, Scotland Yard, Treasury
and Horseguards. I was seventeen when I left school and
started this interesting position in the London area right in
the hubbub of everything.

Two years later I met Ron on a blind date. My friend
had met a Canadian soldier while at a dance in Covent
Garden and suggested to him that next time he came on
leave, he bring a friend for us to meet. The local railway
station was our rendezvous. My friend came with me for
moral support. She was a stout girl, and Ron confessed
to me afterward that when he saw us, he hoped it wasn't
the fat one! I took him home to meet my family that
night. Romance took it's course ending in marriage in
July 1945 and a honeymoon in Cornwall where Ron's
people came from originally.

Ron returned to Canada early in 1946 with me
following in June—very pregnant—on the *Aquitania*.
I had a thoroughly enjoyable trip and was the only one out
of eight in the cabin not seasick. But on the train I
bought apples, made a pig of myself, and then WAS
sick!

It was Dominion Day when I arrived in Timmins, northern Ontario where Ron met me. It had rained, stopped, and then turned incredibly hot. I never expected Canada to be so hot! The different style of housing made an impression, as well as the sidewalks. In those days they were mostly wooden. I remember distinctly the smell of gasoline. Perhaps the heat made it over-powering, but whatever—the street's smelled different.

I was quite nervous when I had to go shopping alone and use the Canadian currency. But after a week or two, I had no trouble whatsoever spending it. I had to use a coal and wood stove for awhile, and thought it quite primitive and it took some getting used to. During summer I used a rangette which I thought was quite a comical set-up. When the top elements were in use, I couldn't use the oven, and vice-versa. For the inexperienced cook such as I, this was some challenge! The old cook stove, I grew to love and was grateful many a cold morning for it's fast warmth. Even cooking on it became a joy once I learned how to stoke it and jiggle the damper.

Our son was born in the October, and that winter I was very excited at seeing my first snow fall—a novelty that has since worn off. Also, I tried to get to the store in snow that had drifted so badly it got into my boots. I was wet through and cried with frustration when back in the house. The moral to this was—wear slacks in deep snow.

I was very homesick, and cried everytime I received a letter from my family, yet I do not recall being miserable. We lived in Timmins for three and one-half years when we decided to sell up and return to London, England. Of course, I was to blame for this. I found Timmins such a small town, in comparison, but now I wish I had just taken a trip home which would have rid my system of the homsickness. We were home only

77

three weeks when I confessed to Ron that I was home-sick for Canada.

By then, his money was tied up, and we had to stay. I went to work as a telephone operator again to help save enough money for our return fares.

I was very happy to get back to Timmins arriving with twenty dollars in my pocket. Ron had returned a month earlier to get settled and find a job.

Barbara Tonkin, Timmins, Ontario

We had one more child, a daughter. Now, of course, both are married with families of their own. When my dad died in 1965, we invited mum to live with us as I was an only child. She accepted, and still does live with us, now a very active eighty-four years.

We've had some "ups and downs" but who hasn't. But I've never regretted meeting and marrying that Canadian soldier—still love the guy!

****

The girl who lived next door to me in England asked me one day if I would accompany her to Aldershot. She was meeting her boyfriend who had asked her to bring a girlfriend for his buddy to make a foursome. I agreed and this is how Tom and I met. It was January 1940 and Tom was in the Canadian Signals, 1st Division, so he had not been too long in England. This date led to many more and we married in April 1941.

It was a small church wedding, and because Tom had to be back in camp two days after, we postponed our honeymoon until his next leave.

Blackpool was teeming with billeted Air Force personnel when we arrived there later on, and not having booked accommodation ahead, the only place we could get was a room with a mattress on the floor!

I had changed my job from factory work to making field kitchens for the army. Later, the country needed girls for the Land Army and I enlisted, staying with them until our son Tom Jr. was born in April 1942.

My husband was in Italy when Douglas, our second son, was born Christmas Day, 1943. In January 1944, I received a telegram from my father-in-law asking if I could get to Canada as Tom's mother was very ill.

Taking the telegram with me, I went to Canada House in London, and arrangements for my journey commenced. However, it wasn't until October of that year that these were finalized. My parents came to the station with us, and it was terrible to part from them. My brother had been killed at Normandy in June, and the children and I were all they had left.

Many brides and children boarded the train for Gourock, Scotland, and we embarked on the *Ile de France* leaving port on October 13. I made lots of friends on

79

Bea and Tom Redford

board; the food was good, and the boys and I were good
sailors.

Arriving in Halifax on October 25, the Red Cross took
the children to nurseries while we went through

immigration. I sent telegrams to Tom and my parents to let them know we had arrived safely, and another to my in-laws letting them know what time we would be arriving. There were two other brides and their children going to the same town, so we travelled together.

We changed trains in Toronto, and by this time we were wondering how much further we had to go, for the travelling seemed endless. The children were getting restless and fretful and who could blame them? I kept thinking of my mum and dad, and wishing also that Tom was with me. The closer we came to our destination, the more nervous I became wondering if his parents would like me.

What a wonderful welcome we received! The Mayor and his council rushed to greet us; the local newspaper crew took pictures, and my new mum and dad were waiting in the station waiting room. Tom's mum, far from well, had asthma very badly, but they greeted us so warmly that my fears were groundless. Riding in the car to the house, I noticed how lovely the town was; the beautiful trees that lined the streets and the well kept lawns. Our new home was lovely too. It looked so big with large lawns and gardens and stately old trees.

The glass doors in the diningroom fascinated young Tom, and I was forever wiping away his finger marks. It was lonely, for Tom was an only child but many friends came to welcome us. I joined the church, the Evening Guild and helped with the Senior Citizens. With the work at home and looking after the boys, my life was full.

The first time I went downtown on my own, I went into a shop and asked for a reel of white cotton. The clerk came back with a bolt of white material. We had a good laugh when I explained what I wanted.

One evening the Guild had a "potluck" supper and we were asked to bring something. I made a lemon pie. On

81

the way to the church my friend said, "What did you make?" I replied, "A lemon tart." She was so relieved when I opened my box and saw the pie. She thought I had made a little tart for myself.

The first fall of snow was very exciting. Dad made a sleigh and took the boys for rides. And I made my very first snowman in the middle of the front lawn. I was so proud of it. That Christmas we had a real Christmas tree—a first for me. We had so much fun decorating it, and oh! how pretty it looked standing in the big window dressed with different coloured balls and lights.

But for all the gaiety I was terribly homesick and missed Tom so much. There was a lot of snow that winter, and one bitterly cold morning at 4 a.m., mum took very ill with asthma again and could not breathe. The doctor came and said she must stay in bed. A month later, dad took a bad heart attack. With mum upstairs and dad sleeping downstairs, things became most hectic and I came to the point where I just could not cope.

The Mayor and doctor sent a letter to Ottawa to see if they could get Tom home. The army authorities sent someone to see me and agreed I had too much to cope with on my own. When Tom arrived home in May, dad had gone back to work, and mum was well enough to sit up. What a wonderful reunion that was! The very first day Tom was home, Doug took his first three steps.

In the December Tom's mum passed away. She had been confined to bed for three months. I was exhausted and expecting another baby. In May 1946, our third son, James, was born, and it wasn't until he was three that I made my first trip home to England. I was so homesick for the sight of my own folk and all things dear and familiar. It was a lovely visit, but as homesick as I had been, I was glad to return to Canada.

While I was away Tom had bought a farm. I hated the loneliness of farm life especially during the winter. The following year I was in a bad car accident and hospitalized for quite some time. My mother came to Canada to stay with us for a period of time and it was lovely to have her.

Our last child was a girl, and we were delighted. The children are all grown now, the boys married with families of their own. We've had our share of illness and anxious moments, but who hasn't?

We moved from the farm and back into town in November 1962 and it was so good to be with all our old friends, to see the old faces which, like ours, are getting older.

The people of Ingersoll made all their war brides very welcome, and we in return, hope we have contributed toward the community that we have, over the years, grown to love so much.

****

Anonymous

When I was eight years old and my brother thirteen, our father died very suddenly. Just after my fourteenth birthday in November, 1940, our mother was killed in an air-raid.

At the time, due to the bombing of London, mum had sent me to stay with an aunt and uncle in Bogner Regis on the south coast of England. My brother Tom had enlisted in the RAF at the outbreak of war and became a Hurricane fighter pilot. I am still proud to say that he was, as Winston Churchill said, "One of the few."

The death of mum was a very bad period of my life. It left me with a feeling of despair when I thought of Tom and I, orphans, with no living relatives other than the ones where I now lived.

Aunt Jessie and Uncle George had no children of their

own, and I knew they loved me as their own daughter. I finished school just after my sixteenth birthday and applied for a position with a small insurance company where I stayed until I left for Canada.

I suppose I was what one would refer to as a quiet reserved girl. I didn't go out very much. The occasional picture show and the odd dance was about my limit. I preferred to stay home and read or sew.

I had become quite friendly with another girl in the office, and one evening during the summer of 1943, she asked me to go roller skating with her. I hadn't done too much of this and thought it would be fun. I was inching my way around the rink when suddenly I was bumped from behind and sent sprawling. This is how I met Steve. He was skating backwards and didn't see me until it was too late. He helped me up and was full of apologies, and although I wasn't hurt, I was shaken up a bit. He offered to walk my friend and I home and after we had said goodnight to her, he asked if he could see me again.

We made a date for the following Saturday evening. We were well suited, or so I thought because, not only was he very quiet, he also enjoyed reading and walking. Steve told me he had lost his mother through cancer a couple of years before the war. Immediately I felt compassion for this rather somber young man and was drawn to him more as the weeks passed. I do not know whether my aunt and uncle liked him; I know they found him too serious for a young man of twenty-one.

I quickly came to his defense and said he was helping to fight a war, and war was a serious business. That Christmas, after my seventeenth birthday, Steve asked me to marry him. I did love him, I was sure. He was such a sad person, primarily because his mother's death had affected him deeply. Also, his father's remarriage to a

84

woman with a totally different personality to that of his own mother, had upset him a great deal. His step-mother had two children of her own, both younger than Steve, and once I remarked how nice it must be for him to have a ready-made brother and sister after being an only child for so long. His reply was, "Oh yeah! So nice that I joined the army as quickly as I could." I gathered from this remark that he didn't like the ready-made family, and was reluctant to probe deeper.

Aunt Jessie declared I was far too young to marry and urged me to wait. Because the routine of medicals required by the Canadian army took time, Steve asked her if she would be agreeable for us to marry on my eighteenth birthday. I didn't want to get married in November. Such a dreary month for a wedding. Aunt Jessie relented, and we were married in the September.

I did not know too much about Steve or his home except that they lived on a ranch outside of Calgary. He never spoke about it except to say that it had been a happy home when his mother was alive. I did write to his father, but never received any answer. I wrote again thinking perhaps the first letter was never received, but again, no reply. Steve's only comment was that his father was probably too busy and his stepmother wouldn't bother. I found this hard to understand and convinced myself that Steve was too critical of them.

When he left for Italy, I missed him very much and found that he too, was a poor correspondent. I had applied for transportation to Canada, and left at the end of March 1945 on the *Franconia*. I loathed saying good-bye to Tom and my aunt and uncle. They had been so good to me and I knew they were heartbroken.

I enjoyed the Atlantic crossing but hated the train ride to Calgary which seemed to go on and on. When I watched reunions between wives and husbands, I wished Steve were waiting in Calgary for me. I had written and told his father of my arrival, and sent a telegram from Halifax. I felt very strange and uncomfortable, but kept telling myself that everything would be all right once I was there.

I didn't know who to look for at the Calgary station and sought a Red Cross booth, gave them my name and asked if anyone was looking for me. The lady said there had been someone earlier and to wait while she paged them over the loud speaker.

A young lad about seventeen or eighteen came to the booth complete with cowboy boots, hat and chewing gum. My first thought was, how typical of a western movie. My second thought, how scruffy he looked. The Red Cross lady told him who I was, and without as much as a smile, let alone a "hello," he picked up one of my suitcases and marched toward the exit. The lady gave me a card and said, "If you ever need help dear, phone this number." Rather astonished, I thanked her and picked up my other suitcase and ran after my "welcoming committee." He was standing by a tin Lizzie of a truck waiting for me. He took the case and threw it in the back alongside the other. We climbed in and off we went. In all this time he had not spoken one word and the silence was most embarrassing. Unable to stand it any longer I said, "Would you mind telling me your name and are you related to Steve?"

"I'm Brad, his half-brother," was the reply. What a surly character he was.

I asked about the ranch, Steve's dad, his sister and mother, and got the briefest of replies. Ruth, the sister, was nineteen, a few months older than myself, and I cheered up a little thinking I would have a friend.

The scenery was desolate with snow still on the ground. Houses were few and far apart. For every mile we travelled, my fears increased, and I began to wish I was back home in my aunt's comfortable house snuggled in front of the fire. We drove down a dirt road for a mile or so when Brad turned into a gravelled driveway that led to a dilapidated wooden house that badly needed a coat of paint.

My heart sank into my shoes as I looked at it. Where was the nice house Steve had told me about? Jamming on the brakes and jumping out, Brad said, "You're here."

A slovenly looking woman seated at a littered kitchen table looked up as we entered. "So yer made it," was her greeting. I tried to smile and act bravely as I whispered, "How do you do?" She ignored me and yelled, "Ruthie. Come 'ere and meet yer new sister-in-law." Ruthie came, a replica of her mother and just as sullen as her brother. I can't describe how I felt at that moment. All I know is, I wanted to run, and keep running until I was home. The place was a mess! It didn't look as if it had ever seen a broom or water. The furniture had once been cared for, I'm sure.

How many times does one say, "Oh! If only I had known!"? I was to say this over and over again during the year that followed. I worked like a slave cleaning that house while those two lazy bitches sat, smoked and drank beer. I thought I would have had a friend in Steve's dad, but in him I saw a broken, defeated, silent man who had taken to drink. In the one time I did get him alone he said he never had got over the shock of losing Steve's mother. And I thought, no, neither has Steve. This second rebound marriage was a terrible mistake and resented by his son. And when Steve joined the army at the outbreak of war and left home, the poor man felt that there wasn't anything left. I felt so sorry for him and told him things would be different once Steve was home. He gave me a strange, odd look and turned away.

There was no family love in this home at all. Steve's

dad hardly spoke to anyone and I couldn't understand why he didn't throw them all out, because Ruthie and Brad fought continuously and Millie, the mother, made it worse with her interference. I didn't know how long I was going to be able to cope with this kind of life, and longed for the day when my husband would be there.

I had become a "maid of all work," and if one wonders why I allowed it to happen, it was because I could not stand to live in filth. If I didn't clean, no one else did.

In October Steve came home and no one was happier than I. If I thought him quiet and withdrawn when I first met him, he was more so now. It didn't seem to bother him that the entire running of the house fell onto my shoulders. My happiness was short lived for he was so distant and would not talk about Italy or anything that had to do with army life. I kept asking him if we could go out for an evening, for I was starved for friendship and the company of intelligent people of my own age. I was told to stop nagging. In desperation I spoke to his dad and asked him for help. "What d'you want me to do?" was the answer I got. I felt helpless and wondered how it would all end.

When I was in the house alone with those two despicable women, they constantly made fun of my accent and criticized everything I did. In front of the men, they ignored me. I would not let them intimidate me, and tried hard not to let it depress me, but for more times than I care to remember, I ended up crying my heart out in the bedroom.

There was no help from Steve even though his relationship with his step-mother, Brad and Ruthie was one of utter distaste. It was hard to believe this was happening.

I wanted so much to get in touch with the Red Cross lady but there was no phone in the house. I didn't drive and when I asked to be taken into Calgary, my request was denied. Millie and Ruth went once every two or three weeks to shop, but I was never invited. I was treated like a prisoner. Once I insisted on going, and what did they do? Stayed home and left early next morning without my knowing.

In November, Steve got a job in a granary and he used the truck for transportation. This cheered me up a bit and I thought we would now be able to move to a place of our own. I clung to that foolish thought with hope although I doubted it would ever happen.

With the new job, Steve didn't seem quite so morose. He even suggested we drive into Calgary to do some shopping. I was so excited, just like a kid on her first picnic. We did have a good day and Steve seemed to enjoy it too. I even bought Christmas gifts: socks for the men; cologne for Ruthie; and a pair of stockings for Millie . . . hers always had a run in them. I was so happy, that calling the Red Cross seemed rather silly. If I could have foreseen what lay ahead, I would have.

My first Christmas in Canada was terrible. I was so homesick, oh! so very homesick, especially when Millie and Ruthie found fault with their presents.

I wasn't given anything, nor was my nineteenth birthday remembered. There was quite a bit of drinking and another fight started. I tried to get Steve away from it but he shook me off and told me to mind my own business. When I stood up and retaliated with, "Don't you dare speak to me like that," he hit me! No one ever struck me before, and I was horrified. I ran to our bedroom and slammed the door. This was it! I had had all I could take. I was shaking and frightened when I realized it was never going to be any different.

Sitting on the chair by the window, I looked out onto fields and fields of snow and my heart broke. I could hear the fight still going on in the kitchen, and I heard dad telling Steve he ought to apologize to me. Steve told him to mind his own business too. I was convinced I had married a mad man. Somehow I had to get into Calgary and phone that lady. But how? My eyes fell onto another farm house about three fields away. I didn't know the people for I had never met anyone in the months I had been in Canada. But I was determined to get to that farmhouse if it killed me. Surely they would have a phone or help me get to Calgary. I had to try.

For the next two nights I slept on the couch. I wanted nothing to do with Steve in his drunken state. Nor did I care who knew it. After Steve left for work on the Thursday morning, and before anyone else was up, I threw what clothes I needed into one of my suitcases and crept out into the icy cold morning. It was still dark as I trudged down the road. My feet were soaking from the deep snow for I had no snow boots. It was further than I had anticipated, but I was determined to get there, especially when I saw the lights go on in the farmhouse. Although my suitcase was not heavy, my arms were aching and I was ready to drop by the time I reached the door.

These people were kindness itself. They took me in, fed me, and listened to my troubles. They had been on very friendly terms with Steve's mother and father, but after the mother's death and the father's remarriage things were never the same. With their help and that of the Red Cross, I arrived back in England in January 1946.

Before I left, I wrote a letter to Steve telling him it was all over and I could not live in the manner he expected of me. The Red Cross lady, as I have referred to her all through this story, for I did not know her name, delivered the letter personally, for I was afraid other eyes would read it first.

He never tried to contact me during the brief stay in Calgary. I thought he might, but was relieved he did not.

With the help of my family, the heartbreak and
hardship of that year gradually eased as the months
passed. I never heard from Steve again, not even when I
started divorce proceedings. Mine was not a story book
romance with the "happily ever after" ending. Perhaps I
was too young to cope; confused compassion for love. I
really don't know. Maybe we were both too young. I
do know we were two people caught in a web of
conflicting circumstance and neither of us could find a
way out, or knew how.

****

Thoughts on Leaving England

We've left our "weald" and "downs" and "fens,"
The moors and northern lakes.
We've left behind the local pub,
"No beers" . . . "sold outs" . . . the daily rub
Of queues, and suchlike mundane things.
Shed a tear perhaps for the home of Kings,
London, the ballet, Wigmore hall.
The costermonger, bomb scarred St. Paul.
To the land of coke, the nickel and dime,
We wend our way . . . may fate be kind.
We follow the lead Columbus gave.
Bride, babe and child, o'er the rolling wave
To Canada.

Author unknown

****

In October 1943, Jack and I met at a forces dance in the Caledonian Hotel, Inverness, Scotland, where my girlfriend and I were on leave from the ATS. Jack and I danced together all evening and went out for tea the next afternoon in a foursome, the other two being my friend and an army pal of Jack's. We said our farewells after tea, thinking we would never see each other again, although I did give Jack my home address. A few months later he showed up there one weekend while on leave, and we got engaged there and then.

Irene Mitchell and ATS Company in England

We decided to get married in August 1944 in a village church close to where I was stationed with the ATS College Staff, in Bagshot, Surrey. Incidentally, before the war, this was the country home of the Duke of Connaught, one time Governor General of Canada. I spent three happy years in that lovely, stately old home and was able to hitch-hike home to London almost every weekend to visit my parents.

When the buzz bombs got too bad in London, my mother, married sister and baby were evacuated to Windlesham, a village close to Bagshot, and my dad commuted every weekend. When I went to see the vicar in the Windlesham church about publishing the banns, he was quite perturbed about my marrying a Canadian serviceman. Seems he had recently married one who already had a wife in Canada and was now "doing time" for the dastardly deed. After the vicar had read all our credentials, we set the time for 2 p.m. August 12.

Preparations proved to be quite hectic. Undoubtedly an ordinary dress would have to do, but my mother had always looked forward to a white wedding for both her daughters. All the girls in my ATS company presented me with part of their allotment of clothing coupons; mother purchased the only piece of white satin to be bought in the village store; a resident offered to make the dress and insisted on loaning me an orange blossom head dress; someone else baked the cake with donations of fruit from various sources, and the village florist promised to make a bouquet out of any flowers that were available. Everyone was so kind to us. We were even invited to spend our honeymoon at the home of a couple whose only son was a POW in Germany. We were truly grateful to those dear people.

A few days before the wedding, Jack wrote from his base in Scotland to say that all leave had once again been cancelled and the wedding would have to be postponed until the following Saturday. I was absolutely shattered! It had been difficult enough getting things arranged without this. When I told my Commanding Officer what had happened, she said with grim determination, "Well! The Canadian army can't do that to us!" Grabbing my hand, she marched us to the switchboard where she told the operator on duty to get through to Jack's Company Commander in Inverness. She then proceeded to give him a dressing down I shall never forget. It was really quite hilarious. With feet planted firmly on the ground, one hand on her hip and eyes flashing fire, she said, "Now look here. We have a wedding arranged for this Saturday. I have given all my company special passes to attend, and whether you like it or not, it's utterly impossible for my corporal (me) to change her plans at this late date."

While this was going on, I was whispering to her, "Don't let him think it's a shotgun wedding, please. I don't HAVE to get married!" So, Jack was rushed by jeep to the railway station clutching a seventy-two hour pass in one hand and his only pair of pyjamas in the other with his COs promise that he would wire him a ten day leave if he could. He did. God bless him!

Jack arrived the night before the wedding, and at 2 p.m. the following afternoon my father, and I in all my finery, were driven to the church. We were met at the door by a little old lady who was replacing the verger who had been "called up." In a bit of a tizzy herself, she didn't bother to check to see if the groom and vicar were at the altar, and she signalled the organist to begin the Wedding March. Dad and I were halfway down the aisle when I noticed Jack wasn't there. In a panic I hissed at dad, "Where's Jack?" Out of the corner of his mouth he hissed back, "I don't know. He left for the church ages ago." The church was full, and I was sure the people were beginning to think the groom had had second thoughts.

We reached the altar steps and stood there like a couple of fools. I felt terrible and wanted to run, when suddenly the vestry door opened, and Jack and the vicar appeared. Jack looked across the church at me and promptly tripped down the vestry steps. I had assumed he knew that I would be decked out in the traditional white, but afterward he said he hadn't known, and the sight of that apparition was a bit of a shock, and he lost his footing. I also found out later why he wasn't at the altar when I arrived. The vicar was still doubtful about marrying us and gave Jack a real "third degree." He apparently insisted on going through all our papers again, and was finally convinced that Jack hadn't any other wives tucked away. The ceremony was all we could have hoped for, and it was a real thrill to step into the bright sunshine and see the long guard-of-honour composed of my ATS Company as well as several male and female officers who had come to wish us luck.

Irene and Bill Mitchell

Jack returned to his home in Vancouver in January 1946, and I followed in June. The journey from Halifax was a bit of a nightmare—so long, and awfully hot. Halfway across Canada the water system broke down, and mothers with babies were told to throw soiled diapers out of the window. Closer to Vancouver, the lights failed, and we groped about in the dark trying to make ourselves presentable to meet our new families.

At 1 a.m. we reached Vancouver (still without lights), the most dirty, dishevelled looking group of brides and children you ever did see! Our clothes and make-up all awry . . . what a beginning!

Jack had managed to get a housekeeping room in an old hotel in downtown Vancouver. Places were hard to get and we felt most fortunate that we had at least one room, hot as it was, and the district very noisy. At first I thought I would never be able to stand it. I wept a lot and thought of my home in England; the cool sea breeze; the green grass and our garden with it's profusion of flowers. But we stuck it out until better quarters became available.

The very first supper I cooked was quite amusing, but not so at the time. I wasn't much of a cook in those days, and decided I couldn't go far wrong with sausages. In the local butcher shop I bought the smoothest, brightest coloured sausages I had ever seen. When I got back to our room, I unwrapped them and thought how different Canadian sausages were from those of war-time England. When it came time to cook them, I placed them in the frying pan, turned up the gas, and blue smoke started to fill the already hot room. I couldn't understand what was wrong, and burst into tears of utter frustration. Jack came home at this crucial moment and said, "What on earth is happening in here?" Through tears I said, "It's these stupid sausages. They're burning and I've only got them on a low burner, I can't turn it down anymore." He started to laugh as he looked into the pan and cried, "Sausages my foot! They're wieners!" I had been frying those lovely smoothed skinned "sausages" in their cellophane wrappers! No wonder the air was blue, and not just from smoke either. Of course I had never even seen or heard of a wiener before, let alone cook them. It took years to live that down.

After that first trying summer, things went a lot more smoothly and we haven't done too badly over the years. I have been back to England several times, and Jack and I have done a fair amount of travelling throughout this lovely continent, but it's always nice to come home again.

****

Charlotte and Ken Farrow
Ontario

Ken and I were pen pals during 1944, and in October of that year he came to see me before leaving for Canada owing to his physical status. This visit started a chain of events that was to change my life and take me thousands of miles away from my family and friends. After five days together we knew we wanted to marry. Ken went back to camp and we only saw each other on two more weekends.

We were married on February 15, 1945, and after a four day honeymoon, Ken sailed for Canada. All told, we had been together for two weeks. To marry after such a short time was shock enough for my mum, but to go all the way to Canada . . . well! I don't think she ever thought I would leave her. But I did on June 7, 1945 on Leeds railway station looking forlorn and dazed. I was so excited at the time that I didn't realize what was happening, but in the months that followed, I was to remember that moment all too clearly.

I boarded a gray ship in Liverpool, and for some unknown reason I was classified as a pregnant bride. I tried to explain this was a mistake, but to no avail. I was treated royally and enjoyed the trip and accepted my good fortune at being waited upon . . . what bliss!

On June 14 I was in Toronto, and a Red Cross member put me on a train and told the conductor to put me off at Dobbington. It could have been anywhere; no one had heard of it. After a five hour journey, I stepped from the train, suitcase and trunk at my side, and not a soul to meet me. I think my heart stopped as I said to myself, "My God! What have I done!" Then the station master's wife came out and asked me my name. Confirming this she said, "Get back on the train dear. Ken is meeting you at Tara." Well, Tara! Where in hell was that? Sounded like something from "Gone with the Wind." The conductor got the luggage and myself back onto the train, and soon we were at Tara, and there was Ken and I was home.

The first day I spent in the barn was quite an event. All kinds of animals were staring at me; I knew they were going to trample me to death—I could see it in their eyes. Ken gently persuaded me to get a stool and pail and sit down between two cows. Boy! What a feeling crouched between two large, warm, smelly cows! They kept turning around to look at me with eyes so big and round, chewing their cuds and wondering what was going on. So started my day as a milk-maid, pail between my knees . . . squeeze, pull, squeeze, pull. Looking at me Ken said, "Once you get the rhythm, you'll be okay." Famous last words! The cow's tail, which had been lying in the wet gutter, suddenly swished around and smacked me soundly on the side of the head. With eyes smarting from wet manure, my knees relaxed, the pail dropped onto the cement floor, milk (the little I had worked so hard for) ran into the gutter, and the cows started jumping around from all the noise and confusion. Well, that was the signal for me to get out of there. So ended my first day.

Charlotte and Ken Farrow

It wasn't so bad after that. An understanding husband
and great neighbours helped me through the first year as
a farm wife. Cooking for a great number is something
I'll always remember.

Over thirty years have passed since I came to Canada
and I still think back to that day on Leeds station platform and see my mum standing there. So many times I
have said, "Oh mum! How I wish you were here." One
sister and one brother and their families have since made

their homes here too, so I do not feel so cut off from my family anymore.

I have never regretted coming to Canada. It is a beautiful country and I've seen a lot of it. But there is still more to see and I sincerely hope I have the opportunity to do so.

****

Elizabeth and Ron Watkins
Cornwall, England

I had no intention of marrying a Canadian or anyone else for that matter, especially a serviceman from overseas. The idea of leaving my family and England to go and live in an alien country was inconceivable. Strange how circumstances can change one's mind. With so many Canadians and other foreign military personnel stationed throughout Great Britain, it was unavoidable to come into contact with them. Although my home was in the west of England, from early 1941 I was working in Edinburgh, Scotland, having been transferred there with the firm I worked for.

I met Ronny one evening in the local pub. A group of us from the office were singing around the piano when a half-dozen or so Canadian Navy type joined us. Conversation was bright and witty; rounds of drinks were bought as we sang, laughed and got to know each other a little. I shared a flat with two other girls, and Ronny insisted on walking us home.

When we arrived at the door, he grabbed my hand and said, "Don't go in yet, please. I want to speak to you." After my friends had said goodnight, I turned to him and said, "Well, what do you want?" Seems he had three more days leave left and wanted me to meet him again.

He appeared so pathetic and lonely that I melted a little and agreed.

After his leave was finished, we corresponded, and when his next leave became due, I took my holidays from work and together we travelled to my home, a small resort town on the coastline of Bridgewater Bay in the county of Somerset. My parents accepted Ronny from the start, and just before our leave was up, he asked me to marry him. I wanted to say "yes" because I loved him, but hesitated for I did not want to go to Canada.

I fretted and worried about this move constantly. Of course, my parents disliked the idea also, but made it clear they would not stand in my way. It was not as if they would be left alone. If this had been the case, my decision would have been easy. But I had a younger brother and sister at home for them to look after for a number of years to come. I discussed it with Ron in my letters. He painted no glamorous picture of his home in North Bay, Ontario. Damn cold in the winter, and stinking hot in the summer, he said. We came to a mutual agreement.

Ron suggested I try it for two years. If, after that time I was still unsettled, I could go home for a couple of months. Hopefully I would then know where I wanted to be. But what if I didn't know, I argued. He calmly said we would cross that bridge when and if we came to it. Perhaps not a very satisfactory arrangement on which to base a marriage, but we both went into it with our eyes wide open.

We were married in 1945, and in February 1946 I sailed on the *Mauretania* for Canada where Ronny was waiting for me. Goodbyes have to be the most sorrowful of happenings, and I cried buckets all the way across the Atlantic. I wasn't much better on the train, and know I looked a sight with my eyes red, puffy and watery when I met Ron in Toronto.

I don't remember much about the scenery from Halifax except that everything was white with snow and looked as bleak as I felt. But I do remember that ride in a truck from Toronto to North Bay. I had never seen landscape so desolate and as each mile passed, my spirits sank lower and lower. This huge land of snow and ice made me feel I was in Iceland, not Canada. Tears stung my eyes again as I thought of dear old England, her green fields, soft rain and most of all, my family. Two years might just as well be two hundred.

I'm sure my darling husband could read my thoughts and knew the inner turmoil I was going through. I wanted desperately to turn back, and how I managed to keep from blurting this out, I'll never know.

Ron told me how excited his family were to meet me; that they were all waiting for me as well as neighbours and friends. He told me the names of some of the lakes we passed, all frozen solid. I was happy to be with him for I had missed him terribly, but oh! I was missing my family so much for we had always been so close.

After hours of travelling, we reached North Bay. I was quite surprised to find it a fair-sized town. Then a new fear overcame me as Ron drove into a driveway beside a large rambling house, with a wide verandah. Now I would come face to face with Ron's parents, his sister and her family. I was trembling so much I could hardly climb out of the truck and my legs felt weak from sitting so long. I needed the support of Ron's arm around my waist as we walked ankle deep through snow to the front door.

Warm arms engulfed me, kisses rained on my cheeks, laughter and tears greeted me. Oh, I was so warmly welcomed into that house that it made up for all the fears and worries of the past few days. I couldn't help it. I burst into tears right there in the hall in front of everybody. Then I started laughing, and at that moment, everything seemed all right.

During the next two years, I tried hard, I really did. Our first child was born ten months after my arrival and how I got through the awful summer heat, flies and mosquitoes, was a miracle. I had a rotten pregnancy, sick all the time, and oh! how I longed for the cool sea breeze of my homeland.

We had our own apartment by this time, and Ron had secured a fairly good position in sales. I should have been contented, but I wasn't. One would think with such a warm welcome, and marvellous in-laws, I would have been, but the home-ties were far too strong to combat even that. I never complained to Ron, but he knew how I felt. He was so good to me, and helped in any way he could. But, at the back of my mind was the forthcoming trip home at the end of two years. Maybe it hadn't been such a good agreement after all. And years later, I could not help thinking, had it not been made, I would have had no choice but to make myself settle down as other brides had to.

When Terry had his first birthday on November 15, Ron, true to his word, told me he had arranged passage for Terry and I to sail for England so we could spend Christmas with my family. I felt guilty at leaving Ron and told him I wouldn't go. But I knew I would. I had to make that journey home and was convinced that being separated from Ron for two months would prove to me that Canada was my home.

How can I describe my feelings at being amongst my family and friends again? Although I missed Ron far more than I thought, I did not want to return to Canada. I told my parents and asked for their help in making my decision. Their reply was negative. As much as they wanted me and their only grandchild, they said my place

103

was with my husband and the choice was mine alone to make. Confronting me was that damnable bridge waiting to be crossed.

In the face of adversity, truth and honesty is the best policy. In a letter to Ron, I told him I did not want to return; that I knew I could never be happy there, and if he wished to divorce me, I would understand. My heart was heavy when I posted this letter for I was sure Ron would seek a divorce. Who could blame him? Therefore, no one could have been more surprised than I when a telegram came saying he had quit his job and was sailing for England within a couple of weeks.

I went alone to meet him in Southampton and feared the worst, for I was positive he had come to claim Terry and take him back to Canada. I shall never forget the first glimpse of his dear face as he came down the gangplank. We ran to each other oblivious of everyone else as we hugged and kissed, laughed and cried.

Ron hadn't come to take Terry away from me—how could I ever have thought such a thing? He had come to stay. I couldn't believe it. But I could believe that he loved me very much to forsake his country for mine.

After a week or so, he found a job along similar lines as the one in North Bay. We lived with my parents until the summer when, very fortunately for us, some friends of my parents were moving and asked us if we were interested in buying their house. This was a God-send, as houses and flats were very hard to come by. We scraped enough money for the down payment and mum looked after Terry while I went back to work to help out financially.

Through the years, Ron has done exceptionally well at his job and became a territorial manager in no time. Our first visit back to Canada was in four years. I felt rather guilty when I met my in-laws again, but I need not have. They welcomed me in the same manner as before. Since then, we have visited them several times, and once they came to England to visit us.

Our parents have passed on now but Ron still has his sister in Toronto, and every second year or so we visit back and forth. Our son is married and now we have grandchildren. They live close by as does my sister and brother. Like me, western England has always remained their home ground, and I can thank the Lord that my dear husband adapted to England far better than I, to Canada. Although I enjoy visiting there and know what a beautiful vast country it is, I must be honest and say, I was too British to ever become a Canadian.

****

Joan and Raymond Gray
Alberta

The Calgary Highlanders were stationed in Bexhill during 1941 and 1942 and billeted in empty school houses. (Teachers and children had been evacuated.) They were a popular regiment in the area, and after the war a street was named in their honour . . . Calgary Road. They certainly looked dashing with their red and white glengarry caps and Argyl kilts.

The local Red Cross organized dances at the Parish hall of All Saints Church in Sidley, and we local girls enjoyed them very much. We danced the "Lambeth Walk," jitterbugged and did the "Boomps-a-daisy"—the latter shocking our parents much the same way as we disapproved of our children gyrating to the "twist" during the sixties. But most of the music played was of a sentimental nature and we danced with these handsome Highlanders to "Apple Blossom Time," "Jealousy" and many others. Many a soldier would get smoochy as he sang, "I Love You Truly."

In the autumn of 1941, I met Ray at one of these dances. When it ended, he wanted to walk me home but some of his pals talked him out of it. Their billets were five miles away and the army had transportation waiting to take them back. We made a date however, to meet at the top of the road where I lived for the following Tuesday. It was pouring with rain that night and as black as pitch. Curled up in front of the fire and reading a good book, I almost decided not to keep the date. Then I thought how unkind it would be not to show up. Rather grudgingly I put on my rubber boots and raincoat and groped my way up the street.

I took shelter in the door-way of a newspaper shop and waited for the bus. It was so dark I could not distinguish the people getting off, so I just waited. Then a Canadian voice said, "Are you there, Joan?"

"Yes. I'm here. Where are you?"

"Here."

"Where?"

"Here."

"Where?"

It must have sounded comical and probably would have looked so if anyone could have seen us groping around for each other in the dark. Our first date was spent walking around as Ray had only enough money to get the bus back.

Ray was away on training a lot of the time so we corresponded more than we met. After eight months he proposed and asked for my mother's permission. His thoughtfulness at asking was appreciated and we were married in October 1942 on a pleasant, mild day. I was a bit disappointed not to see the groom and best man in their kilts. Apparently they were short in supply as many of the men sold them.

We spent our honeymoon in Brighton, and on the very first night a policeman came to our door and asked to see

Joan and Ray Gray, St. Peters Church, England (1,200 years old), 1942

our identity cards. It was really embarrassing as mine was still in my maiden name. He realized it was not an illicit affair as there was confetti all over the floor.

It was not until March 1946, that I and my two sons, David, two years and eight months, and Richard, five months, sailed for Canada.

As we left Victoria station in a bus that took us to the Duke of Aberconway's residence in the west end, most of us were crying as we caught last glimpses of our families. Others put on a brave show in spite of the heart-ache hidden under a smiling face. I will always remember the gracefully curved staircase and marble floor in this lovely home.

In Liverpool, the hospital ship *Letitia* was ready to take us aboard, and as we pulled away from the shores of our homeland, a military band played patriotic and sentimental music. The docks were jammed with parents and friends straining to the very last to hear and see the final farewells, and all faces were wet with tears.

As I had a lively toddler in harness, and a babe in my arms, I was unable to get through the crowd on deck, so I followed some other girls and their children and we sat and talked cheerfully until we heard the strains of "There'll Always be an England." That brought a lump to our throats, and the cheerful conversation came to an abrupt end.

The nine day crossing was a nightmare. The ship ran into a blizzard causing most of us to be seasick. The baby, however, was a jolly little sailor and none the worse for it. One poor soul stayed in her bunk while her baby's pile of diapers grew higher and higher. I would have helped her but I was in rough shape myself and it was all I could do to cope with my own two.

The blizzard caused a few nasty incidents. After it abated, I was on deck to get some fresh air when a beautifully dressed girl walked across the deck. The crew had not had time to scrub down, and she slipped and fell where someone had been seasick. What a sorry sight when she stood up!

Another plump, dark-haired girl was so sick she was transferred to the infirmary. At the end of the journey she was so thin she was hardly recognized. The nurse found her rings in her bed as she had lost so much weight they had slipped from her finger. Two sailors escorted a struggling excited girl to the infirmary also, where her baby was born.

We were a wan looking bunch of brides and children who disembarked at Halifax. The train motion was soothing, and we all slept well. At intervals we took walks along station platforms. The air was fresh and very cold. Snow was still on the ground. The scenery proved to be from one extreme to the other. In eastern Canada there were miles and miles of fir trees, and the prairies were either flat or rolling hills devoid of hedges to which we were accustomed. The huge country and enormous trains were reminiscent of scenes from "Anna Karina," and one felt that Tolstoy and Chekhov would be at home in such an environment.

It was a lovely warm day when we reached Calgary. I had never seen Ray in mufti and must confess feeling a little nervous wondering if he would look like a stranger. But there he was, so trim and smart in a navy pin-stripe suit, carrying a gorgeous bouquet of dark red roses. It was such a happy homecoming.

All his family were there, and as Ray gazed at his bonny baby whom he had never seen, his mother hugged and kissed us all. She was so proud of her grandchildren. They were such a warmhearted, hospitable family who have been kindess itself over the years.

For the first two years we lived in Three Hills where Ray was employed. The people were kind and friendly and gave a lovely shower on behalf of another war bride and myself.

I had to be reminded several times to empty the pail underneath the kitchen sink. It was puzzling at first to empty the dish pan water and then feel it gushing over my feet onto the floor. The "privy" was outside and even on the outskirts of Calgary, people still had wells and outside toilets. This rather amazed me as I thought Canada was so much more advanced than England.

Ray's mother was a music teacher and could play anything from classical to popular music on the piano. Some of the farm children would bring her butter and cream in lieu of payment for their lessons. I was quite amused at this form of requital.

Our first home was a one-roomed apartment with a large cook stove in one corner. The water-man brought the water in a large wooden cart that resembled an oversized cradle. He filled the barrels that were kept in the basement so that the water kept cool. When I needed it, I used a pail and dipper. It was a pleasant apartment, and we were happy there while waiting for our house to be built.

After a bad rain fall one day, I took the children for an outing in the pram. When crossing the street, the pram and I became bogged down in the prairie gumbo. It was like standing in a pot of glue. I pulled my boots out only to get stuck again, and the wheels of the pram wouldn't budge. I thought, this must be how a fly feels on that awful sticky fly paper. Finally, a gentleman saw my predicament and came to the rescue. Another time I remember so well was when a prairie dust storm rolled in. It was so scary and looked as if the end of the world had arrived.

Ray had taken a homestead in the Peace River country before the war, and was now yearning to farm. So toward the end of summer, we sold our house and moved into a couple of granaries before we made the big move. Here I witnessed my first whirlwind that spun David around like a top until his daddy dragged him into the granary. The door slammed shut, some of the saucepans crashed to the floor and a copy of Jane Eyre fell into a bucket of water!

Ray drove to Peace River in an old model A to put the shell of our house up while the children and I waited in Three Hills. His mother had quite a talent for reading tea leaves, and she told me that we would not leave until the first snow fall. Well, grandma was right! Ray came back for us, and the morning before we left, the only dry spot on our pillows was where our heads were. The snow had blown in the chinks of the granary and formed haloes around our heads.

A neighbour was also going to try his luck at homesteading, so he loaded our belongings into the box of his grain truck. After we said our goodbyes, we piled into the model A and headed north. We passed many decrepit

110

looking vehicles on the way. Some had their doors tied together with string and bits of wire; one had it's roof flapping up and down; small trucks carried bedding and sticks of furniture, and it made me think of the characters in the movie, "The Grapes of Wrath."

After Edmonton, the country seemed to get flatter and swampier than that of the rolling prairie. We passed Lesser Slave Lake where the country grew increasingly more isolated as we advanced farther and farther into the bush. The old car developed armature trouble which made it necessary for us to stay overnight in the town of Peace River.

Next morning as we made our way to the garage, a woman, reeking of alcohol and swaying unsteadily, swooped down on my Richard and gave him a loud smacking kiss on his mouth and raved about his beautiful blue eyes. I was horrified and didn't relish her drunken compliment and glared at her icily as I snatched my baby from her unwelcome embrace.

At Eureka, we stopped at a general store for supplies. The store also served as a post office besides being cluttered with pelts, lanterns, axes, pails of lard and traps of all kinds dangling from the ceiling. There was a huge pot-bellied stove in the centre where men gathered to "chew the fat."

Eight miles from Eureka, we took a wagon trail which wound through heavy bush for two miles; then, there it stood, the shell of our new home. We unpacked, set the beds and stove up, and used the top of trunks and boxes for our groceries, as we had no shelves or partitions made.

The next few days, Ray and our very good neighbour were kept busy making them and the one room turned into two bedrooms and a long livingroom. A few days after, they went hunting and brought home a moose. By this time I was used to canning meat, and the moose lasted us several months.

111

We were one of the first families to settle in our district which was named "Deventer." This was a tribute to the Dutch people as the men of the Canadian Infantry had affectionate memories of Holland.

The first years of homesteading were far from easy as there was literally no money in the country. The only cash we saw was the family allowance. The men worked for each other and traded things amongst themselves. We traded the model A for a cow named Jane, a team of horses, Lady and Queen, plus a cream separator so we could learn to make butter. Jane was a good cow and we all learned to milk her; the children and I would each take a teat, her calf the fourth teat, and Jane would stand contentedly chewing the cud. We all became proud of Sam, the first calf we had ever owned. Ray however, took a very dim view of him, as he was spoiled rotten.

During the winters, Ray worked in the local logging camp which the owner was operating on a shoe string. In lieu of wages, the owner would clear and break land for us during the summer. One bitterly cold day about forty below zero, the boys and I were splitting and gathering logs when we noticed the door to the house was open. We investigated, and there was Sam, up on the bed which was slowly sagging under his eight-hundred pound weight, gazing at Raphael's Madonna, hanging on the wall!

Fortunately he behaved like a gentleman and merely left snowy hoof marks on the white counterpane. I yanked viciously at his tail and used some unlady-like language while he trotted around the kitchen table and went out the door which I closed with a resounding bang. A few days later, we looked up from the breakfast table, and lo and behold! there was Sam, gobbling icicles from the roof. In doing so, he poked a hole in one of the windows with his long horns, and upset a five-gallon can of coal oil! By the time spring came, Ray was fed up with his antics.

"That darn calf has got to go if it's the last thing I do!" he exploded one day.

In spite of our tearful pleadings, Ray was adamant. He brought the team and wagon around, and in jumped Sam as cocky as ever. The boys and I watched them go down the trail until they were out of sight. Two hours later back they came. Ray was furious! He had waited all that time until someone had come along and told him the cattle truck was not coming that week.

Needless to say, the kids and I were delighted at Sam's reprieve. He had to go the following week though, and he fetched a good price which bought enough wire for a forty acre pasture fence.

Later on, the family allowance bought two weaned piglets, Jack and Jill. It was such a thrilling moment when Jill had her first litter in the straw pile. Jack was butchered sometime later, and it made me feel sad to see his head on a large platter ready for me to make head cheese.

Water had always been a problem in the Peace country. Luckily we had a creek on our place which helped before we got our two wells dug. One autumn day, I had to chop ice out of the creek as the snow had not yet arrived. I took the old wash tub, the axe and rope, and chopped the ice, loaded it in the tub and hauled it home a quarter mile so that I could do the washing.

It was quite a number of years before we could afford to paint and paper inside of the house. However, we scrubbed the walls with hot soapy water to keep the boards clean. My family have never let me live down the day I put the lid of the copper boiler across the water barrel. I climbed onto it to start my spring cleaning and naturally the lid slowly sagged in two, and I landed plop!

113

right into the barrel with water up to my arm pits. I should have known better at my age.

We had a very bad bush fire one spring. Ray was away with the team of horses working the break down when he spotted the smoke. I saw the flames in the distance, put my three-year-old in his crib and looking him steadily in the eye said, "Richard. I have to go and fetch the cow. You are not to move until I come back." I ran up the trail and was just in time as the flames were edging the grass near her. I untethered her and brought her back to the yard. Ray came with the team, and five-year-old David stood and held the horses for three hours while we slapped the flames with wet sacks and pails of water. We were most fortunate not to lose anything except a fence post or two and a homemade wooden horse the kids had left in the yard.

The following year we applied for correspondence school courses for David. We also listened to excellent educational broadcasts for children over the radio. We organized a meeting at our house in hopes of making educational facilities available in the community. The Supervisor of the school division, who had sixty miles to drive, came and spoke to us. After the meeting we served tea, but as I only had a few cups, the majority of the visitors drank from pint sealers. In those days, all the homesteaders were so hard up that nobody thought anything of it.

Every year we invited our neighbours to a Halloween party. We crammed the livingroom furniture into the two bedrooms, and put the small fry to bed. Some of the local boys had considerable talent, and could play lively polkas, schottisches, jigs and waltzes by ear. Indeed, they taught David and Richard to play the violin, guitar and piano accordian. At midnight, the coffee pot was set on the old wood stove and all the women would help serve moosemeat sandwiches and homemade cake.

114

During the long winter evenings before our two boys left home, there was always music and the sound of hob-nailed boots tapping to keep the right time.

We always made missionaries welcome, and in the summer the Sunday school and church services were held in our house. Sometimes during the sermon, our two big cats came in and made the youngsters giggle as they padded softly over laps in search of a comfortable spot.

Many waters have run under the bridge since our arrival in the Peace River country. We have seen gravel roads built, most of the land cleared, and there are very few homesteads left. There are churches and recreational facilities available to all. With the coming of the water and sewage disposal, the little outhouse which served a useful purpose will be a relic of a passing era.

I am glad to have been a citizen of two countries; proud to have had the privilege of living under two flags. The historical and cultural background of my homeland has enriched my life and given me many wonderful memories.

We have been fortunate too, to be living in such a fine community where people are kindhearted and friendly. It's like living in a large closely-knit family. Most of us came here with nothing but hope, determination and optimism. With sheer hard work we have succeeded in creating farms from the wilderness. We have left our mark in the Peace River country of Canada, paving the way for future farmers in the generations to come.

****

When in England during the war, I was responsible for the operation of War Bride clubs for the Salvation Army Red Shield Services in the following centres: Brighton, Bournemouth, London, Leamington, Lincoln and Glasgow.

I visited the clubs every month and arranged for Canadian personnel to give lectures on Canada and it's customs. We taught the girls Canadian cooking and had them cook Canadian meals; helped them with travelling problems; set up Canadian libraries in their clubs; taught them Canadian expressions that differed from their own such as, "elevator" instead of "lift," "sidewalk" for "pavement," etc., etc.

We took club members on tours; for instance, the Brighton club would go to London and be entertained by them. Many Brighton members had never been to London before, and we thought it was such a pity for them to go to Canada without having seen their own historical Capitol.

I came back to Canada on a ship with several hundred war brides. They became very excited when the train from Halifax stopped somewhere for a half-hour or so. They dashed to nearby stores to buy things that were no longer rationed for them . . . oranges, bananas, candy and clothing.

So plainly I remember one war bride standing outside a Big Chief service station in the hopes of seeing an Indian! Yet another, a guest at a shower who told me she was going to write home and tell her mum about the lovely dishes used at the shower tea, but nothing matched. I tried to explain to her that we didn't have tea-sets as they did in England.

We had marvellous cooperation from the military personnel who were responsible for bringing the brides to Canada. They supplied them with Canadian books, magazines and all kinds of travelling information.

After my husband and I returned home, we rested for a couple of months before we were appointed to Calgary in charge of the Salvation Army Children's Village. On arrival, I was requested to organize another war bride's club, and it served a most useful purpose for several years. By this time, a large percentage of the girls had taken a trip back to their homeland, and had returned and become more settled to Canadian life.

Here in Canada we still had speakers who spoke on various subjects to help the girls. They were experts in their field: cooking; sewing; law and history, talking of the part of Canada in which the girls lived.

After twenty-five years, Calgary war brides held a reunion, and over one hundred were in attendance. The girls had a wonderful time recalling their first impressions of Canada; speaking of the ships that brought them here; and meeting those who were on the same voyage. I was kindly invited and very thrilled to be guest of honour at their reunion, and as I mingled amongst them and listened to them speaking of their lives in Canada now, I thought how far they had come from those frightened young girls of yesteryear to these well-adjusted Canadian women who had contributed much to our society.

Contributed by Mrs. Brigadier Gerald (Francis) Wagner of the Salvation Army, Canada.

****

Anonymous

I worked as housekeeper to an important person in the WVS (Woman's Voluntary Service) during the war and met my husband at a local dance. When we wanted to marry, the Commanding Officer of his regiment visited and questioned my employer as to whether I was good enough to marry a Canadian soldier. Apparently I was, because permission came through.

Arriving in Halifax in the early spring of 1946, my baby and I were met by my husband and driven to our new home. It was quite primitive, with no indoor plumbing. An outside wooden building that had but one draughty hole and a catalogue, served as the toilet.

That was the first of many surprises including job scarcity, food shortages, doing things differently, being misunderstood and called a "limey" in rather a cruel manner.

I had no social life because there was no money to pay anyone to look after the children so my husband went out by himself.

I longed for my family and perhaps I should have left Canada then, but I didn't, and now it is too late. To find work in England after all these years, would be highly improbable, and I have left it too long to change now.

In many instances the years have been happy and still are for many of the war brides. But if I could have foreseen what the future held for me, I never would have left England. When a drinking problem enters a marriage, it is hard to cope, especially when it reaches the point of no communication between marriage partners.

I am an avid reader, watch television, work in the garden but never have any social contact unless I want to gossip with neighbours which never appealed to me. I am alone most of the time and unfortunately, never had the chance to learn how to drive. I think had I lived in a town where I could have caught a bus to get to other places, I would have been happier.

I am not complaining about Canada. This is a wonderful country with so much opportunity for all, and I am glad my children had the good fortune to grow up here.

****

Doreen and Tom Kennie
Ontario

Our house in London was bombed during the blitz and fortunately, we were not living in it at the time. My father worked for a special branch of the Air Ministry and we, mum, dad, four brothers and myself, had been evacuated by the Ministry to Harrogate in Yorkshire.

Mother died when I was seventeen, and it became my responsibility to look after dad and my two younger brothers aged five and nine years. The two older ones were already in the army. I was "called up" for service when I became eighteen, but due to the circumstances at home, I was exempt. Dad was very happy that I wanted to stay with him and run the house. Poor man! He was so lost without mum. I managed very well and was quite proud that I could cope with the rationing and cooking.

With dad busy at the Ministry, I did not get much chance to go out except when he was able to come home early. I had one special girlfriend with whom I went to the cinema and dances and one evening, because she was sick, I went to the local dance alone.

I noticed this good-looking airman watching me and thought he would never ask me to dance, but he did. He took me home, and on our next date he met dad and my young brothers who thought him an angel when he supplied them with candy and chewing gum. Tom was stationed at Topcliffe aerdrome and worked in the control tower. We saw each other a lot and dad was getting a little anxious about my feelings for this polite young Canadian. After a year, we knew we wanted to marry, and I was torn between my love for Tom and the thought of leaving dad alone.

When I confronted dad about it, he said, "I'll never stand in the way of my children." He had tears in his eyes and I felt terrible.

119

We wanted to marry immediately, but first had the army routine to go through. When this was completed, we chose a small wedding because none of my relatives could come from London. Three of Tom's pals and my girlfriend attended but dad could not. He wasn't allowed the time off. The taxi Tom had arranged to pick us up didn't show at the appointed time, so he said he'd go and find one. In the meantime it came, and we piled in and went looking for him. At first we couldn't find him and I was subjected to a lot of teasing from Tom's pals who kept saying he had opted out of our wedding.

Dad arrived home a little bit earlier from the office in time to have some wedding cake and wine and we had a lovely celebration. We had to stay home for our honeymoon because I could not leave my brothers alone, but it was war-time and these things were to be expected. I knew my eldest brother would be home on leave from India soon and the other was wounded in Italy and sent home earlier than we thought, so we celebrated all over again.

Orders came for Tom to report to Torquay, and from there to Canada and maybe Japan. I could not bring myself to believe he was leaving and had decided not to fill and send in the papers for my transit to Canada until he knew exactly where he was going. We all said good-bye at the house and I watched him walk up the road and disappear, then cried for the rest of the day and half the night. To make matters worse, I was pregnant and that didn't help.

My father had met a very nice lady whose husband had died two years before. They became very good friends and married later that year. I was extremely happy for them, and my step-mother was very good to him and my brothers. She had a son in the army and a daughter of sixteen and my brother from Italy fell in love with our new step-sister and married her.

It was August 1946 when I left England with my ten-month-old baby and my girlfriend who had married a Canadian also. Saying goodbye to dad and the family was one of the hardest tasks I have ever faced.

There was a chorus of rousing cheers when we saw the *Queen Mary*. What a huge ship, and oh! so beautiful. It was foggy when we left port, and none of us could see the English coastline through it and our tears.

My poor baby became quite ill and could not keep anything down. The ship's doctor said he would be all right. My girlfriend and I chatted with others about Canada and the different parts we were going to. We also played bingo, and up until then, I thought bingo was a dog's name. Everyone was buying souvenirs to take to their new relatives, and I was annoyed to find out that mine were made in Niagara Falls and not England.

The closer we came to Halifax, the more tense we became. It upset me very much to hear girls saying, "I know I won't like Canada," before they had even seen it. We arrived on August 6 and my friend could see her husband on the crowded dock. They tried to shout to each other, but with all the noise, it was impossible to hear. Her name was called to disembark and it was another sad moment when we said goodbye with promises to write.

At last we were on the train and the size of it amazed me. We were all tipping the coloured porters who were a cheerful bunch. No wonder! We were handing out Canadian currency and didn't know the first thing about its value.

I was still worried about the baby who by this time was too weak to cry. Yet the young doctor assured me he would be all right. The meals on the train were wonderful and I would have enjoyed them had I not been so upset. This doctor was assigned to our coach, but he was more or less occupied with two posh-looking girls whom the other girls talked about angily. "Who do they think they are?" they said to one another.

Two days and nights on the train were enough for me, and I was glad when the time came to send a telegram to my husband telling him what time to expect me in Toronto. I had the prettiest dress hanging up ready to slip into and when we arrived, the excitement was electric. Soon we were kissing and hugging each other and he remarked, "Your English accent sounds funny now."

The ride to Niagara Falls was the longest car ride I had ever had. We were both worried about the baby and I kept saying, "Are we nearly there?" And Tom would reply, "Oh, just another half-hour." There were an awful lot of half hours.

At last we were there and there were more hugs and kisses. I could tell that my mother-in-law thought the baby ill, so she gave him some boiled milk and water, but up it all came like a stream over my pretty dress. After a very long sleep, he was much better, and it wasn't long before he was able to eat solid food again. I guess the travelling was too much for him.

We were made welcome by everybody and there were numerous showers; the gifts were lovely, and I was overwhelmed. Finding a place to store them was a problem as we were looking for a place of our own which wasn't easy to find. I was taken sight-seeing, and thought the Falls the most magnificent sight I had ever seen. I loved ice cream sodas, dill pickles and peanut butter, but found the summer heat unbearable.

Everything about Canada amazed me mainly because things looked so much larger. The first time I saw a robin, I laughed because it was three times the size of an English one. I enjoyed the first winter and bought a warm coat and snow boots. The gaily lit Christmas trees standing in the windows of houses looked beautiful. In the years to follow that was one of the delights of winter —finding the right tree to decorate.

Nobody panicked when our first Canadian-born baby came before I could get to the hospital. After I was placed on the stretcher, one of the attendants knocked over a broom which fell on my head as I was carried out the door.

It was exciting when we moved into our home in the January. The furniture arrived, but the bed did not have the right size boards for the box spring. We slept on the floor for several nights which I thought fun; Tom did not.

The next summer, I found out more about Canada. The beaches were lovely although it was different swimming in lake water compared to the sea. When we bought our first car, we rented a friend's cottage for a weekend. On the way we got hit in the back by a truck, and our car was badly damaged. No one was hurt, but I and our two small sons were shaken up. Tom was calm as an English policeman. Then to top that, the cottage was one long room situated behind a fun fair. The noise was awful!

Our first telephone was installed on the day before Christmas. It took two men all day to install it. They knew the man next door, and kept popping over for some Xmas cheer.

When I got my first washing machine, I caught my hand in the wringer. No bones were broken, but it was a bit squashed.

One summer, my dad and stepmother came for a visit. We had a marvellous time and they were thrilled with everything and thought me a very lucky girl to be living in such a beautiful spot. We took them up north, and it was my first visit there too. One day, my dad found some loose change on the beach and remarked that he thought Canadians rather careless with their money. But I noticed he spent the rest of the week kicking the sand looking for more.

Doreen and Tom Kennie

My first visit back to England was in 1967. What a thrill to see my brothers again. They made such a fuss over me and the three children. Nothing had really changed. It seemed exactly as I remembered it. Saying goodbye again was just as hard and I got homesick all over again and cried for days. Once back in Canada, I soon got into the swing of things. I love my life here and have never regretted coming.

****

I was on ship duty for fifteen months helping the war brides on their way to Canada. One trip stands out above all others. It was on the old *Scythia*, and I'll never forget it. I was slated for night duty and had just gone to bed, and was drowsily sleeping when one of my cabin mates came in and woke me up. "Hey! Are you packed and ready to go ashore?"

"What the heck . . . ?" said I, still half asleep.

"A cattle ship deliberately went across the bay in front of us, and our ship ran into her. There's cattle floating in the water all over the place and we have to turn and go back to port," she said.

I did feel sorry for all those war brides having to pack all over again. Such a commotion getting them all ashore. And of course, the railway had a job servicing a train to get them back to the London centre. We had to wait such a long time.

Another trip out of Liverpool found us Nursing Sisters coping with a group of sick babies. The MO decided the staff should make the formulas. After checking us gals, I was the one elected to do it with a Red Cross girl to help me.

You should have seen us preparing about 350 feedings a day in a room about six feet by six! We used sterilized BEER BOTTLES to put the formula in. On top of this we had thirty-five special feedings to make for the very sick babies.

After filling nearly four hundred bottles, we had to pack them into crates, then carry and place them on racks. An orderly was supposed to be available for this, but half the time we could never find him. The Red Cross gal was so slight in build, that it was impossible for her to lift them. It's a wonder I didn't strain my back lifting those damn crates over waist high. The MO came in one day when I was doing this and took the crate from me, and he nearly did a "heave to."

The babies all got better and we got a verbal "thank you" from the Captain. No Purple Heart for us! They would have given us one in the United States, a country that scattered them around like flies beside a honey crate. But we did our bit, and were proud of it.

Contributed by Anne Munday—Staff Nursing Sister.

Mary and Donald Parrott
Manitoba

In 1942, I was nursing in a small rural hospital near Bracknell in Berkshire, when I met a young handsome Canadian soldier whose company of Royal Canadian Engineers were building a wing onto a Canadian military hospital. After going together for six months, Donald and I were married. Our happiness was completed when our daughter Diane was born just before Donald was posted further overseas.

Mary and Don Parrott

The necessary forms were filled out for our transportation to Canada, and it wasn't long before Diane and I were aboard the *Mauretania*.

The first day at sea was rough and I could not get out of my bunk. Diane, thank goodness, was fine and played with the other children. The nurses in attendance were very good to us all. I couldn't help laughing when one of them gave Diane a banana, and having never seen one before, she tried to eat it unpeeled.

We were on deck when entering Halifax harbour, and I shall never forget the sense of freedom that engulfed me when I saw the blaze of city lights. Many wept at the sight after years of complete darkness.

Not having slept on a train before, the constant clicking of wheels kept me awake the first night, but Diane slept soundly. Passing through New Brunswick we noticed isolated wooden houses and barns and snow-covered fields. One girl remarked, "I'm glad my husband doesn't live around here."

Large crowds were waiting in Montreal to meet their new daughters-in-law and grandchildren, and I could not comprehend that my new home was still over a thousand miles away. Two days later we arrived in Kenora, Ontario. Here, an army officer helped us from the train and told me a plane would take us north to our destination, Red Lake, Ontario.

Meeting us at Kenora were two Red Cross ladies who, after taking us out to lunch, drove us to the waterfront where a small plane on skis was waiting to take off for Red Lake. I had never flown before and was quite dubious about making my first flight in this one. Truthfully, I was downright scared and asked rather timidly if there was another way to get there, only to have the pilot reply, "Only a tractor train, once a month. Don't worry. You'll be there in an hour."

With no choice in the matter, we climbed in, sat on mail bags while a Mountie sat beside the pilot, and away we flew. When the plane began to circle, and I glimpsed the buildings of Red Lake below, I closed my eyes, clutched Diane and prayed silently for a smooth landing on the frozen lake. Taxiing to the Airway office, I was amazed to see vehicles of all kinds on the ice. Never before had I looked upon such a sight; in fact, never had

I seen so much snow and ice in my life, and hurried to the cosy warmth of the office where I appreciated the heat from a huge stove, but not its oily smell.

A huge bearded man who looked like an Arctic explorer in his fur-trimmed parka, entered the room and asked if there were any passengers for the Madsen Mine. The clerk nodded to Diane and me and said, "This lady and child are ready to go." Picking up our luggage, we followed him to his taxi. Once again another journey started, only this time, thank goodness, it was a mere five miles over a snow-covered road.

He stopped in front of my in-laws' house and I was dismayed to find nobody there. He told me to wait while he went to the mine to get Donald's father. A few minutes after he left, Donald's mother came running from a neighbour's house, and dad came from the mine.

The telegram I had sent from Kenora never arrived, so they had no idea I was almost there. After a very lengthy and most unusual journey by land, sea and air, that only cost me one dollar at the very end for the taxi, Diane and I were home.

Once we were settled, there were many things that absolutely amazed me. The heavy tractors and trucks going across the lake made me wonder how the ice ever supported them; the planes landing and taking off on skis, among them the largest war-time Douglas DC3 carrying twenty-five passengers; the fish-packing plant; the workmen sawing the ice into huge blocks, three feet thick (no wonder the lake could carry the weight of heavy traffic) then hauling it into a huge ice-house where it was packed in saw dust. I had never seen ice over one-quarter inch thick in England.

When Donald came back from the war, he, too, worked in the Madsen Mine. His job was to fire the steam boilers for heat in the winter months, then during the summer he worked in the machine shop. He passed

128

his Stationary Operating Engineers examination, and got a job as an operator in the Power House of the Campbell Red Lake mine. After living at the Madsen for four years, we bought a house in the town of Red Lake.

We had four children, and when they were all attending school, I went back to full-time nursing and helped buy our first car and small motor boat. Our children had great opportunities for skiing, skating and all winter sports, as well as swimming, boating and camping during the summer months.

The children all received the public and high-school education in Red Lake, and Diane became a school teacher by taking summer school courses in the University where she received her degree in education. Our only son joined the Armed Forces where he took a mechanics course. After ten years service he left the army to attend Brandon University where he is studying a five-year science course. Our two youngest daughters are nurses in Thunder Bay, and we visit often.

Donald retired after twenty-five years service at Campbell mine, and we decided to move to Brandon to be near our son and his family.

Although we both have relatives in England, and visit them every few years, we would not like to retire there, as our children and grand-children are all here, and home is where the heart is.

****

Iris and Ken Bardwell
Ontario

At the outbreak of war, I was working in the head office of W. Barratt and Company—shoe manufacturers in Northampton. Many war brides will remember their slogan . . . "Walk the Barratt Way," and we used to add . . . "and be crippled for life." Seriously though, they were good shoes. I did not pass the medical when I tried to join the WAAF so stayed with them until I left for Canada.

My future husband was billeted with us in 1942 while attending the Technical College in Northampton. Even when his course was finished, he came back to spend his leaves with me, and we were married the following year.

Ken and Iris Bardwell, October 30, 1943, Northampton, England

Early December 1944, I left my home and recollect the whole family tearfully gathering to wish me well. My feelings were a mixture of sadness and excitement; sad because I was leaving them behind to face the war still lingering on, and excitement at the prospect of going to a new country to settle down in married bliss never to be parted from Ken again.

My sister accompanied me to the railway station, and I remember the two of us queuing up for a drink in a pub to fortify our nerves.

We were allowed forty dollars only for our long journey and my mother's words echoed in my ears . . . "Don't play cards for money on the ship. Keep your purse tied around your waist when you sleep." I guess she knew what she was talking about because I saw some brides lose all their money in a poker game, and there were many incidents of money and possessions stolen from suitcases. Very sad, but true. On the whole I think we got along pretty well considering there were three hundred brides and children packed in such a confined space.

The food was delicious and most of us ended up with dysentery. Personally, I could not resist the fresh fruit which had disastrous effects on my constitution. The name of the ship was the *Louis Pasteur* and we travelled in convoy. One of the other ships was the *Lady Nelson*, a hospital ship. The *Louis* was quite small with bunk beds packed on top of one another in threes. This did not bother me except when the girl on the top bunk was seasick and my clothes and luggage alongside the bottom bunk where I slept, were the target.

Some of the brides obviously did not tell the truth about their advanced pregnancy and aborted during the voyage, and one baby died of pnuemonia on the train en route to Montreal. Another bride spent most of her time crying, which I put down to homesickness. I was later told that just before she sailed she learned that her husband had been killed in battle. I also recall two children who were being escorted to their Canadian grandparents because their daddy had been killed in action, and their mother in an air-raid, the blast of which had blown all the hair off their heads and left them unable to speak. Poor little mites! Such sad things and one will never know how such stories end.

The journey was quite rough and I recall being served a coke for the first time. If you didn't grab the glass quickly, it would travel the length of the bar as the ship heaved and tossed. I thought the taste of this drink very strange and have never liked it to this day.

Before leaving the ship we were interviewed, and when asked for the address I was going to, I realized I didn't have one. Ken had been in the Colonel Belcher hospital in Calgary and I didn't know if he was out of there. My fears were dispelled when I received a telegram on the train saying he was all right and had found a place for us.

I was touched by the generosity of various organizations who provided us with cigarettes, tea, coffee, fruit and cakes on the train. We were told not to speak to reporters because the war was still on. As the train stopped at different stations, we watched the girls being met by their husbands, and those who were not met. One girl remains in my memory because she always ate her meals so quickly. She said it was because she was a nurse and was never allowed enough time for meals. When I saw her get off the train at Qu'Appelle, an Indian reservation, I wondered if she knew the kind of life she was getting into.

In Winnipeg we had to change trains. The troops from the *Lady Nelson* marched as best as they could around the station accompanied by a military band. There wasn't a dry eye anywhere as we watched veterans with missing limbs and eyes marching as proudly as their disabilities would allow. Suddenly one bride in our group with one child in her arms and two hanging onto her skirt, broke away and ran up to a wounded soldier crying, "My husband, my husband." There followed a very heart-breaking reunion with three children looking very puzzled.

Up until then, Winnipeg struck me as being the coldest place in Canada. Most of the women were wearing fur coats and black suede boots, and I thought them very rich indeed.

It was Christmas Eve when I reached Calgary, and Ken told me he had been going to the station for days meeting all the trains. Only then, after the long journey, did I realize what a huge country I was in. The first thing Ken said was, "How many coats do you have on?" The temperature was forty degrees below zero.

Ken had found an apartment in the home of a first world war bride. She has since retired to Victoria, but we still keep in touch. Ken and I would walk around the block every night because I thought the house far too hot and yet, I could not see how anybody could survive in such weather. I would marvel at the icicles forming on Ken's moustache and laugh because he looked so funny. I soon learned to love the cold, healthy Canadian winter.

Settling down was no problem and after a few weeks a member of the Red Cross called to see how I was and if I had any problems. The only one I had was how to iron a man's shirt!

After thirty-eight years, two children and now grand-children, I still love it here, although I still get a thrill when I go back to England for a visit.

****

I served with the Canadian Red Cross overseas, and when I returned to Canada, I organized a War Bride's club that we named, "Always Be Friends Club," (ABFC). Our slogan was:

A - for Atlantic which flows between me and my homeland.
B - for Bride, reminding me of my romance.
F - for Friendship near and far.
C - for Canada, my adopted country.

Contributed by Phoebe Billings, member of the Canadian Red Cross.

****

Anonymous

My life in Canada has been so full and richly rewarding that I find the past just that . . . past. Each year finds me knee deep in projects, and with my job and family affairs, it's a small wonder that the past remains dim.

I have loved this city from the moment I arrived, and did not get homesick for several months. Then suddenly I had the yearning to see my mother, but it was eight years before I did return to England for a holiday. As I then had three children it was quite an expense. My husband said that if I could save the money from the house-keeping to pay for the trip over, I would have to stay in England six months while he saved up enough to bring us back. And that's how I went, and oh! how I missed him and Calgary after just a few weeks away. I was so glad to make that return trip to Canada.

The first time I left England was in May 1946 on the *Queen Mary*. I made friends with a girl from London

War brides party, YWCA, 1946

who was going to Woodstock, Ontario. We have been writing to each other all these years and have seen each other twice. What I recall mostly about the actual trip was that she carried a small "potty" in a string bag for the convenience of her small son's needs. And was she ever a popular soul; no one had thought of that emergency. I can remember too, that she wore a black hat with a veil, and was crying madly. She kept lifting this veil to wipe her eyes, and I wondered why I couldn't cry as well. I did lots of it later believe me. The Canadian Red Cross were really great in helping us on the ship as well as the train, and handed out plenty of diapers and clothing to those who needed them.

When I arrived in Calgary, my husband and I managed to find a two-roomed apartment in an old house. We were ever so glad as places to live were at a premium. It was June, and as the summers in Calgary are super, we enjoyed being together again after a year of separation. We felt most fortunate to have found such a cosy place . . . until the crunch came. An early winter set in that year, and our only method of heat was a black pot-bellied coal and wood stove. We just about froze.

My husband would set the alarm and get up in the middle of the night to stoke the fire. It was many degrees below zero and icicles formed from the ceiling and frost hung from the walls. This cold spell continued until my small daughter and I were forced to move in with my sister-in-law while my husband stayed and looked after the apartment. Actually this dreadful period proved to be a blessing in disguise. With appeals to the Department of Veteran Affairs, we were able to get one of the small wartime houses especially built for service-men and their families. How I loved that wee house and the warmth of it.

I came from the old "shilling in the geyser" era when hot water was at a minimum and the bathroom so cold that one felt it a punishment to bathe in the winter. So, all the beautiful hot water we had in this house was sheer luxury. We moved in the first week of December, so Christmas was quite a celebration.

I really enjoyed the food in Canada after the meagre rations of England. Having a very sweet tooth I sure did enjoy chocolate malts, but I'm a bit wiser about the old waistline now.

I guess I made all the usual errors with saying the things that have different meanings here. I do recall saying that I was "diddled" on the station platform for fifty cents, and a Canadian replied that it was cheap at half the price! I still didn't realize what I had said until I went home and told my husband. Was my face red when he explained.

During the first month in Calgary, I bought a lovely yellow eyelet dress and paid twenty dollars for it. My husband nearly choked when I told him. He was only earning $125 a month at the time. I didn't know the value of Canadian currency then, and to buy without clothing coupons was too much of a temptation.

When I gave birth to twins, we could not buy a twin buggy for love nor money, but did manage to find an old fourth-hand one. We had no washing machine at that time either, but I managed and enjoyed the babies to the fullest.

I do feel that the bride clubs started by different organizations when we first arrived, helped us to settle down to the strangeness of it all. We know that misery loves company, and I guess it was one place where we could air our beefs without it doing any harm. We all knew what it felt like to be so far from home, and in new surroundings.

My way of getting to know people was simple. I was well-known in those early years for inviting other war brides to my house for tea. My approach was, "Oh, are you English?'' when it was obvious from their clothing and speech that they had just stepped off the boat. Never did I say, ''You must come over sometime for tea.'' I set a definite date right then and there, gave them directions on how to find my house, and through this I am still friends with them all. They have all told me that it was the matter of setting a firm date, and making them feel at home, that did it.

After twenty-five years in Calgary, I organized a war brides reunion which was a huge success, and my life here in this wonderful country has been the same.

****

Pam and Dalton Clost
Ontario

I was sixteen years old when I met Dalton at a local dance held every Saturday night in the little town of Maidenhead, Berkshire. My friends and I, at one end of the hall, were eyeing the boys we would like to dance with and Dalton and his friends were at the other end looking at the girls they would like to ask. Because Dalton was not very tall, he was looking for a short girl and I fitted that description. But when the music started, he was too shy at first to cross the hall to ask me. He finally found the courage, and that was the beginning of our romance.

It was very short because three months after, Dalton was posted back to Canada. He sent me my engagement ring and I planned to sail as soon as possible. My still young mother however, became pregnant and I decided to stay with her until her baby was born. I'm glad I did because the baby turned out to be twins and she was glad of my help.

After sixteen months of correspondence, I sailed first class to Canada where Dalton met me in Montreal. I stayed with my future in-laws for two months, then on July 25, 1947 we were married.

Pam and Dalton Clost

I went through a few embarrassing experiences at first. When people asked what part of England I came from, I would innocently say, "Maidenhead." Believe me, I soon cut that out and said, "Berkshire." Before we were married, Dalton went into the drugstore to ask if any pictures were ready for Miss Shaw. The druggist said no, but there were some for a Miss Shore. Dalton said, "That's them!" So much for my English accent.

When friends in England heard I was leaving for Canada they said, "How will you put up with all that cold weather?'' It wasn't the cold that bothered me. God! With only one little fireplace to warm our house in England, the central heating was a blessing. It was the terrible humidity that I could not stand. I didn't know a person could perspire so much!

Dalton was the eldest of twelve children, and one day when I entered the kitchen for supper, I was shocked to see the whole family eating corn on the cob. This was fed to the animals in England and the only time I ever saw it was when I used to feed it to my grandfather's pigs. Believe me, I had a hard time eating that supper.

After our marriage we lived in rented rooms with borrowed furniture. We did buy a cupboard that cost three dollars and a two-burner stove with a toaster in the middle. The lady downstairs from us cooked on a wood stove, and the pipe from it ran up through our bedroom. Talk about heat!

Our first baby was born while we were there, and after one month she became quite ill. I was a proud and stubborn eighteen-year-old, and not having my own mother to talk to, I would not consult anyone else. When I realized how sick she was, it was too late and at two-and-a-half months, we lost her. I became pregnant right away, and just before our second girl was born, we moved into our own home that Dalton had worked so hard to build.

When I was pregnant for my fourth baby, my father died and Dalton and I brought my mother and brothers to Canada. It had been ten years since we had seen each other and what a wonderful reunion we had.

Through the years we have had our share of tragedies but on the whole life here has been very good to me, and to my brothers. Dalton has a very good position with a construction company, and I work in an accounting office. We own a lovely home and summer cottage, and personally, I do not think any of these wonderful things would have happened if I had not met that young soldier at a dance so many years ago.

****

Anne and Ossie Grist
Saskatchewan

When I was eighteen, I applied for canteen work and was accepted into the NAAFI in Aldershot. Like most young girls in a strange town, especially a military one, I was at first scared to go out alone. But after a few weeks, I went out with the crowd and fitted in like an old shoe.

British and Canadian forces used the canteen and they appeared to get along very well together, but at times it was quite noisy, especially when they came back from manoeuvres.

It was here I met Ossie. I had seen him in the canteen several times with his buddies, but did not dream he had been in England long enough to know the English currency so well. Hoping to get to know him better, I tried to pull a "fast one," and took all his money for his lunch without handing back any change.

Being polite, he never made any fuss but waited until another customer came in to buy lunch, and while my back was turned, took the customer's money. I asked for it back and he said, "That's what you get for not giving me my change." And as he says now, I have been taking his money ever since.

We went to dances whenever we could and talked a lot about Canada. Two other girls from the canteen married Canadian soldiers and we have remained great friends with one couple.

I awoke to rain on my wedding day, but the sun was shining for us when we came out of the church and I

141

Anne and Ossie Grist

touched the uniform collar of a British sailor which was supposed to bring good luck.

My young daughter Linda, aged seven months, and I, sailed on the *Franconia* from Liverpool for Canada on March 28, 1945. Up until then I had not thought too much about leaving England, but when the ship pulled away and I saw the last of a tall church steeple behind the docks, I realized that I could be seeing England possibly for the last time. We were on the Atlantic for twelve full days, some foggy and some stormy. I think the Captain and crew deserved a good pat on the back for getting us safely to Halifax.

The lights of Halifax harbour shining on the water looked so beautiful. Everyone was singing, "Don't fence me in," a hit song of the time, and to this day it never fails to touch my heart when I hear it.

The Red Cross took over throughout the train journey and were absolutely wonderful. They brought me a bassinette for Linda and were so helpful to everyone. In Montreal we were allowed to send telegrams, and in Ottawa I saw a huge clock that reminded me of Big Ben in London. A reporter from a Toronto newspaper took a picture of Linda and myself, and I had copies sent to my family in England.

We arrived in Winnipeg one very hot morning and as I had on a flannel suit, I thought I would cook with heat. The station was crowded with everyone pushing and shoving and I didn't know what to do because my husband's people lived in Portage La Prairie and I had no idea if anyone was there to meet me. I took a chance and got off the train leaving Linda on it. I realized after what a stupid thing it was, but at the time I did not think I was doing anything wrong. I found my way to a Red Cross booth and asked if my mother-in-law was waiting for me. She was. She had been there with her two daughters and a niece since the early hours of the morning.

When I saw her I thought what a lovely lady she was, and we took to each other straight away. One of my sisters-in-law said, "Where is Linda?" When I said she was still on the train there was great concern as the train was ready to leave for Edmonton. I explained that I could not take her off unless I could prove we had a place to stay. The Red Cross gave us permission when they knew we were staying with Ruth, my sister-in-law, and between tear drops and laughter, we were a happy bunch of people.

A taxi took us to Ruth's house where her son was frying a pile of bacon and eggs. I couldn't help telling him that one could not buy that much bacon or eggs in England in six months let alone for one meal.

Everything seemed strange, and leaving home and the long journey suddenly hit me like a ton of bricks, and I had to shut myself in the bedroom for a while. Later, when I felt better, Ruth gave me two airmail letters. One was from my brother, and the other one I had written to the in-laws telling them I was leaving England. All over it were thick pencil marks where the censor had crossed things out and written: "THIS PERSON TALKS TOO MUCH!" I could have crawled into a hole!

Sunday we arrived in Portage La Prairie where I was to stay with Ossie's parents, his sister Rachel and Don, her husband, until Ossie came home. I remember so well the beautiful house plants and snowy white lace curtains. There was a bucket of water sitting on the cupboard and Don lifted what I thought was a small saucepan, and took a drink. I said, "Don't you have any glasses in this house? Why do you drink out of a pot?" They laughed and explained it was called a dipper. The next surprise was the "biffy" out back. Rachel showed me the way and told me to call her if I needed anything. It was so dark and spooky. Rachel came looking for me and asked if I were okay. I said I was, but I couldn't find the chain! That was the second laugh.

I helped Legion members make up parcels for the boys who were still overseas. On the way there once, a plane from the nearby airport flew over and I immediately hit the dirt. Rachel laughed and said it was a friendly plane. It took quite a while for me to accept the fact that they would do us no harm.

My mother-in-law was the most rewarding person and I had the pleasure of loving her for ten years before she died. Anything I said or did was all right with her, although when put to task, she could hold her own.

My father-in-law was a staunch British Canadian and very exact in everything he did; a painter and decorator by trade, the house was spotless inside and out.

Ossie arrived home on Dominion Day, and it wasn't until 1948 that we bought a three-roomed house with no inside plumbing—just pumps outside—and oh! how it took a lot of patience and experience to thaw them out during those bitter cold winters. How I hated going outside to the "biffy" those dark winter nights.

There wasn't too much work around, but Ossie did get a job cutting the brush in the park for the city. At night he would come home crawling with wood ticks and not knowing any better, thought they were bed bugs which terrified us. How relieved we were when the barber told us what they were. We were about to burn everything we had—which wasn't much.

Once, the chimney caught fire in the wood stove and I ran outside for help. The fire chief gave me a good talking to, as I had left two children asleep in the back room. That winter was the worst I have ever experienced. We had a battery radio in the house and it was so cold that a new battery in a cardboard box broke in half.

Shortly after, Ossie was offered a job managing a general store in a small town some thirty-five miles away. We had to find a house to rent, which was not easy as there weren't many available. We found one that was filthy dirty and I sat in the middle of the floor and broke my heart. I said I was going back to England as I was not used to living in such a place. Ossie assured me everything would be all right if we stayed and worked together. I stayed.

A very strange thing happened while living in this town, and to tell the story I must go back to the time before I left England. A neighbour of ours in my hometown of South Tottenham, found out I was going to Manitoba and asked me if I would look up her aunt who lived there. Not realizing that the entire British Isles could be lost in practically every Canadian province, I said I would. She told me her name was Mrs. Fred

145

Salmon, and I never gave it another thought. Visiting the store that Ossie was managing, I met an elderly lady inside and our conversation ran something like this.

"Hello. Are you the new manager's wife?" asked the lady. I replied I was.

"Oh. I can tell you are from England. What part?"

"South Tottenham," I replied.

"How very strange. I am too. In fact I have relatives still there." She paused, then added, "Where in Tottenham?"

"Seaford Road," I said. She became quite excited as she declared that she too came from Seaford Road. I looked at her and said, "Your name wouldn't be Salmon would it?" It sure enough was, and I told her that her niece was our next door neighbour. She came to tea one afternoon and we had a wonderful chat. I introduced my small son to her and said, "Percy. This is Mrs. Salmon, dear." He studied her very carefully for a moment, then said, "Did you come out of a tin can?" Talk about kids getting you hung!

We moved back to Portage La Prairie one stormy January day, and it was not too long before our life really changed for the better. A man offered Ossie a job in Saskatchewan. We talked it over, and as the saying goes, "Go west young man, go west," we decided to venture. Our life was so much better in all ways from then on, that it made all our first experiences worthwhile.

We had three children, all married now with children of their own. I went back to England in 1967 and 1972, and believe me, I'm quite contented here and thankful that I was able to make Canada my home.

****

Ballad of the Brides
by Gwyneth M. Shirley

There were six hundred war brides who sailed away
On an old troopship one winter day.
For Canada bound, after World War II,
From England they sailed, to start life anew.

At first, all went well. They feasted each night,
Exclaiming with wonder, unused to the sight
Of white bread and oranges, sugar piled high,
Rich gold butter and ice cream with pie.

But, alas! two days later a boisterous sea
Swept up the ship with sadistic glee;
Way below deck, it was hell—plain hell—
Tossed like toys on the turbulent swell.

Six hundred war brides, prostrate and pale,
Bewailing the day they ever set sail—
Bonny Scots lasses, Irish colleens,
French girls and Dutch brides, still in their teens.

Six hundred war brides with mal de mer racked—
Bunks close together like cheap coffins stacked—
Lost between two worlds; a limbo where love
Seemed more remote than the stars up above.

Homesick and seasick, each girl in her bed
Found time to think and found time to dread
The uncertain future and life in a land
She never might love or understand.

Ten days, ten nights on that hateful sea
And then . . . a strange tranquility!

A silence, unearthly, around them lay;
By noon, thick fog obscured the day!

While fate stepped in, played a cruel trick,
The children were suddenly taken sick.
So near and yet so far from land,
Still as a statue the ship seemed to stand.

Too weak to cry, the babies lay,
More feverish every passing day,
While Red Cross nurses, four in all,
Tried to cope with every call.

The ship ached in every bone.
Oh! You could hear her timbers groan.
But through the fog she groped her way,
Detached, suspended, steeped in grey.

At last, a vast expanse of sky
And raucous gulls a-wheeling high,
While on the waves, a welcoming sign:
Dark strands of seaweed intertwine.

The cry went up, "Land, land in sight!"
Look where the distant sea breaks white
Against a bleak and barren shore—
Surely untouched by man before.

And then the sun's reflected light
Sparkled on window panes so bright.
"A house, a house" . . . with wood piled high
And frozen washing 'gainst the sky.

The *Aquitania* docked with ease
And standing in the chilly breeze

Six hundred brides one thought did share,
"It's Halifax, we're really there."

The quayside, bright with colours gay,
Bedecked with flags to mark the day,
Bustled with life. The cheeful sound
Of drums reverberated round.

Army officers, shouting commands,
Mingled with citizens shaking hands.
Sally Ann ladies, served cups of tea,
Coffee and sandwiches, all quite free.

Mounties in scarlet stood stiff as starch
To rousing strains of the Wedding March
While one brass band broke in to play
"O Canada" on such a day.

And war brides awaiting sang along
Not sure of the words but liking the song.
Their voices floated across the sea;
Their story passed into history.

This was the last war bride crossing of the *Aquitania* in
January, 1947.

Reprinted with permission of *Legion Magazine*.

****

There was a self-service café in the Woolworth's where I worked in Piccadilly, the main shopping centre of Manchester. Vern came into the café one day with two army buddies who already had dates for the evening. One of them asked me if I would like to date Vern to even it up. I said if he couldn't ask me himself, why bother. Vern was very shy, but did pluck up the courage to ask me. We were both very young, Vern seventeen and I fifteen. Although we were just kids, we went out regularly, and when he left he asked me to write him.

I left Woolworth's and went into a factory that made plastic tubing for aeroplane radios. I stayed there until I was seventeen, then joined the Land Army until Vern and I were married. I never really considered marrying anyone whose home was so far from mine, but I did when I became eighteen.

We had planned to get married in the October, but the army decided to send Vern home sooner than we expected. He was on leave when the signed permission for us to marry came in the mail on Friday, September 28, 1945. The next day we were married in the Registrar's office at 11 a.m.

There was some tearing around that day, I can tell you. I managed to buy a suit, hat and shoes. Vern had his uniform cleaned, and that was it. No frills or fripperies. Vern never put on any act. He told me he helped his dad on a farm, and farming was what he intended to do when he got home; that life on the Island was a good deal different from the life in the big city of Manchester. He was honest with me, for which I was grateful. I was fortunate in that respect; some girls were not.

Vern was waiting for me in Halifax when the

Joyce and Vern Norring

Aquitania docked on April 10, 1946. I was able to leave the ship almost immediately, and in my haste and excitement, left my one pair of good shoes on board.

The following morning we left for Prince Edward Island, and Vern said when he left there, the weather was good. When we arrived however, his father met us with a long wooden box sleigh. I didn't know whether to laugh or cry when they wrapped fur robes around me to keep me warm. Snow blocked all the roads so we travelled through fields. At the tender age of eighteen, I had no idea what to expect. It certainly wasn't snow!

I was cold and scared when we reached my in-laws' farm, and to complicate matters, I could not understand them very well as their Danish accent was quite prominent.

We stayed there a couple of months until we got our own farm, and then life really was an experience. The farmhouse was huge and surrounded with woods. Bats flew around at dusk and I often wonder how I ever stood it. I was pregnant with our first child and had the habit of falling quite often, much to the concern of the neighbours. But I laughed it off as one of those quirks of pregnancy.

Our toilet was a two-seater in a small building at the back of the house, and I do mean back; it was about one-quarter mile away. We had five children by the time I was twenty-six, so I had my hands full.

During the cold winters the children had to use a "potty," and it was emptied into a five-gallon can that we used as a "slop pail." Sometimes Vern would be away at the store getting supplies, and I would undertake to empty it. Knee deep in snow, and in some places up to my hips in drifts, I would drag this pail. With one leg down in the snow, I would cross-wise the other trying to get a foot hold. The more I dragged that darn pail, the further away the outhouse seemed to be. What a chore! By the time I got back to the house, my legs were raw and wet from the cold.

The local hall put on a movie once in a while and sometimes Vern and I would go. One night when we came home, Vern lit the oil lamp and we got ready for bed. As I turned down the bed covers, four mice were running around in our bed. Vern chased them all over while I was roaring blue blazes. I don't think I slept very well that night.

152

Our first child was a boy and a delight to us both. Even so, I was very lonely that first year, and shed many a tear for my family and England, and I often wondered what I had let myself in for. Money was scarce in those days, and sometimes we would get butter sent to us in payment for the cream we had shipped. We had no modern equipment so everything was done the hard way. It was thrilling when years later the electricity was installed.

Once, when the children were still babies, Vern asked me to drive the tractor while he picked potatoes by hand. The twins were asleep, the two eldest playing, so I wrapped up our baby daughter and took her with us. It was some job driving that tractor and holding the baby while the snow blew in my face. Every now and then we would stop and Vern would light a fire for me so I could warm my hands, then off we'd go again. It was experiences like this that either made or broke you.

In 1954, Vern worked very hard trying to get into purebred Holstein cattle. We had two old barns, and he and other men put them on blocks and moved them together to make one long barn. They put in a cement foundation; stalls for the cows where they were to be milked; pens for one, two and three-year-old calves, and upstairs a new hen-house. The other part of the barn held pigs, and over the loft, all the feed. They all worked very hard to get this done before the summer ended, and Vern was mighty proud of the project.

On September 10, just one month after it was finished, hurricane Edna blew in and flattened it all. Luckily we had left the cows out all night as some of the stanchions that held them at milking time had twisted.

The neighbours rallied together pulling timber away to see if any animals were buried. Some pigs were already dead and others squealing with pain had to be destroyed on the spot. We lost fifteen pigs. But the most pathetic of all was when our eldest son, then eight, got up in the morning and, seeing all the turmoil around him, started to cry as he ran and found a litter of kittens we did not know we had. He held them so tightly in his arms and asked our permission to bring them into the house so he could look after them.

How does one feel at times like these? I felt completely numb and Vern could not believe that this happened after all the hard work he had done. The garage where we housed the tractor had to serve as a milking shed, and of course the cattle were reluctant to enter. But they had to be milked and put back into the field so that we could work at the pile of lumber that had been our barn.

Neighbours are wonderful, especially in times of distress. They started canvassing and holding bean suppers and dances to help us rebuild. The response was fantastic. Not only did they help money-wise, but men gave their valuable time to help us rebuild and bring in our crops. Everyone was so kind, and we were full of gratitude.

Harvest is a busy time. We grew thirty acres of potatoes and most of the help came from Cape Breton. Vern would try to have enough potatoes dug and stored, then on rainy days they would grade them ready for shipping. I never knew such large amounts of food could be consumed in one meal. It seemed all a body was doing was cooking meat and vegetables, serving, and washing dishes. Sometimes I would be asked to help outside as well when they were shorthanded.

It was during these times that I would get so tired and depressed, for after the evening meal, there were five children to get ready for bed. The hours were long, so little wonder I never gained any weight. But I chalked it all up as being a wonderful and interesting adventure.

We never went out much, never had the money. Anyway, Vern was a firm believer in . . . "We brought children into the world and it's up to us to look after them." We never asked his family or hired a babysitter to help.

We gave up the farm a few years ago and moved into a small bungalow, and oh! what a difference. We still lead a quiet life. Vern works for the CN Ferry service so I am alone a lot. The children are all married with their own families to bring up. As kids, they loved the farm and the animals. It was a hard life, but what we accomplished was well worth all the hardships.

****

Hilda and Hal Jenkins
New Brunswick

It was a lovely warm July evening in 1945, and I wanted so much to take the bus to Windsor, but my friend Margaret and her sister suggested we go into a club. Margaret got into conversation with three Canadian soldiers, and soon we were introducing ourselves. Before I realized it, we were all walking down the street to the local dance hall, and I found myself paired with Hal. He had been wounded in Holland with shrapnel in his shoulder and lung, and had been in the hospital near Slough where I lived.

We saw a lot of each other, and when we knew we wanted to marry, I recall there was a lot of red-tape to go through. When all these preliminaries were over, we were married and our reception was a very happy one. Dad, who was a Welshman, sang for us, and my uncle played the piano, and we all enjoyed ourselves with what

155

Hal and Hilda Jenkins

little we had.   Margaret, too, married one of these
soldiers, and he was our best man.

Leaving my mother and two younger brothers in
December 1946 for Canada, was one of the hardest things
I have ever done, for dad was killed a month before from
a bicycle accident that ended his life at the age of fifty-
four.   It is very hard to put into words the way I felt the
night I stayed in the London hostel before embarkation.

Margaret and her baby son were travelling with me and my six-week-old daughter and really, it took all my will-power to stay there and not return home to my mother.

When the *Samaria* docked in Halifax on December 18, Margaret and I said goodbye, for her husband was waiting for her there while I boarded the train for Moncton. What a different world I was in! From a large bustling city to a small town surrounded by thick woods. And oh! so cold.

Hal was in hospital with T.B. and had to stay there for eighteen months before he was able to come home. He was allowed to meet us and take us to stay with his sister and her husband, and my father-in-law. We settled in quite well, but I missed Hal very much.

One day when my sister-in-law was away, Hal's dad asked me to make pea soup. There I was with my thoughts on how to go about it. In England we bought peas-pudding, but I had never heard of just pea soup. Well, I thought, I best get started and opened two cans of peas, put them in a pot, added some water and placed them on the wood stove. When Hal's father came in from the barn, he looked into the pot and said, "What kind of mess is that?" I replied that it was the nearest thing to pea soup I could think of . . . needless to say, it got thrown out! I soon learnt how to make it the right way.

During the first winter it amazed me to see how dazzling the snow was when the sun was shining. I thought the family foolish when they asked if I would like to walk on the crust, and thought they meant bread crusts. Once outside I discovered what they did mean.

When Hal came home, he was unable to work for two years. He then got a job with the Fraser Company in Plaster Rock. We were able to buy a house nine miles from there, and in 1953 it burned to the ground. We built again on the same spot, but sold it in 1955 and

157

moved back to England. We stayed with mum for seven months but, to my great disappointment, Hal could not settle. Back we came to Plaster Rock and bought another house. When we were renovating the inside, this too got burnt and we had to redo it. I was lucky to save photographs and personal things that could not be replaced.

We were happy with our family of four daughters and one son, although tragedy struck when we lost our daughter from pneumonia at the age of fourteen months. As the children grew up, we all enjoyed the outdoor life and camped and boated as often as we could.

Hal was town foreman with the Public Works until his lung collapsed in 1970, then he was unable to continue. He was hospitalized again and unable to work anymore.

We have been back to England several times, and I consider myself extremely lucky. I really love to get back home to my family and friends and to the house where I grew up. I have been fortunate, too, that my mother has been able to visit us in Canada.

Since last winter, life has become very confined for us as Hal is now bedfast. Sickness is very distressing and sometimes I feel like giving up. But who can help what life has in store for them? I am just thankful for the happy years Hal and I have had together.

****

Gloria and John Brock
Saskatchewan

Like a lot of war brides, I met my future husband at a dance. I was born and raised in Hyde Park, Leeds, in Yorkshire, and one night in August 1944, I met John at the Mecca ballroom. We became engaged on October 9, just before he was sent to Belgium. All the wedding arrangements were left to me, and as I listened to the banns being read in Hyde Park parish church, John heard them in a church in Belgium. He flew over for the wedding which was on May 26, 1945.

A few of his friends from the air force base attended, and we had a large reception after which we all went to the White Rose hotel where my parents had booked entertainment for the evening. Everyone helped me with the rationing coupons so that I could buy wedding and going-away outfits.

John was expecting to leave for India when I left England. I took one look at the ship I was to board and said to myself, "This boat will never make it. It's much too small." I was wrong, however. After ten days of tossing, sea sickness and thick fog, the *Letitia* berthed in Halifax, June 29, 1946. I was expecting our first child, and after such a long journey was sure I would lose it.

The porters on the train were absolutely wonderful and did more to help than anyone else. One of these boys bought fruit for us and provided reading material. On my birthday, when a group of us were sitting together, he sang for us. He even made sandwiches for a birthday treat. They were only jam, but it was the thought and kindness shown that counted.

The seat I was given was on the left side facing the engine. After I had been in Canada a few days, people began asking what I thought of it. My reply to this was: "I sat on the left side of the train and it looked pretty good to me. Someday I hope to sit on the right side and see the other half." This always brought laughter.

Reaching Regina in ninety degree weather and wearing heavy clothing, was very uncomfortable. Unfortunately, my trunk with all my clothes continued on a journey to heaven-knows-where, and I did not receive it for a long time.

Leeds is a very large industrial town, and I went

straight to a small farming community of about five hundred, and that's stretching it a little. John was still overseas and my new home was with his parents. I was quite scared about this. Supposing they didn't like me . . . what would happen? I think I had someone guiding me because I was so warmly welcomed. My mother-in-law was, and still is, a gem of a woman. She helped me tremendously with her kind understanding ways. She had raised a large family and knew how strange everything was to me, and how I felt.

Whatever she was doing at 4 p.m., she would stop and have a cup of tea with me because she thought that everyone in England did this. When my baby was due to arrive, it was she who got up and took me to hospital. If I had to choose my own mother-in-law, I could never have found better. At the time, I told myself that this was her home and I was a guest, and as long as I remembered this, I could adjust.

My father-in-law was a very hard-working farmer whom I respected very much. He knew the farming business inside out. I never realized that a farmer had to be an engineer, seed inspector, vet and lawyer all rolled into one. Until I came to live on a farm, I'm afraid I took farmers for granted as having the best of both worlds.

The people in the community wanted to give me a shower. Now this to me was rain or water, and in no way were they going to pour water over my head. There were six war brides to be "showered" I learned, and I thought I must not spoil it for them. So off I went to the church basement, and what a sight met my eyes! Tables were decorated beautifully, and gifts covered them from one end to the other. I just could not believe it. I was really in a rosy haze that night.

John came home in late August, and I decided to bake a cake for the occasion. I mixed all the ingredients until

160

the batter was smooth and creamy then placed it in the oven to cook. When I took it out, it would have made someone a good door step. I asked my mother-in-law what I had done wrong. She asked me how much baking powder I had put in. Baking powder? I thought it was self-raising flour that we used back home. I didn't know one had to use baking powder. So much for that cake.

One thing I didn't care too much for was the fact that some people wanted me to join a particular church. They meant well I'm sure. But I was left with the impression that if I didn't join, I would be left out of things. If John had asked me to go to this particular church, I very likely would have, but I found one of my own denomination and I joined it.

The church held only sixty people, but the way they worked to keep that little church going, impressed me very much, and I felt that this was for me. I helped in both churches whenever asked, and now people and times have changed so that the two churches work hard at supporting each other. Whether they see it or not, it has given them a better understanding of each other and their devotion.

John and I had three children, and our lives have been interesting. We started with nothing, and I mean just that. We didn't even have a tree. Over two hundred we planted by hand and pail-watered each one. Now when I look outside and see them, I feel very proud. We built our house from an old one; had no table so sat up to the sink counter on saw-horses. Later, John made a table out of plywood, which I still have. Our one big buy was a monster called a coal and wood range which I'm sure resented me and tried many times to break my morale. We also invested in a radio, as we needed some kind of entertainment.

We fixed each room in the house one-by-one when we had the time and money. I remember we lived our first

161

six months on three-hundred dollars. It was hard as the baby's needs took a large portion of it, and I tried not to let John see how homesick I was.

Life has not been all good; neither has it been all bad, and John has always said he could not have made it without me "digging in." With this kind of husband, and knowing what I know now, I would still do it all over again but I would make a better job of it.

****

Anonymous

In a sleepy village in the province of Gronigen, Holland, on May 13, 1945, I met Ray. My girlfriend and I were out walking and he was riding a bicycle, trying to show he could ride every bit as well as the Dutch. He smiled, and said "hello" and stopped to chat, then asked me if I would like to go for a walk that evening. The language was no barrier because I had studied English for six years. Our romance blossomed and we were married on December 13 the same year.

Just before I left Holland in August 1946 for Canada via England, I received a telegram from my father-in-law who was a lieutenant in the Canadian army and on leave in London. He said he was coming to Holland to meet me and my family. Very disappointed, for I would have liked him to meet my family, I had to wire him back to say I was leaving for England immediately. He wired back again and said, "Meet you at Tilbury docks London." I was very eager to meet him but alas! army rules were that he was not allowed near the ship, and I was not allowed to leave it. So somewhere on that crowded dock was a man waving frantically to all the war brides, and I was waving to the crowd, but so was

Field Marshal Viscount Montgomery and Archbishop of Canterbury
with Dutch brides

everyone else waving too. We did not meet until he was back in Canada and discharged.

Many things about the voyage I have forgotten and would like to turn the clock back and do it all over again. I do remember having for breakfast one morning a bowl of cornflakes. Not ever having seen them before, none of us knew milk and sugar should be added, so we ate them dry. We all thought it was rather odd food, then.

Field Marshal Montgomery was on the *Mauretania* as well, and seven other girls and myself occupied a cabin next to this great man. We were all sorry not to get even a glimpse of him.

The trip from Holland to England was rough and stormy and I was never so glad to see land. This reminds me of one poor girl on the *Mauretania* who really looked grim from seasickness. "How can I meet my husband looking like this?" she kept saying. In every crowd there's a joker, and we were no exception. This particular war bride suggested to her that if she could bathe her face in good salty sea water every day, she would look absolutely radiant. The poor girl fell for it and just about drove all ship personnel crazy begging them to get it for her. Suffice to say, it cured the seasickness. A case of mind-over-matter perhaps.

Ray and I stayed for a while with his family, then later, with the help of the Veteran's Land Act we purchased a small fruit farm near Niagara Falls, Ontario, and have been there ever since.

I adjusted to the new way of life in Canada very well, and loved this country right from the beginning. The subsequent years have been happy and I am proud to say I am a Canadian.

****

164

My father is Canadian and was in England during the First World War. He was admitted into the hospital for jaw casualties and my grandmother was the nurse who looked after him. Through her, he met her daughter, my mother, and they fell in love. When dad was sent back to Canada, he had to save up the money to send for my mother, and she arrived here in 1920.

Three of us kids were born in Canada, and in 1929 my father had to take mother back to England for she was very ill. We settled in Farnborough where dad built a military laundry, the largest at that time. It was called the Hampshire Steam Laundry Ltd., and was on Queen's Road. I am sure many a serviceman will remember it, even if it is only for shrinking their socks!

In England during the first war, my father had made friends with a George MacDonald, and they stayed friends throughout the years.

When the Second World War started, George's son, Deane, came to England and visited us. Then in October 1942, Deane's cousin Stuie (my husband) came over and Deane wrote to him and told him to go and see my father at the laundry as he was an old friend of his dad's. Actually, Deane had just returned to Wales after spending his honeymoon at our place.

Dad brought Stuie home for supper, and we found that our birthday's were the same day with Stuie being three years older.

After I had finished school, I went into the Royal Aircraft Establishment as a stenographer and had the experience of typing manuscripts about the first jet planes when they were top secret. Besides working for the RAE, I spent time with the Civil Defence, ambulance division, for which I had to have a St. John certificate;

one night a week at the Toc H, a service club; one night fire-watching at my dad's laundry; and any spare Saturdays, I worked sorting salvage, bottles, bones, papers and so forth. A very dirty job, but I think we were all fired with enthusiasm.

In between these duties I had fun at dances and in the shelter dad had built under our two-car garage. He outfitted it with a small-sized pool table and dart boards, and many a good time we had down there. One complete wall was covered with names of servicemen, mostly Canadian like my dad. It was great having so many men around.

Then I started dating Stuie, and we were married on May 1, 1943. Deane was a Flight Lieutenant by this time, a spitfire ace, and was best man at our wedding. He died for his country six months later.

There are probably very few brides who cannot remember their first trip to Canada. Although I was born here, my own remains quite vividly in my memory. The Canadian Red Cross and those responsible for our transportation were simply marvellous. The efficient system was practically faultless.

Stuie left for Canada in September 1945, and at that time we had one daughter, Diane, aged eighteen months, and a baby due in February. I had hopes of following him in time for Christmas, but not so. Our travelling papers did not come until July 1946, and instead of two children, there were three. I had twin girls.

Luggage, kept to a minimum, was a problem with three children to clothe, especially since I had to have enough formula for two to last throughout the journey. Now that I have grown children, I realize how my mother must have felt watching me and three children leaving for a strange country. After all, she had also been through the same situation.

In Liverpool our children were whisked away from us

Peggy and Stuie McEwen

much to the horror of Diane who thought she was losing me forever. The mothers were taken through customs and had to fill out forms, forms and more forms. A good hour later I reached the cabin where the twins were yelling lustily, and Diane, poor little soul, had fallen into a sobbing heap beside them.

We were on a hospital ship and were sixteen women and eighteen children in one cabin. Every morning at

10:30 there was a cabin inspection. What a rush and commotion to get it straightened in time! I met on board another girl who had a three-year-old and thirteen-month-old twins who had just started walking . . . and I thought I was busy!

There were two periods during the day when the tap water was fresh and what a rush to get our washing done. We had a "love" of a steward who took it all and dried it for us in the engine room. When the weather was fine, we sat on deck in a circle with the children in the middle so we could keep our eyes on them. This way they shared their toys and played together.

Diane's evening meal was brought to her in the cabin everyday at five o'clock and she ate while I bathed and fed the twins and got them ready for bed. At six, she came to the diningroom with me for she wouldn't let me out of her sight. After she was asleep at night, I went with the other girls to a movie or to bingo. Sometimes we just sat and talked about our families and wondered what our new homes would be like.

After four days at sea, I became seasick and didn't care whether I lived or died. The nurses looked after the twins, and I don't remember what Diane did . . . probably pestered everyone in the cabin. The stewards came every evening and fed me soda crackers and gingerale whether I wanted it or not. One time I tried walking on deck and had to rush to the rail. I heard Diane crying but was helpless to do anything. Someone kindly took her to the ship's office and I managed to get there to claim her. The twins stayed healthy until the seventh day, then they developed dysentery which plagued almost every baby aboard. I was glad to see the journey end.

On the train the Red Cross nurses fell in love with the twins and took over, giving me a much-needed rest. Reaching Toronto, I found no husband waiting. I

168

almost cried with sheer frustration and exhaustion. I asked for Stuie at a Red Cross booth, and the lady told me he was there somewhere. It seemed an eternity before my name came over the loudspeaker and Stuie came flying around the corner to grab me in his arms.

Diane did not remember her daddy for it had been almost a year since she had seen him. It was heartbreaking for him. Stuie's mother and dad were so good to us and since my own mum died in 1954, I have just one "mum" and she is great. We lived with them for two months and mum taught me a lot. Three days after we arrived, she took to her bed . . . just the strain of preparing for our arrival. I had to do the cooking and decided to make a pie. The filling was lovely, but the dog wouldn't even eat the crust. We ground it up for the chickens. I cried, and mum said, "Never mind, Peggy. I'll teach you to bake." And she certainly did.

Some of the presents that were given me at a kitchen shower, I still use today. I was so shy that night with thirty-odd girls, all strangers, ogling at me. It was their way of welcoming me to Canada, and was much appreciated.

I was never really homesick. From age thirteen I had been away to boarding school and this tends to toughen up a person. Only once I remember being homesick and that was the first Christmas here. We were living in the village of Drayton, Ontario, and Stuie's parents lived on the other side of it. The family gathered there, and I had Diane, the twins and was pregnant, and felt very downhearted.

Carol was born on May 30, 1947 and snow was still lying in the fields for that winter had been especially hard. We hadn't told my parents about my being pregnant because my grannie was sick and mum had enough problems. But when they received the cable saying, "Fourth girl arrived," mum was over within a month.

169

This was another reason why I wasn't homesick. I was too busy . . . also my parents came to see me every year.

I recall being horribly fascinated when Stuie took me to a friend's farm for supper. This family had huge young men and they ATE; huge helpings, and all kinds of pie for dessert. I was astounded at the amount of food consumed, and didn't realize that they had put in a twelve-hour day in the fields.

Like others, we were poor for the first few years and had only an old truck for transportation. Driving back from seeing Stuie's parents who had moved to Dundas, we had four flat tires, the last of which Stuie said, "To hell with it," and took it to a garage.

We had apple trees in the garden, and one day when

Peggy McEwen and five daughters

170

we were cleaning them up, one of the twins sat on a tub full. The other tub had just a layer of apples floating on top of water. The other twin came along and sat on it. Was she ever surprised!

We buried our dog, Pat, in that garden. Or I should say Diane did. She was only four-and-a-half, and conducted a real service. Since she had been staying weekends with some Catholic friends of ours, it was liberally sprinkled with "Hail Mary's."

I have had, and am still having, a wonderful life in Canada. Stuie has always been my "back-bone," and has been at my right hand always. He has helped with the children, the canning and preserving. Now it is thirty-six years, five daughters and fourteen grandchildren later, and he still says things to make me feel like a bride. What more could I ask for?

****

Vera and Gilbert Giberson
New Brunswick

My uncle, who immigrated to Canada after the First World War, gave Gilbert, who boarded with him, my parents' address in Kensington, London, when his regiment left for England in 1942. Uncle had never mentioned anything about Gilbert, so his visit was a complete surprise. Of course, it led to our going out together for a couple of years until we were married in July 1945.

Prior to my leaving for Canada, I worked in Cadby Hall for the J. Lyons Company preparing food for restaurants. Thinking I was not "doing enough" for the war effort, I left. An American firm located in East Acton was hiring girls for war work, and I found myself spraying parts for radios. Quite a difference from working with food. The Duke of Kent visited us here a week before he was killed.

I left for Canada in May 1946 on the *Ile de France* along with two hundred other war brides, two hundred civilians, and eight thousand troops.

I thought Halifax a dreary dismal place, and many of the brides wanted to turn back right away. However, we "stayed with it," and I have often wondered how they are now. On the bus from St. John, New Brunswick, to my destination point, a small but pretty town, I met a very drunken sailor who bought me my first hot-dog and said he was glad I was a "limey." Why, I never found out.

Gil and I lived with his mother until we built our own eight-roomed house, where we still live today. Life was far from easy in those early years. I had four children in four years, and it was always a struggle to keep them in clothing and food.

It seemed at the time that people in this area always ate homemade beans every Saturday. When Gil asked me to make them, I hadn't the faintest idea what to do. He will never forget the little hard rocks I served him that evening so long ago. Neither will I! Same with buckwheat pancakes. Mine turned out like slabs of cement until I learned I had to add the baking soda and powder to the flour.

Gilbert has worked at the Fraser Lumber Mill since leaving the army. Two of our children are still at home. A son, since leaving the navy, also works at the mill; our other son and his wife are both in the forces; one daughter at home; the other married and living in Manitoboa.

Although life here was hard at first, it has been a good life and much easier these latter years. My mother is now eighty-two years old and I have been able to visit her several times. England will always be home to me although I am proud to be a Canadian citizen.

****

Pat and Tommy Thompson
Yukon

Tommy was a bomb-aimer with the Royal Canadian Air Force when we met in Darlington in November 1943. He had not done his first op. over enemy territory when he asked me to marry him shortly after. I suggested we wait until he had finished his tour of operations which was thirty-four trips. However, he talked me into marriage after his thirteenth, and May 11, 1944 was our wedding day.

Our honeymoon was almost disastrous which I blamed on wedding-day excitement. At the end of this story, a poem I wrote for Tommy on our thirty-first wedding anniversary tells what happened.

The night he completed his tour of ops., and came home to tell me all was accomplished, was a night to remember. We were so happy it was over, and relieved.

Tommy left for Canada in November 1944, and I followed two months later on the *Mataroa*, a New Zealand ship that was replacing the *Ile de France* which was in New York undergoing repairs. Sailing down the Clyde out of Glasgow, I remember the dock workers singing "Will ye Nae Come Back Again." To say we were all crying buckets is an understatement. In convoy for seventeen days on the stormy Atlantic, I kept asking myself a hundred times a day, what I was doing there.

My twentieth birthday was celebrated en route, and though the food on board was rationed almost as badly as in England, the chef put on his best show. The steward arrived in the diningroom with a large covered silver

173

Pat and Tommy Thompson

platter which, to everyone's amusement, held one small cup cake with twenty lighted matches. To me it was wonderful. There we were, in the middle of that cold, cold ocean with everybody singing in that friendly warm atmosphere, "Happy Birthday."

I'll never forget the waiter on the train when he asked, "One egg, or two?" My fellow passengers and I wondered if we had heard correctly. Arriving in Toronto, I saw Tommy and his family walking down the platform. I was so scared and nervous I hid behind a Red Cross lady until my name had been called several times. Then tears and greetings came as we met again. I put my arms around a stout lady who informed me, "I'm not your mother-in-law, just a neighbour."

I soon settled in with Tommy's family. The amount of food on the table at meal times never ceased to amaze me. I wrote home three times a week and told my mother how wonderful Canada was and sometimes had to tear up the letter because the ink was so blurred from my tears.

When we settled in a home of our own, I made my first enemy . . . a cantankerous cook stove! Tommy chopped the kindling every morning before leaving for work, telling me to use it sparingly before adding the coal and logs. Usually before 9 a.m. all the kindling was gone and I was thankful I had brought lots of woolies with me. Finally, I hit upon the idea of stocking up with empty toilet tissue rolls and filling the insides with floor wax. They burned beautifully, and often I could get the coal to catch from them.

Tommy's favourite of my blunders was when we were at the market and he said, "Pat. Let's buy one of these." Fearfully I looked at the watermelon he was holding and said, "Oh no! Tommy, I don't know how to cook it," much to the amazement of other shoppers.

My mother-in-law gave me a good-sized enamel pot complete with lid. It was just the right size in which to store the bread and biscuits. Imagine my embarrassment when she came to visit and saw me taking bread out of a chamber pot!

I cannot say that I liked Canada at first. It took me a long time to adjust. I still love England which will always be home to me. But, I also know my place is here, and it is where I belong.

Now, three children and seven grandchildren later,

175

with numerous visits back to England, I've come to the conclusion that homesickness never leaves, it becomes a part of life. Nothing can compare with the northern England sense of humour; the pubs with their nightly songs, laughter and friendly atmosphere; visiting my mother in the same house where I was born; the same neighbours who still can call the "sure thing" over the backyard wall for the horse racing of the day. But then, my ties are here and there are the grandchildren who say "Ta-ra" as easily as they say "bye-bye."

Would I do it all over again? Of course I would. I cannot believe the years have flown so quickly, and I hope God blesses us with many more.

Thirty-One Years of Sheer Bliss!

Thirty-one years today my dear
Since we made our marriage vows.
The memories of that sunny day
Come back to me fondly now.
Remember we set off for London town—
I had never seen that city
And as the train began to move
You said, "Honey, where's the 'kitty'?"

We had seventy pounds saved up, you see,
To spend on a grand honeymoon.
And to keep it safe, in a secret place,
It was home in my own bedroom.
My heart took a thump;
In my throat was a lump
As I had to admit my terror
That, in my excitement,
I had left it at home
And that was my first marriage error.

176

Well, love conquers all
And we had a ball on our thirty-two
Shillings and sixpence.
The bombs were hailing;
The sirens were wailing
But we didn't give a damn, for
We dined on chips along with fish
And sometimes, chips with Spam.

My heart would dance,
As I thought of the ranch
Of which you had told me so often;
Of the great gopher spread
Of which it was said
Was bound to make us a fortune.

To sum it all up,
Let's lift up our cups
And drink to the good times we knew.
We don't need the ranch;
All I need is a chance
To round up my days with you.

Happy Anniversary, Tommy.

****

There were six hundred war brides on the ship I was on when returning from overseas. One humorous remark I overheard in our sleeping quarters was another airman remarking how old the brides looked. Some wise guy spoke up and said, "If you ask me, I think they must have missed the boat from the last war!"

Contributed by an anonymous veteran airman.

****

My home was in Acton, west London, nearby
Hammersmith. I'm sure there are many war brides and
Canadian servicemen who remember the Hammersmith
Palais and the good dances they held there.

I very much wanted to join one of the services, but my
dad was against it, and in those days one did as their
parents told them, so I worked in an aircraft factory. I
met my husband in Hyde Park one day while he was on
leave. This meeting led to many more, and then
marriage. After our wedding, I wanted to join the
Canadian service (CWAC), but Dusty was more against it
than my dad, so I gave up trying. Instead I worked in
the Canadian Records Office in Acton until I left for
Canada aboard the *Queen Elizabeth* on May 4, 1946,
arriving in Halifax four days after on the first anniversary
of VE Day.

My two-year-old son, Glen, had been exposed to
chicken pox prior to sailing, and I was in a panic lest he
broke out and we would be kept in Halifax. He most
conveniently waited until we arrived in Woodstock,
Ontario. Glen absolutely refused to use a strange toilet.
As the hostel we stayed in before sailing was so close to
home, I made a quick trip back and got his "pottie."
My, but that thing got a lot of use among Canada's
young new citizens. When the *Queen* pulled out, I
remember thinking, "Oh! It's just too far to jump now,
even if I could." It seemed so final when one had no
idea of what lay ahead.

My husband had decided to buy the home farm from
his parents, and I hadn't a clue as to farm life. I asked
him what they used for lights, having visions of paraffin
lamps, and he said they used hydro. I was none the
wiser not knowing what hydro meant. I had dozens of

Ethel and Dusty Millar

new relatives and they were all gathered to meet us and made us so welcome. Poor Glen! His daddy was a stranger to him; he had only seen him twice. When bedtime came he went to kiss his picture as he'd always done. His daddy soon set that right.

The abundance of food amazed me. And the sausages! Oh, the joy of having something left after cooking them. One had gotten used to losing half of the English kind after they were cooked.

We stayed with the in-laws for a few days, then moved to our new farm. Surprise number one! The kitchen needed papering. Dusty had done the painting, but I found out the women did the papering. Oh joy of joys! My mother-in-law and various other relatives descended on the house one day and went to work. I was given the lovely job of cutting the borders and pasting paper. I had never papered before. My dad always did ours. The kitchen was huge, twenty-five feet long by fifteen feet wide, with more windows and doors than I had ever seen in one room. I did eventually learn the fine art of wall papering, but never will I forget my first attempt at papering the ceiling. It was catastrophic!

I was determined to learn farm life, but my introduction to threshing was really something. Never had I seen so much food, or seen it vanish so fast. My mother-in-law cooked all this on a wood stove, and the heat was fierce. Another surprise was my cook stove. It must have been six feet in length, with a reservoir at one end, and a warming oven on top. After getting used to dampers and drafts, I conquered the brute. It sure baked great pies. There were many burnt offerings before I got the hang of it. I was so happy when a furnace and electric stove replaced it, although I would probably get a fortune for such an antique now.

Stove pipes were another necessity of life. As far as I know, the woodwork in the upstairs hall of the old farmhouse still bears the scars from the day Dusty threw a length of pipe in disgust when it refused to go back together after the annual clean out. This was a miserable job. One put bags over the ends of pipes to prevent soot from falling out (one hoped) and took them outside to empty the year's accumulation.

Farm life was so different from anything I'd been used to. I was quite scared of cows. Dusty worked until we got the farm going, so we only had one cow—a real gentle old pet, really, but looking at her big horns, I was not convinced. She wouldn't stay around. Kept going across to dad's cows, for company, I guess. Dusty tethered her in the field and I was supposed to take her to the barn for water. There was no way that I was going to untie her, so I carried buckets of water to her, and she sure could drink!

Later on we had more cows, but until we put water bowls in, I gave them all pails of water. That was a sight to see. I was too scared to go between enormous animals, so lifted the pails over the stalls. Today, farm wives have a lot more conveniences.

I learned that cows can be very stubborn. A heifer was missing at milking time one day, and we found her under the apple tree. I'm sure she was tipsy from eating the apples. It was autumn, the barnyard muddy, and the fallen apples had fermented. We pushed and pulled that brute for an hour trying to get her into the barn. We had new cow stalls installed, and the cows, being creatures of habit, did not like them. Dusty was fairly patient with me. At times when I would do something dumb, he'd throw his hands in the air and say, "Oh, what did I do to deserve such help!"

My first big responsibility was three hundred day-old chicks. I guess by now Dusty thought I was ready. I had been told they must not be too hot or cold; have food all the time; and not to let them crowd. Believe me, I wore a path down to the brooder house every half-hour. I was so proud; only three passed away.

I had so much to learn when I came to Canada. Even recipes didn't seem to work out the same. Different flour, I suppose. Chickens for instance: this was an eye opener when Dusty brought in plucked chickens for me to clean. I saw two openings (one where he'd chopped off the head), and asked him from which end I pulled out the insides. That was good for a big laugh on his part. Worse to follow. These particular chickens were for a dinner I was to cook for some of my new in-laws. I did manage to clean them, but not knowing chickens had a crop to store grain, I didn't take them out. When my sister-in-law offered to carve these darn chickens, to my horror there sat these little bags of grain. Thank God they were intact!

We had this immersion water heater, only I didn't know you placed the thing into the pail. It looked like a

181

stove burner to me, and I was trying to put the pail on top of IT.

Bringing in the hay one time, I went too close to the corner that Dusty had to unload and unhook the wagon, the loader and horses to get me out. He always said I didn't go in close enough; well, I did that time. When we first had the tractor, what a time I had learning to drive it. Having never rode anything more mechanical than a bicycle, it looked easy enough until I tried to back-up.

The school house was the centre of our social life. The first dance we attended I found it quite strange to see all the men sitting along one wall, and the women, the other. When they did not remain in couples and groups, it seemed rather odd. The annual Christmas concert was held in the school, and each year before school closed for the summer, we had a grand picnic. I think when pupils went to larger central schools by bus, a great deal of community life was lost.

I'm a great one for putting the kettle on for tea as soon as anyone visits, and found this was not a generally-accepted habit here. So, for a long time I thought people didn't like me, as they never offered a cup right away.

The first Christmas here was such a lonesome one. I wasn't homesick, just "mum" sick. I had heard so much about sleigh rides that my brother-in-law got the team out and took us for a ride. On the way back as we drove into the lane, one of the horses just fell down and died. I did not know he was an old horse and not too healthy. I felt awful and took a lot of ribbing from everyone about how I'd killed the poor animal.

Looking back over the years has been fun for me. A lot of water goes under the bridge in over thirty years. We worked hard but it was a good life. Farming has changed a great deal through the years.

I was one of the more fortunate war brides whose

parents came to Canada and made their home here. When I went back to England for the first time two years ago and found it changed, I was glad to get back to Canada and my family.

****

Joan and Alex Stodgell
Manitoba

I had a commercial course at Pitman's College after leaving school and worked as a typist until August 1940 when I changed my job to that of a phonogram telephonist at Cable and Wireless Ltd., in London's west end. The work was very interesting and I enjoyed it.

I met Alex in a rather round-about manner. My girlfriend, Margaret, had a penpal who lived in Swan River, Manitoba. This girl gave Margaret's address to a young neighbour of hers when she knew he was leaving for England. This young man visited Margaret, and one Saturday in May 1944, she asked me to make a foursome as Roy, her friend, was bringing his army buddy along.

We met Roy and Alex at Finchley railway station and they took us dancing. Shortly after this, they both left for the second front. Margaret heard from Roy a few times while they were in France, but it was December before I heard from Alex who said he would be in England on leave in January. He came to my home, met my parents and brothers and we went out together several times. After he returned to France, he wrote regularly and we became engaged during his next leave in July 1945. His regiment returned to England in September, and the earliest date we could get married, according to the permission papers, was October 3. Margaret was

Joan and Alex Stodgell

bridesmaid, and Roy, best man. We honeymooned in
Scotland then a month after, Alex returned to Canada and
I followed in June 1946.

There were about two thousand war brides and chilren
aboard the *Queen Mary,* as well as Prime Minister W.L.
MacKenzie King. He gave us a welcoming speech in the
lounge the first night at sea. I cannot remember it except

for one sentence, quote: "When I look around me, I must say that I admire the taste of my fellow country-men" . . . unquote.

During the time we were waiting for the ship to leave Southampton, some of the girls were having misgivings about the big step they were taking. One girl in particular had a sudden attack of homesickness and was determined to get off the boat with her baby daughter. A Canadian officer talked with her for over an hour telling her that if she didn't go out to Canada, at least to give it a try, she would always regret it. Eventually he persuaded her to stay.

I made friends with another bride name Olive whom I never saw again after we left Halifax. On the train my travelling companion was a girl from Scotland, Mary and her three-year-old daughter. The journey was exciting and tedious. The kiddies were fractious from being confined to limited space, and it seemed as if everytime the girls would try to fill their babys' bottles, the train would give a sudden lurch, splashing milk all over.

The Red Cross nurses were very kind and helpful as were the ones who met us in Winnipeg. I waited on the platform for Alex and started to get concerned that maybe I was stranded in a strange country, for, I could not see him anywhere. Suddenly I caught sight of him wandering up and down the train looking for me. I waved and called, and we were relieved and happy to see each other. Members of his family were waiting, and after I had met them we got into Alex's car and drove to the home of his aunt. There, I met my mother-in-law who was in her late seventies and with whom I stayed for the next seven years.

My sister-in-law took me shopping the next day for some new clothes. I also sent a much-needed food parcel home to my parents. Two days later we left for the farm. Alex carried me over the threshold, and I saw my new home for the first time. There were oil lamps for lighting; a wood stove for cooking; no plumbing; the water came from the river that flowed close to the house. Beautiful spruce trees surrounded us, and oh! how lovely they looked in the winter covered with a fresh fall of snow. I shall always remember my first winter in Canada for I had never seen so much snow.

Our first son, Dennis, was born in March 1947, and I returned to England with him early in 1949 and stayed until the May. Goodbyes were said once more, and I was destined never to see my parents again. Alex's mother passed away in January 1953 two weeks before our third son was born. He entered this world ahead of time one cold February morning. Alex hitched up the team of horses and we travelled by sleigh two miles to our nephew's place where we left the other two boys. We used a neighbour's car to drive to the nearest hospital and the baby was born that evening.

As the years passed, we increased our herd of cattle. The boys were all in school by the time our daughter was born in 1961. We had electricity installed in the old house in 1953, and in 1965 we had our first telephone. It wasn't until 1971 that we left the old place and moved into a modern house on the same farm. We now have plumbing and central heating, a television, and for the last five years a gravel road right into our property.

Two of my brothers have visited us here, and in 1973 I and my daughter made a trip to England. It had been twenty-four years since I had seen my other brother and the rest of my relatives. We stayed for a month then headed back to Canada and home.

I certainly found life on a Manitoba farm very lonesome at first, and I was awfully homesick as I'm sure most of the war brides were. However, I'm quite happy here and would not go back to England to live.

****

A small coal mining town in southern Yorkshire called Cudworth, is my place of birth. The closest large town is Barnsley situated three miles to the south, and here is where it all began.

In March 1944, I went to Barnsley to meet a girlfriend as we were going to the cinema. For some unknown reason, Martha never showed up. While waiting for the bus that would take me back to Cudworth, I walked along Regent Street.

Looking in a shop window, I was startled when a voice behind me said, "Excuse me. Could you tell me where I can buy a cup of coffee?" I turned around and there stood the man who is now my husband . . . Victor James Simpson. This was his first visit to Barnsley, having just transferred to Cawthorne Camp with the army.

My mother, that wise lady, allowed us to become engaged a month later with our promise to wait a year before marriage. She said, "Canada is far away, and I want you to be sure." In the November she gave in and said we could start the wedding plans. I was nineteen at the time.

I had to obtain references from our vicar, my employer, and someone who had known me practically since birth. We were married by special license February 3, 1945 at St. John's Anglican church in Cudworth.

The following month Vic returned to Canada, and not until 1946 did I receive orders to prepare to sail from Liverpool on the *Scythia*. Two or three times these orders were cancelled because the *Scythia* kept running into trouble. My mum was beside herself with worry and she kept saying, "You are not going if all they've got is that old tub!" Finally, I received a telegram informing

187

Gladys and Vic Simpson

me I would be sailing from Southampton on the
Aquitania. What a relief!

It was almost traumatic leaving my mother, family and
home. I know the tears fell all the way to London from
my native Yorkshire. We were loaded into army trucks
and taken to hostels. This was April 23, 1946. A band
was playing when we boarded the ship, and I wondered,
as I'm sure every bride did, if I would ever see my
family and England again.

The crossing was without incident except for the usual quota of sea sickness which fortunately did not affect me. I never missed a meal. There were 1,002 war brides on board, 200 children, service personnel and other passengers, including Kurt Meyer who was being taken to Canada for crimes committed against Canadian servicemen.

It was raining sheets when we docked in Halifax on May 1, so I felt quite at home. The first impression for me was the size of the train and everything else. The train looked gigantic and the wide-open spaces intimidating. I fell in love with the houses painted in a variety of colours.

I was very warmly welcomed into Vic's family. He had the same number of brothers and sisters that I had left in England. My mother-in-law was also English and she took me to see the shops. So many goodies, but a bit saddening when one thought of the situation back home.

Things went happily for the remainder of the first year until the last day of December. I found a lump in my left breast and was quite alarmed when a minor operation found that I had breast cancer. I was twenty-one years old. There were several weeks of treatment, then in April 1947 I had a mastectomy. After five years without recurrence, I was allowed to start a family. While waiting, I went to work in a textile plant, and Vic worked for the railroad. We had a tiny three-roomed apartment and were very happy. In January 1948 my mother passed away. This was a terrible shock and hard to bear. I was deeply grateful for my mother-in-law who was a rock to lean on, as was my husband through all my troubles.

During that summer, we went on a camping trip and camped near a small lake. Vic decided to take me out in a canoe. Half-way across the lake a wind started to blow, and much to my dismay the lake got quite choppy, and to my disgust I became SEASICK! I never got sick crossing the Atlantic, and there I was on a silly little lake. It took a long time to live that down.

For my first driving lesson, Vic took me along a country road. I took the wheel and he told me to turn into a farm lane. I turned all right! I continued driving right into the wheat field. Got out of there in a hurry!

Once on a fishing trip, the men had been fishing all day without as much as a nibble. I thought I'd try my luck. After a few minutes of casting, I landed a lovely black bass. Needless to say, this didn't make the men any happier.

During the years I have lived here, there are many incidents I have experienced, happy and sad: the building of our first home that Vic designed and built himself, as with our present home; the joy of our daughter's birth in 1953; the death of my dear mother-in-law whom I miss very much; my husband's youngest brother who, at the age of twenty-six, died from drowning; my many friends and the fellowship of the Overseas Women's Association. We still meet once a month.

England will always have a warm place in my heart, but Canada is my home, and I love it.

****

Anonymous

My sister worked in Edinburgh, Scotland, during the war, and was introduced to two Canadian soldiers by the father of her girlfriend who had met them in a public house. My sister married one of these soldiers in 1944, and the other one, Len, was their best man. Because the

190

rest of the family lived in Essex, none of us attended the wedding. We met my sister's husband from time to time, but it wasn't until she moved back to England that Len and I met . . . three years after he first met my sister.

It was April 1945, and although I knew instinctively that I need look no further for my Prince Charming, there was not enough time for a courtship and marriage. We saw each other for three days only on that leave, then Len returned to Holland for the four months before his repatriation leave. When I received his letter about this leave, I was convinced this meant his immediate return to Canada. Thinking I would never see him again, I lay sobbing on my bed until my sister came to the rescue and explained repatriation leave would be in England.

Len and I became engaged on VJ Day, September 2, 1945, and he departed for Canada later that month. I, of course, was not a war bride in the true sense. I had to pay my way to Canada, and was informed that passage was available on the *Aquitania* in December 1946 . . . fifteen months after Len had left. We sailed Christmas Eve, and I shared cramped quarters in the hold with thirty other war brides (something I have never figured out as a paying passenger.) The Atlantic storms made the crossing rough, but I came through fairly well.

We left Halifax New Years Eve, and the train ride to Montreal passed quite quickly. But by the time I arrived there, I was exhausted. I'd had little sleep during the past two nights because of train motion, the building excitement and nerves. Having kept my tummy pretty well under control all the time on board ship, I was appalled when I spent practically the whole trip from Montreal to Ottawa in the washroom being sick!

I reached Ottawa at an unearthly hour—5 a.m.—and since I had no idea of my time of arrival, no one was there to meet me. A friendly traveller's aid lady directed me to the telephone, and after placing a call to my fiancé, I sat down and waited.

Quite suddenly the magnitude of what I had done, hit me; I had left my family, friends, familiar surroundings and travelled thousands of miles to marry a man I hardly knew! The length of time we had spent together could be counted in days, and not very many of them at that. I wondered in desperation if I could get a train back to Montreal, retrace my steps, find the sanctuary of the *Aquitania* and return to the life I knew.

In those days, the wooden benches in the old Union station provided a haven for the derelicts of the city. At 5 a.m. that bitterly cold January morning, they were all around me as I sat, scrunched up in a corner, luggage at my feet, and tears streaming down my face. When I saw Len walking through the station looking for me, I was even more convinced that I had made a horrible mistake. I didn't know this stranger in a civilian suit . . . with a moustache yet! I cowered even farther into the corner deciding that if he didn't see me, he would go home, and I could go gladly back the way I had come. Len was not so easily discouraged. He found me, and in a short time, my fears started to slip away.

I stayed with Len's father, a dear man who came to Canada as a young man from Bedford, England in 1905. The day I arrived, the city was recovering from a major snowstorm, and the banks looked like mountains to me. How quickly I became used to them.

We were married in two weeks in a quiet ceremony in St. Luke's church, Ottawa. My father-in-law gave me away; a cousin was my attendant, and Len's friend, best man. I was terrified, as there was no organ music, therefore nothing to cover up the sound of my knocking knees.

Following the ceremony and a meal, we left by train for Montreal. In the hotel suite that evening, I was in the bathroom sorting out my toiletries when I leaned back on what I thought was a wall. It was the shower curtain and I landed on my head on the hard floor of the shower stall. I suffered a few cuts on my head and wondered if I originated the saying, "Not tonight, dear, I have a headache!" We spent a few days in New York city as well, then came back to a rented room.

Later we moved to a winterized cottage on the Quebec side of the Ottawa River. Without electricity and running water, it became quite a challenge for me to go armed with axe and pail to chop holes in the thick ice for water.

One can never anticipate, or be prepared for, the differences in life-style in a new land, yet, when asked by friends in Britain in what way they differ, I found it hard to put into words. The land itself is so vast and varied, and the weather, perhaps, is the easiest difference to explain. I'm sure we all heard how cold it was in Canada, but experiencing it is far different from picturing it.

During my first full winter in Canada, I was fooled by bright sunshine and clear blue skies and went out one day without covering my ears. One ear felt cold and painful for awhile, but after a time I no longer felt it. I was stopped by an acquaintance and taken into the local tavern so that I could "thaw out." My ear was frozen and like a solid piece of ice. I'm sure had I tried to bend the lobe, it would have broken off. I was given bad advice and told to rub snow on it. With no feeling in it, it was impossible to tell how hard I was rubbing. As it thawed, the pain was such that I nearly passed out. When I got home, I was horrified to discover that my ear was about twice its size and the lobe cut into shreds from the hard rubbing. It became infected but did get better, and I never ventured out without them covered again.

I've had my share of feeling homesick, and could have sailed back to England on the *Queen Mary* from the tears

193

I shed during that first year. I found it easy to fall into the trap of seeking out other British people, but I learned a valuable lesson in that first year. I was introduced to another war bride who lived nearby, and it didn't take me long to discover that our geographical background was all we had in common.

I realized that just as I could not relate to everyone I met in Britain, I would not find all expatriate "Brits" compatible in Canada. I still have friends with roots in Britain because we often have the same interests, but that shared interest is just a part of our friendship, not the nucleus, and I treasure the association of my Canadian-born friends just as much.

Having worked in London, England, for a few years, I had become accustomed to the British theatre. I missed this when I came to Ottawa and frankly, was amazed that the country's capitol had not even one proper theatre. The opening of the National Arts Centre was a welcome event. Prior to this, the only "culture" I was exposed to, and did not participate in, was the gathering of the masses at the local tavern . . . especially on Family Allowance day!

We have been in our present home for over twenty-five years now. Before coming to Canada, I imagined I would learn to skate and ski; I have done neither, but I do mix a mean batch of cement; and can use a hammer and saw with a fair amount of proficiency. This house, the result of "blood, sweat and tears," represents a lot of hard work and sacrifice, but was well worth all of it.

****

Brenda and Ivan MacArthur
New Brunswick

Many London firms were evacuated to different parts of the country soon after war started, including the one

194

for which I worked. In Redhill, Surrey, one very large mansion house served as our office, while in nearby Caterham, the staff were housed in two large houses that had been converted into hostels. We drove back and forth in a special bus to the office each day, and I remember one morning when reaching the office how horrified we were at seeing the beautiful lawn and sunken garden replaced with an air-raid shelter. We did not realize the importance of this at the time, and it was not until the male staff were gradually "called up" for service, their hostel closed, and the usage of this shelter, that the seriousness of war dawned on us.

Caterham, a military town, was swarming with Canadians, and a corporal with the Carleton York Regiment working with the medical officer at the Regimental Aid Post (RAP) was to become my husband.

Absent from the office for a few days with the "flu," my friend Heather and I, when feeling better, walked into town. On the way the driver of the RAP truck, whom Heather knew, stopped to chat with us. Seems the other soldier in the truck asked the driver if he could arrange a date with me through Heather. The outcome was a triple date with another girl from the hostel, and a third chap. We had no idea what these fellows were like and hoped they were a decent sort. The evening turned out very well and Ivan, my date, and I met regularly after that. When he asked me to marry him I protested, saying that it was impossible for me to go to Canada and leave my family.

I wrote my mother and asked if I could bring Ivan home to meet the family. She agreed. She was also heartsick and worried at the thought of her youngest child even entertaining the idea of marrying a Canadian let alone go to a country we knew nothing about. Ivan broke through her quiet reserve, and with her blessing we were married in September 1941. Our first son was born

195

Christmas, 1945, England—"Janey Canuck" Club

in July 1942. Ivan left for Sicily, and we didn't meet again until one cold snowy day in 1946 in New Brunswick.

As we prepared to sail from Liverpool aboard the *Mauretania*, word came that a terrible storm was brewing in the north Atlantic. So bad was it, that the *Queen Mary*, due to leave with her quota of GI brides, postponed her sailing time. I suppose the powers that be must have thought the Canadian brides were made of sterner stuff, for we sallied forth regardless. Needless to say, it was not long before most of us fell ill.

Robert was now over three years old, and we shared a cabin with three other brides who also had one child each. One girl made herself quite objectionable throughout the voyage, lashing out at all and sundry. How we avoided a quarrel with her was really amazing. When we arrived in Halifax, we could not believe how cold it was under the brilliant blue sky and blazing sun. How unlike the dreary English winter sky with its watery sun.

The husband of the girl I had befriended, was meeting her in Halifax. We eagerly scanned the dock to see if he was there. When she saw him she exclaimed, "What on earth is he wearing?" We had never seen the Canadian-type red and black checkered jacket before, nor the winter boots which we all thought were for the old and infirm. Shy and embarrassed, she hid from him, but we coaxed her out of hiding, and soon she was waving happily to the handsome young man who eagerly awaited her.

That evening as we went ashore to board the train, it happened! I tripped and tore the sole of my right shoe, and when I walked down the gangplank, all one could hear was, "clipperty clop, clipperty clop," as the sole flapped up and down. So much for a graceful entry into my new country!

197

Robert and I were in the New Brunswick section of the train, and when a black porter walked through, young Robert could not believe his eyes. He had never seen a black person before and I tried to explain as best I could the difference between black and white people. I thought that was the end of it. But oh no! When the porter returned, he piped up and said, "I know why you are black and I am white . . . .God made us that way."

Arriving in Saint John early in the morning, those like myself, who had to travel further, were taken to a Salvation Army hostel and made very comfortable. A kindly young man took some of us shopping and I was able to buy another pair of shoes. Our English clothing was hardly adequate for such cold weather and deep snow. I reached my destination that night, and saw Ivan for the first time in three years.

A Red Cross lady insisted we stay overnight with her even though Ivan had booked a room in the hotel. She asked Robert who the gentleman with us was, and he replied, "My daddy." He didn't really know for he was only ten months old when his daddy left England for Sicily. But she took this as suitable identification and said, "Well, if you are okay, I'll leave you. But here is my phone number should you want anything." Poor Ivan! I really think she disbelieved he really was my husband.

There she was, bright and early next morning to see us off, giving Robert a gift box of small toys. She really was a very kind soul.

Like my friend on the boat, I too was embarrassed by Ivan's huge snow boots. When the train stopped at a station, I anxiously watched everyone's feet to see what kind of footwear they had. Everyone wore these snow boots but I still felt they were for old people. Finally, I mentioned it to Ivan. He laughed and said within a

Red Cross Christmas party, Saint John, New Brunswick, 1946

couple of days I would feel the need to wear the same. Of course I did after nearly freezing off my feet.

Meeting us was my sister-in-law, the local doctor's wife and another Red Cross lady. Again, Robert was the proud recipient of a box of toys. We were whisked off to the doctor's home for tea where his kindly wife said, "I have a real treat for you with your tea." Guess what it was. CREAM in my tea! I could hardly drink it, but she really thought it was a treat, so I downed it.

The next ride to Ivan's home seemed non-ending and running through my mind all the way was the horrible thought that if Robert took ill, how would I get to a doctor. Of course, I realized after that it wasn't far from civilization, and as we stayed only long enough for Ivan to find accommodation in the city, the dreaded thought never materialized.

We were soon meeting the rest of the family, and when shown to our room, much to my dismay, there was a hole in the floor. I nearly died from embarrassment when young Robert, in his high-pitched English voice said, "What a funny house. There are holes in the floor." Ivan had quite a time convincing me that if I insisted on covering it up with my suitcase, the heat would not come through the room.

Some of my luggage had gone astray, so next morning Ivan said he would take me shopping. I was amazed to see him so casually attired, and asked him to please dress up. When we arrived in the small town, I soon understood why the casual dress . . . nobody dressed up for shopping. This casual way was one of the harder things for me to accept. But I eventually did.

We moved into our own apartment in Saint John and Ivan continued his work as a Psychiatric Attendant. Later he received his diploma as a Registered Attendant, and became Ward Supervisor.

Robert and I visited England when he was ten years

old, and the following year Ivan and I had our greatest joy since Robert's birth. We adopted a beautiful baby girl whom Robert received with open arms and promptly named Susan. During the years I fostered many children. Rewarding work, but heartbreaking when the time came to part with them. When Susan started school, I worked as a sales clerk part-time. I wanted something better and enrolled to take a secretarial course at night which enabled me to find the position I still maintain.

Ivan's health began to deteriorate due to a war disability, and he took an early retirement from the hospital. He tried easier work, but the doctor was against this and he had to give it up.

I have been fortunate and visited England several times—once with Ivan, where we revisited some of the places where he had stayed and where we were married.

I think the biggest obstacle I had to overcome at first was the horrible feeling of never seeing a familiar face. Then suddenly it dawned on me . . . I was seeing familiar faces, and that's when the overwhelming sense of loneliness began to abate.

The Red Cross organized the Overseas Wives Club which helped to alleviate the feeling of isolation. Here we made enduring friendships that have lasted over the years.

Now, after more than thirty years, I can look back at the rough and good times, and feel glad I was young when I undertook the severe change in my life.

****

When the air-raids on London became very heavy, my aunt, who lived in Scotland, wrote and asked if I would like to go and stay with her. Without knowing her, away I went to spend one year, returning home in November 1941. While I was away, my older sister had joined the Women's Air Force, and was stationed in Cumberland where there was also a lot of Canadian air crew. I was working in the office of a Cable and Wire factory when my sister came home on her first leave.

We decided one evening to go to Marble Arch to see a stage show. The show was "sold out" so we walked to Leicester Square hoping to get into a theatre there. On the way, my sister suddenly turned to me and said, "Wait for me." Off she ran leaving me standing there. The next thing I knew she was heading for three airmen who were walking ahead of us. To this day I don't know how she recognized them from behind, but she knew them well as they were stationed at the same camp as herself.

One fellow had plans for the evening, so we went with the other two to see the pictures, "One of our aircraft is missing." They were due for leave in June, and were invited to spend it at our home as it was always open to servicemen and women during the war. Earl and I began to write to each other and he spent all his leaves with me. In May 1943, we got engaged, and a year later we made plans for a September wedding. Arrangements were completed with the minister; I bought my wedding dress and a dress for my bridesmaid. Earl returned to northern Ireland where he was then stationed, only to return two days after because he was being posted to Nassau as a radar instructor. This meant we had to get married right away. I was able to get the rest of the week off from the office, and Earl saw our minister and obtained a special license.

I gathered up what clothes I could and mother tried to get some food together for a small reception. Earl was able to get in touch with his friend to be best man, and my sister got leave to be my bridesmaid. We were married at 4 p.m. on May 18, and two days later, we said goodbye. And that was the last we saw of each other until March 1945 in Montreal.

I applied for passage to Canada in September and the following March I received word to be ready to sail. I don't think I had any apprehension about leaving, although I admit, I shed quite a few tears at the thought of leaving mum and dad. We left Liverpool on the *Rangitarta* in a convoy that took eleven days to reach Halifax. One girl I got friendly with was going to Ontario, so we travelled together as far as Montreal where she was to be met by her in-laws.

While I was sitting on the train waiting to continue my journey, I was paged. As my friend had said she would like to have me meet her in-laws, I assumed this was why I was wanted. Imagine my surprise to find Earl waiting for me. He had arrived in Montreal the day before from Nassau, and after making a few inquiries, found out that I was due the next day.

We had a seven-hour stop-over in Montreal during which time we saw quite a bit of the city. Back on the train, Earl was the only male, apart from the crew, among all us war brides. When we reached Winnipeg, we got off and stayed over for a day. Earl phoned home that night and learned that all his family were there in preparation for the coming Easter weekend. I really got cold feet then, and persuaded him to stay over two more days.

We reached Regina on Good Friday, and arrived in Yellow Grass Saturday night. The whole family have been wonderful to me; I could not have asked for better. I was given a tremendous welcome and felt at home right away. The community gave me a bridal shower, and about 150 people attended. It was absolutely terrific. Everything was really appreciated since we had almost nothing to start a home.

Life in a small community was quite a change from life in London. I've had my share of homesickness, and there were always the times when I would liked to have been with my family. But I adjusted and settled into my new life without too many problems. Perhaps it was because I was just eighteen, or maybe it was knowing that I could not afford to go home even if I wanted to. There are no regrets; life has been good; nor would I change a thing.

****

Vera and Albert Edwards
California

My folks immigrated to Canada after the First World War and I was born there. We lived in the Rosemount area of Montreal, and Albert lived next door to my girlfriend. He and his pals used to make an ice rink in the winter at the back of his house so they could play hockey and we girls used it for a skating rink only to be chased away by all the boys.

I had visited England once with my mother when I was seven years old, but when I was thirteen in 1936, we went back to live because mum was homesick.

I kept in touch with my girlfriend, and when war started, Albert was in the first contingent that landed in Scotland. My friend sent me his address and I wrote to him. As I knew Albert was engaged, I asked him if he could get me a pen pal. He said he'd write to me himself as his engagement was then broken.

204

In the August he came to see me, and at Christmas 1941 he asked me if I would get engaged. We were running home from the cinema in an air-raid, and I said, "Okay." I was so intent on getting home before the planes came over, that the importance of his question didn't really register. He had only kissed me twice, and both times very hurriedly when he went back from leave, so it came as a shock when I realized what I had answered to.

The following April we were married and traditionally one is not supposed to see one's intended before the wedding. Albert and I, however, rode by bus, on top and in front, to the registry office. When we came out after the ceremony, another couple were going in. Both their families were engaged in a big fight and we got out in a hurry. We went to a small pub in Romford for a drink. When visiting England a few years ago, we went back there and told them we were there in 1942.

I had my heart set on sailing back to Canada on the *Queen Mary* when I left in June 1946. But when I saw the ship I was to sail on, it could easily have been a tug for the *Queen* herself. I was so disappointed. It was the troop hospital ship, *Letitia*.

My daughter was fifteen months old, and our sleeping quarters consisted of a cabin with twenty-nine bunks, all of which held war brides; at the side of each bunk was a fish-net hammock for each child. These must have been used for the troops' gear. When one baby woke up crying, they all cried. It was sheer bedlam for the nine-day voyage. Most of us were sick and we were without help of any kind. We came over like cattle.

Montreal had not changed, as I was old enough when I left to remember it. I did not like it, and I don't think I ever did. I loathed the conflict between the French and the English even as a child and never liked living in that environment. The extremely cold winters and piles of snow, I detested intensely.

We moved into a veteran's housing unit in 1946, and our son was born in the spring of 1947. We stayed in Montreal until 1955, then moved to the United States. The primary reason for this move was our son had allergies, and doctors recommended a warm dry climate.

Our choice was Texas, but I didn't like it because it was too dry and the desert depressing. Albert had a good job and we lived there for five months. One day I took a month's subscription to a Los Angeles newspaper. Each day I checked all the jobs suitable for Albert, marked them, folded the paper neatly and placed it beside his plate at suppertime.

One day, Albert said, "I'll answer one ad just to shut you up!" Well! The man paid his plane fare to California for the interview, and while he was gone I got everything packed. Talk about luck. He got the job.

We have been in California ever since, and for me it is the only place on earth to live. It is a pleasure to be able to see green trees and grass, flowers in bloom, humming birds at the feeder, snow-capped mountains, and oranges growing all through winter.

My parents left England again and came to live here and stayed many years. Then they returned to England to live out the remainder of their lives. I have visited them often, but have not returned again to the land of my birth. Having lived here most of my life now, California is where I call home.

****

Ross and I met early in 1944 at Paisley (Scotland) ice rink where Vera, my friend, and I had gone while on a weekend home from school—Rothesay Academy.

We were wary of these rather forward Canadian and American servicemen. However, my future husband picked me up, literally, as I had ungraciously fallen on my bottom. I was really quite good on skates, but when I spied this good-looking young sailor, vanity to show off proved my "down fall." Anyway, he kindly assisted me, we chatted for a while, then he asked if I would be there the next weekend. I was!

After a short courtship during which he met my parents and I started corresponding with his, I had graduated from school and returned home to Glasgow to either further my education or look for work.

Time was running out for Ross and me. We were very much in love; the war was coming to an end; and his return to Canada was imminent. We were so young, I seventeen, he twenty-one. Everyone was quite skeptical when we decided to marry.

My gentle mother was very happy for us both. My Da was another matter. An aggressive Scotsman, strong and somewhat distant of "women's things," he liked a man who enjoyed a good drink. Neither Ross or I drank, so my quiet gentle Canadian had a formidable task to ask for my hand in the usual manner of old Scots tradition.

The big night arrived. Mother and I escaped to the kitchen (we were really listening outside the closed parlour door). Ross and Da's voices filtered through indistinctly. Ross abruptly appeared as we scampered back to the kitchen. He looked surprised and pleased as he had expected to run the gamut of questions. Da had simply hmm'd a few times and said, "Well. That's fine

207

young man.'' The real story came later. Ross inadvertently had chosen a night an important boxing match was being aired on the radio—my Da's only real sport interest. Da was deaf in one ear due to an operation a few years previous, so he was listening with his good ear to the radio, and poor Ross was giving his all for my hand to a somewhat "deaf ear."

No one was more surprised than Da when he saw us hugging and laughing as we went to thank him. All ended well and our joy and future happiness was toasted. My dowry was also discussed—a matter of some honour in an old Scottish family for their only daughter. Ross was surprised, but Da insisted, and so it was settled. My husband left for Canada in June 1945. He had signed on for the Pacific war zone, but it ended before his processing had finished.

I thought the waiting would never end for my turn to sail for Canada. The war brides list was a long one but come it did and I was scheduled to sail on the *Ile de France* from Southampton on March 26, 1946—my husband's birthday. A tearful farewell to my parents, relatives and friends as the train pulled out of the Glasgow station bound for London. I did not see my brother James before I left, as he was still away in the army. The big moment came to board the huge ship lined with thousands of men returning home, and I was terrified at what I had done. But, in that instant I knew I was strong enough to go ahead. The trip was wonderful. Good food, not a lot, but more than I or any other bride had seen for a long time; crowded cabins; communal bathing with salt water showers; and men everywhere.

We were allowed to speak only to officer rank and had to be in our sleeping quarters by 11 p.m. Guards were stationed outside our quarters with fixed bayonets all night . . . probably needed as there were a couple of thousand troops to four hundred wives. There were a

Margaret and Ross Roche

few incidents of wives being caught on deck after curfew, but we never got any further details.

We docked in Halifax on a bleak April morning, but to me it was Canada and looked beautiful. Entrained, I was fortunate to get a roomette with a girl going to Vancouver. My only purchase on the ship was a box of one dozen Cadbury chocolate bars and I intended to eat them all. My knowledge of steam heat was limited, and I deposited them on top of the radiator. Next morning . . . a chocolate mess!

Finally, after many stops, clanging bells, flickering lights . . . Ottawa, my future home. My journey seemed so vivid to that moment, then, almost complete confusion as my in-laws welcomed me to Canada; the Red Cross hovered over me; I said goodbyes to other girls; thanked the wonderful Canadian troops who had helped and guided us, lost and frightened, to this wonderful moment; then our joy, almost too much for both of us, as Ross and I met again. He looked different in civvies, heavier too. I can never explain how I felt.

The first years were not all sweetness and light. Our first home was a winterized cottage with outdoor plumbing, and there was very little money. My wonderful mum and dad Roche were all I could have asked for . . . kind, considerate, patient and loving. When carrying our first child, my mother-in-law was dying. My father-in-law was grief-stricken, and my own parents were so far away, and there were few people to turn to for comfort except each other.

There were times when the loneliness became almost unbearable. One Christmas we did not have enough money to buy toys. How could we face our little three-year-old boy and explain? I prayed. Ross bought a ticket in a variety store for some local charity, his last dime. He won the draw and Christmas Eve a huge stocking full of toys was delivered to our door. Dickenish, maybe . . . faith and love, definitely.

The years have flown with their changes: births; deaths; our measure of joys and sorrows. Many, both here and in Scotland, gave dire warning that this marriage would never last. Well, here we are thirty-seven years later, and we thank God for His blessings during our years together with our two sons, one daughter, and two grandchildren of whom we are so proud.

****

There wasn't a girl in the dance hall who did not want to dance with him. Week after week it was the same, and I was no exception. He was extremely good-looking, and he knew it. He was hardly ever with the same girl more than twice but whoever it was, he seemed to treat her like a princess.

I was madly in love with this soldier and wished he would notice me, but he never knew I existed. When the band played an "excuse me" dance, there was one mad rush to dance with him. No girl ever got to dance more than two or three steps when she was excused by another. I knew his name was Eddie. Quite a common, ordinary name, and to me he looked as though he should have been named something far more pretentious. Now, when I look back on those early teen years of mine, I cringe at my ingenuousness.

The night we really met for the first time, he came to the dance alone. I'm sure every unescorted girl in that hall, and there were a few, had the same idea in her head as I. But I was going to be bold and carry it out. Stupid me!

The last girl he had dated, I knew slightly. I also knew she had joined the Women's Auxiliary Air Force and had left for camp during the week. Before I could stop myself, I went up to him and said in my happiest-go-lucky voice, "Hello Eddie. Where's Julie tonight?" knowing full well where she was. I just about melted when his brilliant blue eyes gazed into mine and his soft voice drawled, "Hi, honey. Where have you been all my life?" And without further ado, he took me in his arms and waltzed me around the dance floor. My legs could hardly move for I was in seventh heaven. I was positive it would not last. But it did! He danced with me all evening, took me home, behaved like a gentleman and asked me for another date. I couldn't believe this was happening to me, and had I any sense or awareness of the outcome, I would have said NO then and there.

But I didn't have any sense. Who does when at seventeen you think you are in love with the most wonderful man on earth? Our dating became regular and I was the envy of all my friends. On my eighteenth birthday he took me to London for a night on the town. We had a marvellous time. Eddie was always a gentleman; his uniform, immaculate; and he was never without money. This puzzled me sometimes because I knew army pay was not that great, but I would never have dared mention it.

I was an only child. My dad left my mum when I was about four years old and I did not remember him, so it was nice to have Eddie around the house on weekends. He acted like a sophisticated man of the world, and mum and I were fascinated by his charm. Mum worked hard and looked older than her forty-two years. She was a dressmaker and tailor by trade and had built up a good business over the years. It had been hard work and the long hours had aged her and I hoped that, now I was working in the local council office, she would ease off a bit.

Our courtship, if one can call it that, was stormy to say the least. We would fight over trivial matters; break-up! Eddie would be seen with another girl; my heart would almost break; then the next thing I knew we would be together again. After two such stormy years, we were married. Soon after, Eddie went to Europe. Lonely months followed until the war was over and he came back to England for his repatriation leave. He left for Canada and I followed five months later. The hardest thing I ever did was say goodbye to my mum. I wanted her to come with me and oh! how I wish she had. But she wouldn't give up her home and business and I could not blame her.

I sailed early summer 1946 on the *Queen Mary*. I really enjoyed that voyage. The less said about the miserable dirty train ride the better. In the heat of a Canadian summer, it left much to be desired. I was excited about meeting Eddie's family and brimming with happiness at the thought of seeing my husband again. Only once had I received a letter from my mother-in-law. A very formal one that didn't say too much except that she and Eddie's father were shocked that their son had married. Apparently he had never told them and their only way of knowing was when the army allowance stopped. Nor had he spoken to me about his home in Montreal very much except to say I would like it because it was so much larger than the little bungalow mum and I lived in.

The Montreal station was packed with people, but there was no sign of Eddie. I had sent two telegrams: one from England when I left, the other from Halifax telling him of my estimated time of arrival. I looked into all the faces around me and felt so alone. I watched happy reunions and became increasingly agitated as time passed and the crowds thinned. A Red Cross lady came forward and asked who I was waiting for. She took Eddie's name and address and told me to wait. By now, I was almost in tears, and the feeling in the pit of my stomach is something I have never forgotten. Somehow I knew he wasn't coming, and yet I kept thinking up excuses. He never received the telegrams; they were away on vacation; perhaps he had been delayed; or maybe he wasn't coming at all.

While this alarming thought was in my mind, the Red Cross lady came back with a rather grim expression on her face. My heart jumped into my throat when she said she had telephoned Eddie's home and spoken to his

213

mother who had said Eddie was not there, neither did she know about any telegram or my arrival. The outcome of this was that the Red Cross lady, whom I shall call Miss Heaney, arranged with Eddie's mother for me to visit her the next morning. I was practically hysterical now and determined to find my way there that night. There wasn't a hope in hell of my doing so as long as Miss Heaney was with me.

Exhausted, and in a terrible state, she took me home with her where I could, she said, relax and get some sleep. How I longed for my dear mum. I thought I would never stop crying, or get to sleep. But I did. That dear lady was kindness itself.

The next morning I felt a little better and told myself that everything would be all right once I saw Eddie. Only, I was puzzled why nobody knew I was arriving. I kept saying Eddie must have known and surely something was radically wrong. Miss Heaney told me not to worry and once there, we would soon find out. I was very thankful she was with me, for with the changing of trams, I never would have found my way to the Town of Mount Royal.

I was not prepared for what awaited me. First, the size of the house and the grounds surrounding it filled me with awe. I was sure we had the wrong address, but Miss Heaney assured me this was the place. My second shock was a maid answering the door. I must have been staring at her with my mouth agape for she gave me a haughty stare and turned to Miss Heaney who, upon seeing I was at a loss for words, explained why we were there.

If the size of the place filled me with awe, it was nothing to what I felt when I faced the stern formidable woman that was my mother-in-law. I had absolutely no idea that I had married into a very wealthy family and instinct told me that she regarded me as a nobody who

214

had tricked her son into marriage. Gradually pieces of the unsolved puzzle fitted into place. Now I knew why Eddie always dressed so immaculately; why he always had had so much money; why he had been able to buy me the expensive diamond engagement ring. I was bewildered, shocked and very dumb!

Before I had any chance to greet this woman, she told me without preamble that Edward (not Eddie) was away on business for his father; that I would not be allowed to see him again; divorce proceedings were being handled privately by the family lawyer; and I would be well compensated before I left Canada.

I argued and pleaded with this cold woman who was so intimidating. I told her that Eddie and I loved each other, that I wanted to see him, to talk with him. No one could have been more hostile. She said I was not good enough for her son, not in the same class (and I thought England was the country of class distinction). My British reserve snapped, and I made things worse by screaming at her. Now I don't even remember what. I was crying hysterically as Miss Heaney and this horrible woman spoke to each other in low tones, then Eddie's mother left the room, and the same disdainful maid ushered us out of the house.

We took a taxi-cab back to Miss Heaney's, and I sobbed all the way. I'm sure the driver must have wondered what on earth was wrong. She made some tea, calmed me down enough to tell me what had transpired between Eddie's mother and herself. They had been horrified to learn of his marriage to a nobody, so Eddie was given an ultimatum; marry the girl his mother wanted him to and enter his father's business, or stay married to me and be disinherited. He chose the former.

It was so very hard to comprehend all that had taken place, and although I could not see it then, I did realize later on that what happened was for the best. Had Eddie

215

chosen me, I'm sure our marriage would have been a disaster, and there may have been innocent children involved.

I returned to England and mum. Facing everyone was not easy but their kindness and love helped me regain my sanity. I received the final divorce papers along with a cheque for a very substantial sum of money which disgusted both mum and me. Her solicitor returned it.

I did re-marry a few years later, this time really to the most wonderful man on earth . . . to me. I've led a full life, had four wonderful children and now, the joy of grandchildren.

My short marriage to Eddie, the brief encounter with his mother, the short stay in Canada, are but dim memories. It is an unpleasant part of my life that has long been over and although never entirely forgotten, remains obtuse.

****

Vera and Earl Bateman
Ontario

Birmingham was where I was born, but when very young, my parents moved to Sussex, a few miles from Devil's Dyke.

During the war I joined the Land Army and worked on a farm near Fletching. There was an army camp there, and one day some Canadian soldiers came over to help the farmer bring in the hay. One of them was Earl. When they moved away, we wrote to each other and met as often as possible. We were married in August, 1943.

Upon receiving notification of my sailing date, my mother tried desperately to get me to change my mind.

She knew Earl would be good to me but we now had two sons, twenty-two months and six months old, and she hated to see us leave. But we had to go, and in October 1946 we boarded the *Letitia* whose name during that voyage was changed to the *Empire Brent*. The boys were good little sailors; but I cannot say the same for myself.

On the train from Halifax, I was issued with an upper and lower berth. Rather worried that my eldest son might get up during the night and fall out, I took both boys into the lower berth with me. The next morning when the porter made up the berth, he did not say anything to me about not using the upper. The second night after everyone had gone to bed and I presume the porter thought all were asleep, he came and climbed into my upper bunk. I was so scared I never slept all night. Some of the girls said I should have reported him, but we were nearly in Toronto and my only thought was to get off that train and be with my husband.

I did not feel as if we were going to strangers, because Earl's mother, sister and I, had corresponded for some time, and I felt as if I already knew them. I hardly recognized Earl—he looked so different out of uniform.

We lived with his parents in St. Davids, and a few days after my arrival, I was given a shower. I am sure everyone who lived there turned out for it. Never will I forget that memorable evening. Nervous and overwhelmed, I couldn't speak, and Earl had to say the "thank you" for me.

Not long after, our eldest son developed a bad cold that would not get better. A check-up found he had a heart condition. This was a terrible shock and when he was nine years old he had open-heart surgery. It was successful, and now he is married with three healthy children of his own.

Earl's people were good and kind to me although I was

homesick at first, but I gradually settled down. Having never lived in a city before, I enjoyed living in the rural area of Ontario.

My in-laws urged me to go home in 1958 because my mother was very ill. It was wonderful to see her and my brothers and sisters again. But oh! how things had changed. Mother and one brother and his family had moved to Partridge Green, and where their other house had been, there now stands a block of flats with a pub right across the road. I was happy to see them, but somehow it did not seem like home anymore. I began to miss Earl and the children and was happy to get back to Canada.

When a telegram came in 1960 to say mother had passed away, my sister-in-law, who came to me after I had phoned her the news, suggested I go home again. But I did not. I wanted to remember mum as I had seen her last.

In 1972 Earl and I went back and visited relatives in England and Wales. They gave us a grand welcome, and we thoroughly enjoyed our trip.

We now live in the Fort Erie area where we bought a house with two acres of land to give us something to do when we retire. I have no regrets that I came here and am proud I have my Canadian citizenship.

We have made many friends over the years, and I have wondered often if there are any war brides in Canada that I might know from my early days in England. Whether there is or not, I would like to wish all war brides happiness in their remaining years.

****

May and Nick Nichols
Ontario

The first servicemen to arrive in the south coast resort town of Bournemouth where I lived, were Americans. Then came the Royal Canadian Air Force personnel who were billeted in luxury apartments over-looking the English Channel.

I was the first girl bus driver in Bournemouth and quite proud of the fact that I could manoeuvre those heavy vehicles around tight corners.

My dad's youngest sister and her husband lived in Canada, and I was anxious to find out exactly where the town of Fonthill was. Every chance I had to speak to Canadian boys who boarded my bus, I would ask them. After inquiring for the umpteenth time, an air force corporal replied, "Yes, I do. It's in the fruit belt of Ontario, not far from Niagara Falls." It appeared he was stationed there prior to his leaving for England.

What excitement at home when I related this news. I was told that if I saw my "Canadian boy" again, I was to ask him more about Fonthill. It was quite sometime before we did meet again but it led to a dinner date on my first free evening. We met regularly after that, and sometimes he would ride on the bus until I was finished, then at the end of the line, I would point out several beauty spots such as the Isle of Wight and westward to Swanage and Weymouth, and across the English Channel to France.

On my evenings off, we would go dancing, especially if Guy Lombardo and his Canadians were playing, as Nick liked this band very much. He had already asked me to marry him before the war ended. I had not given him an answer as leaving my family to go and live so far away was a big decision to make. Then suddenly, he had to leave for the north of England to await final orders to leave for Canada.

I was able to get time off from work to go to the station to say goodbye. It was a very sad morning indeed as many couples were saying tearful goodbyes. As the train pulled out, Nick shouted, "I'll let you know, if possible, when we are sailing." A few days later I received a telegram saying he was leaving from Southampton on the Tuesday and could I be there so we could see each other once more. Well, this really knocked me sick, for I had not made up my mind whether to go to Canada or not.

I was granted the day off to go to Southampton not knowing what time the boys would arrive, or what time they would sail. I watched train after train come and go and the boys marching straight to the *Ile de France*. No one could get near them for everything was barricaded and they were not allowed to fall out of line.

They were all aboard and I hadn't even seen Nick. After a time, they all came out on deck, then I heard a yell. There he stood with several pals waving along with him. We stood staring at each other for so long that I could hardly see through my tears. Over and over again I kept asking myself why I hadn't married him. Now it was too late. Only then did I realize how much I loved him and wanted to be with him no matter how far away I had to go.

Someone beside me was sobbing her heart out and I tried to console her, and when I looked back at the ship again, I couldn't believe my eyes, for there was Nick coming down the gangplank. He rushed to me saying, "I begged for just a few minutes ashore before we sailed, and they gave me ten. Aren't I lucky?" In those few minutes great plans for the future were made, and I promised to go to Canada as soon as I could. That was February 1946.

Neither of us realized all the red tape there was to go through: passport to get; medical and doctor certificates; letters signed by my future mother-in-law, their family doctor, minister, and MP all proving to the immigration that I was going to a good family and that Nick was working. Finally, the great day came when I boarded the *Queen Elizabeth* as first-class passenger on Main deck, June 25, 1947. It had taken sixteen long lonely months of waiting.

I shall never forget the splendour of that trip; the thrill of finding that my dining-room companions were a Duchess, a wealthy Texan and his wife, and none other than the English actor, John Mills and his wife. She was the sweetest of persons, and I shared a hymn book at the church service with her as there were so many there. John Mills was going to America to make the film "Great Expectations." They were such wonderful people, and we took snapshots of each other when on deck.

One morning as I was taking a photo of them standing by the rail, a gust of wind blew everything and everybody. John grabbed his wife around her waist just as I clicked the camera. The picture came out great and I treasured it very much.

Taking the elevator to the dining room one day, I was surprised that the operator was a gentleman I had often seen on my bus in Bournemouth. He had lost a leg on the battlefield and now had an artificial one, and looked so smart in his Cunard uniform.

We arrived in New York during a stifling heat wave on the thirtieth of June. Oh! It was so hot. I had on a long-sleeved silk blouse under a suit and I thought I would die. Everyone else was wearing the skimpiest of dresses and shorts.

As we docked, once more I was searching for a certain someone, only I was on the deck this time. I knew Nick was waiting for me, and I was relieved when we found each other.

The size of Grand Central station amazed me. It was like a city itself. The sky-scrapers held me in awe. The next few days in my new home were hectic. We were married on July 7, and spent our honeymoon at Niagara Falls. The firm where Nick was employed gave him a six-week leave that gave us time to get settled into our own home.

There were lovely "welcome home" parties and showers, and a presentation dinner and dance for us in the church hall where I met so many kind people. It was quite touching to find that my husband was held in such high esteem by everyone.

After the church dinner, we promised Nick's brother that we would stay with him and his wife overnight. It had been a busy exciting day and around 11 p.m. my sister-in-law suggested we get some sleep. The long sweeping driveway of their farm led right to the highway, and the bedroom Nick and I had, faced it. We were just dropping off to sleep when all hell broke loose. I thought there had been an explosion or fire as lights were flashing on and off, and the noise of honking and hooting was terrible. Also, people were trying to climb through our window. We jumped out of bed, grabbed our dressing gowns, and rushed out of the room just as someone fell right through it.

I was terrified as we rushed through the living room and into the kitchen. Nick, all this time, was trying to tell me all was okay, and that it was only a joke. Lights were on all over the house, and I noticed the dining-room table laden with food. My in-laws had not been to bed at all, and told me I must open the door and ask them all in to eat, or the racket would continue all night. It was called a "shivaree."

I received more beautiful gifts, and it was quite a

Mr. and Mrs. O. Nichols, Niagara Falls, July 7, 1947

night. The farmyard was full of cars, trucks and tractors
all lined up side by side. And that's how they had driven

up with their lights flashing and horns hooting. No wonder Nick's brother insisted we stay overnight!

We were also invited to Nick's employer's home where I met more people. He was extremely kind, and drove us around the next day alongside Lake Huron and I was thrilled with the lovely scenery.

Throughout my years in Canada I have, of course, spent many happy times in the village of Fonthill with my aunt and uncle. And I cannot help but feel, had it not been for them I would never have met Nick or seen this lovely country. Life for me has been happy here, and I owe this to Nick, my wonderful in-laws, and the many good people who have become my friends.

I am very thankful to my dear husband who has always been so willing to spare me to go "back 'ome" to visit my loved ones nearly every year. At the end of these visits, the parting is not nearly as hard when I know there is another loved one waiting at home for me.

****

In 1960 I worked for an air-force sergeant in Alberta who during the war was in the Royal Air Force in England. He met a Canadian army gal there, and later they were married. His wife repatriated to Canada with her unit, and he followed on a ship that was full of war brides.

As the only male he was dubbed the "male war bride." My imagination tells me this must have been quite an embarrassment for him.

Contributed by George Babak, CFB Petawawa, Ontario.

****

My father's first reaction to the hordes of Canadian soldiers tramping through town was, "Don't you [me] bring any of them damn Canadians in this house!"

One Sunday, soon after this emphatic statement, he came home from his "lunch hour pint" at the local and asked mum if she had enough dinner for two more. In walked two young Canadian soldiers. After they had thanked mum and dad for their first English home-cooked meal, they left. Of course, I kidded dad for doing the very thing he had said I must not. His excuse was, "Poor little buggers. They were standing on the corner looking so lost. If I hadn't brought them home, they would have got mixed up with the wrong kind of woman!" That was the first of many Sunday dinners we shared with young, "lost looking" Canadian soldiers.

I met Jack this way. He came with a pal who had been to dinner before. My parents took an instant liking to him and to this day mum thinks the sun rises and sets on "her Jack."

We were married in October 1941, and my aunt gave up her flat so we could spend our first weekend alone. But the next morning I wanted to go home. I made Jack wait around the corner while I knocked on mum's front door. (I was too shy to be seen with him.) When mum opened the door, I burst out crying and said, "Oh mum! I don't like it!" And there was poor Jack poking his head around the corner wondering what all the fuss was about.

We managed to get that straightened out however, and left to spend a few days in Bournemouth. From there, we headed for London and another hotel. As I was unpacking our suitcase, I told Jack I had forgotten to pack his pyjamas. The laugh was on me, because when I looked for my nightie, I had forgotten that too. Both of

225

them were still under the bed clothes in the Bournemouth hotel.

Leaving England in April 1945 was an event I have never regretted although the journey started very badly with the death and burial of a baby after four days at sea. The mother, a girl from my home town of Sutton Surrey, collapsed, and I looked after her two-year-old son while she was in the sick bay. We became very good friends during the long tedious voyage but, once on the train, became separated. I have thought about her many times, wondering how she got along in Canada after such a tragic beginning.

Many times in England, I would sit and listen to stories Jack and his pals told about Canada. One thing fascinated me very much: their going into a drug-store to buy a soda. I often imagined myself doing this and couldn't wait to try. Alas! A complete flop! After much discussion and embarrassment trying to explain what I wanted, I was presented with a glass of COKE with a lump of ice floating on top. I thought it very unpleasant and was dreadfully disappointed.

I had no trouble learning the currency or spending it. Until I learned east from west, I invariably found myself going the wrong way on a street car, thus finding myself miles away on the wrong side of Toronto.

The first party Jack and I gave, there was a stunned silence when I asked a friend who was staying the night if I could knock him up in the morning. Embarrassment again—until the other guests burst into gales of laughter.

We had two boys; the eldest is married and has twin boys of his own. Our second son was born with a spina bifida, but enters all wheel-chair games. He won two gold medals and one silver medal at the 1978 games in Brazil, and competes all over this continent, and a few years ago, in Europe. There is not a thing he won't try.

He water skis, plays baseball, drives his own car, plays guitar and sings.

Jack and I saved our money and bought a grocery business in a small Ontario town which we ran successfully for ten years. During this time we invested in a lakeside cottage in the Kawartha Lake area of Ontario. We loved it there so much that we decided to winterize it and live there permanently. We sold the grocery business and moved. Jack is now assistant manager in a liquor store, and I am head-cashier for a local food chain.

When I first came to Canada I was desperately homesick and missed my parents and sister very much. Mum had visited Canada often but dad would never come. My sister and her husband visit frequently, and I go home fairly often, sometimes with Jack when we can manage time off together. But Canada has been my country for many years, and I thank God for it.

****

Olga and Lloyd Rains
Ontario

In 1940, my country, Holland, was invaded by the Germans. I was fourteen years old and in grade ten, high school. Although I started grade eleven, the school system was changed by the Germans and my parents would not allow me to finish. My father was a banker and we also owned a cigar store, so I helped out in there. This didn't last too long as we were forced to close. There was nothing left to sell. Everything went to the German army, even our food and clothing.

When I was sixteen I found an office job, hated it, left, and started working in a dress shop. I liked this and took sewing and tailoring courses at night. Before long this stopped because the Germans started a 6 p.m. curfew. The curfews imposed upon us were punishment for interfering with German soldiers or demolishing their equipment and refusing to obey their orders. The hours were often changed but never later than ten o'clock.

Things grew steadily worse over the years. We had to part with most of our belongings: blankets, silverware, copperware, radios; they even wanted our dog. One day I made the mistake of wearing my watch to work. On the way home, I was approached by a German who said he wanted it to send home to his girlfriend. When I refused, he forced it from me.

One day they rounded up all the young girls who were out walking. Filling two trucks they took us to the basement of the town hall and asked us question after question. We were kept overnight standing with our backs to a cold brick wall. Once in a while they slapped and poked at us. Apparently a Dutch girl had pushed one of their soldiers into the canal where he drowned. They did not find out anything, so released us in the morning. The resistance of the Dutch people was something the Germans could not tolerate, and at times they became very brutal and we had to be very careful what we said or they would take a family member for hostage.

In 1944, my sister and I went to a friend's farm near the Belgium border. We liked it there because there was lots to eat. But this was short-lived as the allies were closing in and the fighting started. We had to return home to north Holland and were on the last train before the bridge on the river Rhine was destroyed.

Planes were shooting at the train thinking it was full of Germans. I will never forget the face of a tail-gunner as he pointed at us. I grabbed my sister and we jumped out of the moving train rolling down into a dirty muddy ditch. We lost our shoes and walked the rest of the way home, covered in mud.

That winter was the worst of all. Most of Holland had been liberated by then except a few provinces in the north where I lived. There was no food, and people were dying of starvation in the streets; no electricity and no fuel. We had an old wood stove and burned all our furniture. The only food we had was what we could scrounge ourselves. It took a lot of wheeling and dealing to get a small bag of flour or a few vegetables and then we had to walk twenty miles to get them.

I became very ill with diphtheria. There was no serum so the doctor could not do very much. My father paid six guilders for ONE egg so that I would have something to eat. After six weeks of isolation and the loving care of my parents, I got better. I didn't realize it at the time, but now that I'm older I think back to the close calls I had, and thank God for sparing me so that I could meet my wonderful husband.

Our liberators arrived about May 8, and oh! joy of joys! There seemed to be parties everywhere, and the food! It was hard to take at first after the muck we had been eating.

It was at a friend's party that I met Lloyd. I had learned English in high school, which helped, and I managed to make myself understood. It wasn't long after that he asked me to marry him. He applied for permission and after a lot of red tape with forms, medicals and blood tests, we were married on December 24, 1945.

Lloyd's brother who was stationed in Germany was able to attend the wedding which was carried out in traditional Dutch style. The groom calls on the bride an hour before the wedding to bring her the bouquet, and together, in a horse-drawn carriage, they drive to wherever the ceremony is to take place. In our case it was the City Hall. All our guests were transported in like-manner. The reception was enjoyed by all,

Olga and Lloyd Rains (Holland)

especially the food supplied by the Canadian army.

In January 1946, Lloyd left from Nymegen for Canada and I followed in the August of that year. The *Lady Rodney* took other war brides and myself from Holland to England where we boarded the *Mauretania*. I was very impressed with this lovely big ship and the delicious food we were served.

My destination was Sault Ste. Marie, a small Ontario town. My first impression was one of primitiveness;

Dutch War brides on the "Mauretania" in Halifax, August 24, 1946

hydro wires above ground; huge steam trains and wooden houses. In Holland all trains are electric and the houses, brick.

The beauty of the Ontario northland took my breath away. I loved the wide open spaces and the distances between towns—the nearest one to us was Sudbury, two hundred miles away. I found Canadians more reserved than my own people and found it strange to see the streets deserted on a Sunday. In Holland, everyone went out on a Sunday whether it be to the theatre, a restaurant or just walking.

The furnace heating system in the basements of houses appealed to me—what a pleasure after the cold houses of Holland. I only knew the metric system and found it hard to shop for groceries. I remember another Dutch war bride and myself spending hours trying to whip table cream thinking it was whipping cream.

Meeting my husband's relatives for the first time was quite a challenge. They all stared at me as if I came from outer space. It didn't take long for me to understand them and the Canadian ways. After all, I had to. I was in Canada and it was up to me to adjust, not them.

Lloyd has always been self-employed, mostly in the motel business. We had a motel in Orillia for seven years after we moved from Hamilton. We gave this up and moved further north to open another. I did get lonely at times but Lloyd helped me through these difficult periods. We love the northland and are very happy and expect to stay here for as long as we can.

****

Liberation 1945

by
Lini R. Grol

When the nights
   were dark and lonely
   and filled with fearful sounds,
The silence deepened in the homes so cold
Where no fathers were around.

When every footstep
   in the night
   startled the women in fear,
For these steps that came so close
Told them of death being near.

When mistrust grew
   and bitter words
   chilled every heart and room;
When lowliness and lawlessness
Filled all hearts with gloom.

When starvation hovered
   in every home
   and no heart had left a song,
We cried and prayed: "God let freedom come
And send your sons along."

Oh, the sun shone bright
   that glorious day,
   one day in early spring,
When finally the Canadians came
And made all Holland sing.

Special permission granted by author

233

During the early war years I worked for the Ministry of Food packaging dried eggs for the armed forces. As I was in charge of a department, I was exempt from further war duties until 1942 when all supplies were exhausted. I then became eligible to join one of the services. I volunteered for the army, and on January 1, 1943, became a recruit in the Auxiliary Territorial Service (ATS).

After basic training, I was sent to the Royal Army Corps of Signals where I underwent further extensive training which resulted in my being sent to Tangmere Aerodrome in Chichester as a plotter.

Esther (Terry) Green

George Green

A friend and I went to a dance one evening at the YWCA. There I met a Canadian soldier who, after

234

dancing with me, invited me to have a drink. Rather shy, and a non-drinker, I declined. But as my friend was enjoying herself with other girls from the base, I asked him to escort me back to my barracks.

George was very nice, and when we reached barracks we said goodnight, and for three weeks never once saw each other. Then he came one day and asked if I would go out with him. These dates became more frequent until one evening he said, "Hon. You are the best little woman in seventy-seven counties. Will you marry me? I love you but, you must remember if you do marry me, you will either freeze to death or starve to death in Canada."

After I accepted his unusual proposal, we had to apply to our commanding officers for permission. The weather was extremely cold the day we were wed in the Borough of Hackney town hall. For months London had been bombarded every night, and February 19, our wedding night, was the only night the Luftwaffe stayed away, much to our relief.

When the *Mauretania* left England in February 1946, I shared a cabin with several other brides whose company I enjoyed. One was a woman who, although may not have then been in her forties, certainly looked and dressed the part, even to her nightly undressing of fleecy-lined knickers. A puzzled young steward who had observed her leaving the cabin several times, said to me, "Who is she? Is she a war bride?" I replied she was. He let out a loud guffaw and exclaimed, "Blimey. She gave up blushing long ago!"

George met me at the station in New Brunswick and I had never seen so much ice and snow. It remained until May when George took me to see a house which he wanted to buy for us and the family we hoped for. We did buy it and brought up four children of whom we are

235

very proud.

In those first years I learned how to can food, bake bread, churn butter, garden and cook on a wood stove.

George worked as a carpenter for many years, then in 1957 became the maintenance man for the Canada Customs until he retired in 1972 due to ill health.

One of the first novels I read was "The Egg and I." It seemed as if I had written that book, for the adventures of the heroine were like mine, including the first skunk I had ever seen.

My dear George who passed away September 17, 1973 at the age of sixty years, never saw our youngest son graduate from college, nor our little grandson. But I'll be ever thankful that he gave me a wonderful family and a happy life in Canada, and I have never froze or starved since I arrived.

****

Constance (MacDonald) Dulong
Ontario

I worked in London for the Midland Bank, overseas branch. In May, 1939, I was chosen for the position of bank teller on the liner, *Queen Mary*. This thrilled me very much and I was eager and excited to start this new venture. Alas! Hitler's "antics" put a halt to the procedure. I was so disappointed and upset by this turn of events that as the war progressed with all the bombing, rationing, black-out and other inconveniences, I was determined to get out of England one way or another. I was thoroughly fed up and how I was going to accomplish this, I had no idea.

My girlfriend and I were having dinner in a pub one day. I noticed a Canadian soldier watching us and after a while he came over and asked if he could buy us a drink.

He said he was stationed in Epsom, Surrey, which was near my home and we started to see each other quite regularly.

We were married in January 1943, and five months later Stuart left for Sicily. The next time we saw each other was in March 1945 when he came on leave, and for the first time he saw our little daughter Constance, whom we nick-named Cherry because there were three in the family named Constance. He went back to Holland until July, then back to England where he worked in the Repatriation Office on Charles 11 Street in London until he left for Canada in March 1946.

Two months after he left, I had a miscarriage. Stuart was so worried about me, that he came back to England as a civilian on a "flat top" that was bringing grain to the Port of London. Cherry and I left on the hospital ship *Lady Nelson,* September 3, and Stuart followed two weeks later on a ship that carried civilians and misplaced Canadian soldiers.

The *Lady Rodney* left Southampton two hours before we did and ran into a fierce storm. They radioed the *Nelson* not to leave port. The advice was ignored and we sailed. Exactly one hour after we had eaten a beautiful roast chicken dinner with all the trimmings, fruit, and gobs of whipped cream, we ran into this storm. Need I say anymore? Cherry remained in her bunk for nine days, apples and soda crackers her only diet. On the tenth day she felt better and was allowed up.

When we were passing the coast of Newfoundland, we were on deck. I turned to get Cherry and found she was missing. The ship was searched from stem to stern, and for three hours I was in a complete panic. The Captain came to the terrible conclusion that she had gone down one of the ladders and when the ship lurched, must have been thrown overboard. I was hysterical, and even more so when I got the wonderful news that she had been found. She had gone to the kennels where the army dogs were kept on a lower deck. Somehow, she had found her way there and was sitting on the floor talking to them. After this terrifying experience, I was glad when we pulled into Halifax. The first thing Cherry said when she saw land was, "Look mummy, there's a tree."

The *Lady Nelson* also carried veterans headed for Westminster Hospital in London, Ontario. It was heartbreaking to see them behind nets, absolute vegetables, and some looked so young. Just a few years before they had been strong and healthy men.

The train looked as if it had been taken out of moth balls just for us. It was so dirty. Some of the girls got off on the wrong foot when they called the coloured porter, "Snowball." I'm afraid that did not go down too well with him. The girls didn't mean any harm. Most of us could count on one hand how many coloured people we had met in our lives.

We stopped in Moncton and were allowed off to buy anything we needed. One girl, not realizing that in Canada trains run on the same track both ways, proceeded to get on a train with the engine facing the other way, and so went back to Halifax while her two children headed for Montreal with the rest of us. Those poor kids! We helped the Red Cross to take care of them and once in Montreal the Red Cross took over completely until they were reunited with their mother.

There was a two-hour wait in Montreal, and we were told we could get off the train providing we remained on the station. It was here that I had my first feeling that we Britishers were not wanted. I had bought Cherry an ice cream cone and took her to a washroom to wash her hands and use the toilet. There were two young ladies in there and when they heard Cherry flatly refuse to use the toilet because the door was broken, one said to the other, "We should have all these limeys sent back with their

238

high and mighty ideas." I ignored them both and went in search of another washroom.

In Toronto, one girl was met by her mother-in-law who greeted her by placing a mink stole around her shoulders, and giving her a brand new baby carriage for her baby. From there to Chatham, we stopped at every station to let girls off. One, looking out the window exclaimed, "Oh! What ocean is that?" Of course it was Lake Ontario.

The scenery disappointed me for it was so flat. My in-laws greeted me warmly, and made me feel at home. Cherry had a few bad moments when other children made fun of her accent, but it was soon overcome. I adjusted to my new country easily enough and we stayed with Stuart's parents until January 1947 when we moved into a veteran's housing unit where our three other children were born.

My mum and dad came to Canada to live in 1951, and I, an only child, was glad to have them here. Through the years, they helped us in many ways. Dad passed away in 1958 and my independent mother lived on her own until recently.

In 1960, Stuart had a bad stroke and was unable to work anymore. For a year, he was in and out of hospital then died early in 1962.

Life was a struggle with four children, but one always seems to manage. A few years later I met and married a fine man. We bought a farm through the Veteran's Land Act, and have lived there ever since.

Life sure has not been all easy. But this country has been good to me. I have never been back to England or wanted to for that matter. I never felt homesick which may sound unusual to many. I was determined to like Canada and become a good citizen. I succeeded with the first; I hope I have with the second.

****

239

I was closely associated with the movement of troops and war brides during and after the war. On June 14, 1946, the *Queen Mary* brought to Canada some 1,700 war brides and children with the returning Prime Minister of Canada, The Right Honourable MacKenzie King. It was my custom to address the war brides on each voyage before reaching Halifax, and on this particular crossing the Prime Minister addressed them as well. This was my address:

" . . . You have been given a sincere and hearty welcome to Canada by our Prime Minister; a message that must have warmed your hearts as it did mine in extending to you on behalf of the Government of Canada such a fine welcome and hope for your future happiness in the land of your adoption.

"The shores of Canada are looming up on the northwestern horizon . . . the first lap of your long trip is almost over . . . the culmination of long months of waiting for transport to the New Land, which years ago your forebearers founded in the true pioneering spirit of their time. As early settlers, their industry and great determination developed a country that today commands such a high position of importance among the great nations of the world.

"You are a part of the many thousands now taking up new homes in Canada . . . wives and sturdy children of Canada's fighting forces, men of honour who offered their all in the great cause for which we fought.

"When I see the lovely children on this ship, I cannot help but think of our Prime Minister's speech when he said, quote: 'The tiniest bits of opinion sown in the minds of children in private life, afterwards issue forth to the world and become public opinion; for nations are gathered out of nurseries, and they who hold the leading strings of children, may even exercise a greater power

240

than those who hold the reins of Government. . . . '
unquote.

"The shores of Canada are ahead . . . the dawn of a
new day and a new adventure. . . . "

The part of the Prime Minister's speech was added to
all speeches I gave to war brides on subsequent voyages
and a copy of these were available to all.

There were approximately 69,000 war brides and
children who crossed the Atlantic during and after the
war; they made new lives for themselves in this great
country of ours.

Contributed by Lieutenant-Colonel W. Evan Sutherland,
OBE, Officer in Charge, Ship's Conducting Staff.

****

Sylvia and Carson Stevens
Ontario

Just before the war started, the personnel in the
laboratory firm where I worked, mentioned that the work
we were doing was not essential to the war effort and the
possibility was that we young girls would be "called up"
for the women's services or other war work, and if we
wanted, we could go ahead and do this with their
blessing, so to speak.

Electronics interested me and I applied for work with
His Master's Voice (HMV) which is now RCA. They
had a huge place in Hayes, Middlesex, now Heathrow
Airport, and I was given the chance to take a six-month
course which would place me in the research department
if I passed. I did pass and stayed with them until the last
year of the war when the place got a direct hit with a

land mine. There were twenty or more of us girls in the air-raid shelter, and only two of us survived.

I remember my mouth was full of dust from the debris around us, and my clothes all torn. There was a large hole in the wall which I thought we could crawl through to safety. But because the gas main was hit, flames were on the other side of it making it impossible for both of us.

We were rescued after what seemed hours, and once out on the street were given a weak cup of tea. It was far from funny at the time, but I do laugh now at that awful tea. It was so weak it was almost colourless. And oh! so sweet! I loathed sugar in tea, but tea is the English cure for what ails you . . . and I drank it.

As far back as 1914 there were many families from my home town of Milton Regis in Kent, England, that immigrated to Kent County in southwestern Ontario; perhaps they thought they would feel more at home there because crops were similar. These families left many relatives in Milton Regis and in later years went back there to visit. One of these was an elderly gentleman who, in 1931, came for a visit bringing with him two much younger friends. One was about sixteen years old, who many years later was to become my husband. The elderly man knew my family very well, and this was how I came to meet Steve (Carson).

Steve stayed for a few months then returned to Canada. We corresponded and he made two more trips to England before the war broke out, then he joined the Canadian Army, and in January 1940 he was back again.

As my family knew most of the families who had immigrated, and saw them when they came for visits, I got to know Kent County, Ontario, very well. Also through corresponding with Steve and his family for a number of years, my knowledge of the area was such that when I arrived here in 1946, the only things that surprised me was the size of the trains and the unpopulated areas.

I knew all about the weather, humidity, the crops that were grown, and had heard so much about everything that it was as if I had been there all my life.

Steve was stationed in the south of England with the Essex Scottish regiment, and in August 1942 he was taken a Prisoner of War during the raid on Dieppe. At first his parents were notified that he was missing in action, then later the news came that he was in Stalag V111 B prison camp where, amongst other difficulties, they were chained for eighteen months. He was only allowed to write a certain amount of letters during a period of time, so when I received one I would immediately wire his parents and they would do likewise. Over the years, my future in-laws became more of a family to me than my own.

In December 1944 when the Russians surrounded Budapest, all POWs were force-marched until they were liberated in May 1945. If their captors knew the Russians were advancing in the direction of the march, they turned their prisoners the opposite way; if the British, Canadians, or Americans were advancing that way, they marched them in another direction. And so it went on and on for five horrible months. They were so poorly clothed and starving to death, that only ten per cent survived, and Steve was one.

He was taken to hospital in the south of England, and after his release we were married. He left for Canada and, once home, entered Westminster Hospital in London, Ontario. I followed him on the *Lady Rodney* in May 1946. On board were the Dagenham Girl Pipers, who piped us into Halifax harbour. The band on the dock stood in awe as they listened to these girl pipers; they were absolutely marvellous. Coming over, all the brides put on a concert for the crew. There was a lot of talent amongst the girls, and one Scottish bride recited a monologue that would put many actresses to shame.

Steve met me in London, and we drove to Chatham where we stayed with his parents until we found a house of our own.

The terrible prison diet and those last five agonizing months of marching, had left their mark. It had ruined the health of all those brave men who had survived and Steve was no exception. He was very handicapped, and never able to work. He could walk only very slowly; he read a great deal; spent many hours with his stamp collection; and kept up a correspondence with families in England with whom he had been billeted.

Steve loved England, and fortunately we were able to visit there despite his ill health. All through the years he was in and out of hospital and never once complained. No one ever knew he was suffering. We had one son, and I kept working until a couple of years ago. For the last years of Steve's life, we lived in a small town near Chatham. He enjoyed the country air and would sit on the grass, for he could not bend, and help me weed the garden.

The years were not easy, but together we made the very best of the life we had, and that was good. Steve passed away in April 1976; he suffered greatly during his last year. But now he is without worry, without pain and at rest. And I miss him so.

****

Olive Kitcher
Ontario

A town between the south coast of England and London was where I was born. It was a regular "bus route" for the German bombers as they flew to the

Capitol. We were surrounded by anti-aircraft guns and many a bomber dropped their bombs in and around our town if they were caught in the search-light beam that made them a good target for the ack-ack guns.

I worked in a factory that produced transmitters and receivers for planes. I learnt to operate many huge machines that in peace time were operated by men only. I really enjoyed my work.

Servicemen from different countries were arriving regularly in Britain, and getting to know them was quite exciting for the young English girls. My girlfriend was going out with a Canadian soldier who was with the Canadian Medical Corps stationed at a hospital near our home town. There was a dance there one Saturday evening and she asked me if I would go with her friend's pal to make a foursome.

At first I declined, but after assuring me that my "blind date" was a very nice chap, I agreed. I was the last one to think this soldier would become my future husband. For the next few weeks we went out quite a lot, and he came home and met my family. They liked him very much, and on Christmas Day, 1944, we got engaged, much to my father's disapproval. He did not want me to marry a man from another country.

We were going to wait a while before marrying, but after the New Year there was much talk that the unit might be shipped out. We applied for permission as soon as possible and a lot of pleading and talking ensued to get my dad to sign the permission form, as I was under twenty-one. But he did sign and everything went through and we were told we could marry after May 5. This was a blow because we knew the unit would go before that date. We took matters into our own hands and married on March 3, 1945, knowing, of course, that we would probably get into trouble.

Things didn't work out too badly, however. My

Olive and Les Kitcher

husband lost a month's pay, and I did not get the wife's allowance until after the legal date. We did have a lovely wedding in spite of war time restrictions. It was a lovely sunny day and we were so happy even if we couldn't go on a honey-moon because my husband could only get a weekend pass.

A few weeks after, the unit were told they would not be leaving for overseas after all but would remain in England to tend the many wounded that were coming back.

February 1946 my husband had seven days leave, then they were shipped back to Canada and I followed three months later.

How sad I felt when walking up the gangplank. I looked back at my homeland and had mixed feelings about the new life I was starting and the old I was leaving behind. Would I ever see England and my family again? It was such a big step to take for such a young heart. But there I was, watching the shoreline gradually fade into the distance, and the only life I knew, with it.

The *Queen Mary* was a beautiful ship; the meals delicious; and crew most helpful. I made quite a few new friends, but one thing worried me. Every girl I spoke to and asked where in Canada they were going, but none were going to Timmins in northern Ontario. I thought maybe I was going to the North Pole.

A band welcomed us in Halifax, and after we were checked through immigration, we were put onto a train and I was in the Ontario section where I met five other girls who were going to Timmins.

I was quite relieved and very happy that I would have company all the way. My first encounter on Canadian soil was when the train stopped at a small station in New Brunswick and a Red Cross lady said we could get out and stretch our legs. There was a store nearby, and espying some oranges, the first in years, I bought one-half dozen and was charged one dollar. The money and the prices were all strange to me, and it wasn't until I got back on the train I was told I had been badly over-charged. They were only twenty-five cents a dozen at the time. I never spent anymore money en route!

We changed trains in North Bay and what a slow train that was! I told the porter to be sure and tell me when we came to Timmins as I did not want to go past it. He laughed and said not to worry as Timmins was the end of the line. All I could see from the train window was bush, bush and more bush. End of the line? Where in God's name was I going?

As we neared Timmins, I became quite scared wondering if I would be accepted into my husband's family and if I could adjust to this new life. My fears were needless. I received such a wonderful welcome

247

from the family and their friends. And I was warmly accepted everywhere I went.

My in-laws owned a lovely house with all modern facilities, and I felt so much at home because they were my kind of people having come from the north of England in 1925.

Although I liked Timmins, there was a lot to get used to. The climate especially—extremely cold in the winter with tons of snow, and very hot in the summer with hordes of mosquitoes. When I started to shop on my own, for some time the sales people had a hard time understanding my accent. I asked one if she had any lace, and she replied in a puzzled voice, "I'm sorry. We do not sell 'lice' here." I was mad at the time for I thought she was being smart, but I laughed over it later. The buying of groceries for two weeks at a time instead of daily, amazed me. And asking for a "roast" instead of a "joint" took months.

I hated the old cook stove and burnt more food trying to get the hang of using it. My husband loved raisin pie so I decided to surprise him and make one. He was surprised all right! I used about three pounds of raisins, but didn't soak them first (didn't know I had to) and when I opened the oven to take the pie out, the top crust had come off, and the raisins were all over the oven like hard black bullets!

When we bought our first house, I was very thrilled. It gave me much pleasure furnishing it, and one of the first things I bought was an electric stove. No more cook stoves for me.

A war bride from the First World War invited all the new brides to her house so we could meet each other. From there, we started what we called "The War Bride Teas." There were about twenty of us who met every second week for about the first eighteen months, then the children started coming, some moved away, and we disbanded.

My first trip home was in 1954, and although I was homesick for my family, I would not have wanted to live there anymore. It was not the England I had left. So much had changed. Although I still love my homeland, I am proud to be Canadian. My life in Canada has been very good; but who knows, if it had not been for a fine husband, in-laws, and friends who went out of their way to make me welcome, I might not have stayed. I can truthfully say, I have never regretted marrying that Canadian soldier whom I met on that "blind date" so many years ago.

****

Marjorie Willis
Alberta

I was a teletype operator with the Woman's Auxiliary Air Force during the war and stationed at Linton-on-Ouse. One of the corporals on my watch was fed-up, homesick for Canada and his wife and family. One night he invited my friend Doris and myself to a show (movie). In Signals, we were sort of apart from the rest of the WAAF who looked upon us as over-privileged because our spare-time did not come under Admin, but our own Signals Officer. So we tended to stick together and our married friends were not separate from us. We all chummed around together and thought nothing of it.

The show finished at nine o'clock, and the three of us caught the bus back to Linton. When we got as far as Newton-on-Ouse, we found there was a dance in progress. Doris and I decided we'd go, and our married friend continued back to base.

Here I met the tall blonde man who kept calling me "blondie," a name I loathed. Our first date was a real flop. All he did was complain what a dowdy place England was, and moaned in general about it, the war, and all the twits he worked with. I was so darned mad by the time we got back to camp that I said "goodnight" and walked off before he had the chance to ask for another date. I told the girls in my Nissen hut that I had never been so cheesed off about a date as I was that one, and sincerely hoped I would never set eyes on him again.

My reprieve didn't last long. He came round to Signals next day and apologized for being such a bore and asked if I would let him make up for it on another date. Obviously, I did! We were married in 1944, and I left England for Canada in February 1946.

My worst moments leaving England occurred firstly at the train station, and later as the *Aquitania* pulled slowly out to sea. I was one of hundreds of war brides to board a special train at York station to start us on our journey to Canada to join our husbands and embark on a new life.

We had been advised to say our family farewell on the home front, and I was glad I had. A lot of parents accompanied their daughters to the station, and it was heart-breaking to see the tears and hear the promises: "I'll write every week, mum." "I promise I'll come back in two years." A few of the parents ran along the platform as the train began to move, still holding onto their daughters' hands, hoping these promises would be kept.

For the first hour of the journey we were all very quiet, and I suppose we needed this time to accept what was happening before turning our thoughts to the future. Then we began to introduce ourselves, made friends as we gradually got to know each other, and the laughter echoed through the train. The worst was over!

250

After one night in London, we travelled to Southampton to board the good old "Acky." The first pleasant surprise came the next morning when we found our allotted tables in the dining room, picked up the day's menu and found such things as bacon and eggs, lamb chops, steak, and all the butter and sugar we wanted. This was a real treat after rationing where we thought we were lucky to get one egg every two weeks or so. With the abundance of food, it was like offering a man a gallon of water in the Sahara! The medical officer did a roaring business in indigestion tablets, that is, for the two days the ship sat in dock. After that, I would say two-thirds of us didn't care much WHAT was on the menu.

The day before we sailed, we watched the *Queen Mary* pull out from her dock with her quota of war brides and returning troops.

There were two thousand brides aboard the "Acky" headed for all parts of Canada, from Prince Edward Island to Vancouver Island. The next afternoon our turn came to sail and with it, the second bad moment. Most of us were on deck holding our wee ones, and as we slowly pulled away, a lone band was playing, "Til We Meet Again." The only people on the dock was a couple who had travelled from Scotland to see their only child off to Canada. There seemed to be a dead silence on the ship, broken only by the noise of the engine, the slapping of the sea, and the screeching seagulls. I can only speak for myself at that moment. I had a lump the size of a baseball in my throat, and no amount of swallowing could get rid of it. All I could think to do was take my small son's wrist and flap his hand around saying, "Wave bye-bye to England, David." What a futile idiotic thing to do, really, but it helped from breaking down. I watched dear old England disappear slowly, and wondered, as I'm sure everyone did, whether I would ever see it again. I haven't yet. Poor old England—rationed to the eyebrows, tattered and torn and half blown apart for six years, but still flying the good old Union Jack and still grinning and bearing it.

The first evening at sea was great. Nice calm waters, hardly a ripple. This was going to be easy. Look out Canada, here we come, full of lamb chops, steaks, bacon and eggs. Not so at all!

The next day we sailed into a nice thick "pea-souper" FOG! The ship did not plunge, nor did it roll from side to side; it just went "uupp and doown" like an elevator, as the ocean rose and fell. After a while our stomachs went up and down with it, and many of us were very sick. I could not face the dining room at all, and while I munched on crackers, David lapped up all his meals with a disgusting appetite.

Our cabin was complete with port-hole, and at diaper-washing time, which I could not face either, the port-hole came in mighty handy.

The day before we arrived in Canada, we were asked to go down into the hold of the ship and verify that all our luggage was in order. I didn't feel too well, and decided no matter what, I was absolutely NOT going into that horrible hold. My name was called over the speaker and I was told to report to the Commanding Officer immediately. I obeyed the order but told him flat out that he could fling my luggage overboard if he wanted as I refused to go down below. I expected to be thrown into the brig, or put out to sea in a rubber dinghy, but the dear man remarked that I did look a little green, and handed me a few tiny red pills saying, "Don't tell a soul about them. I only have a small amount."

They had been given to the troops on the landing crafts on "D-day." Perhaps they were placebos; I really don't know, but within an hour of taking one, I felt marvellous. My only problem, as was everyone else's,

252

was to walk around in a normal manner. As the ship went down in the swell, one's foot searched for the deck, and it was like searching for a step that wasn't there. Then, as the ship came up, one had the feeling that a knee would come up and clobber one's chin. We must have looked like drunks trying to walk a straight line.

The next morning our long-awaited moment arrived. Our Captain informed us that if we went to the portside, we would very soon see the coastline of Canada. The fog had lifted, visibility was normal, and oh! there it was! A very thin line on the horizon. Oh happy day! Canada at last, and best of all, dry land!

As we grew closer we could hear strains of music, and as we pulled into dock the band was playing, "Here comes the bride." The dock was packed solid with people; troops, dock hands, men, women and children, all waving to us. They shouted, smiled, and called out messages of cheer and welcome. It was overwhelming to say the least. They began to throw streamers at us, and before they were through, the whole side of the ship was a mass of garlands. We had streamers draped over us from head to foot. What a sight! And oh! what a wonderful welcome.

Despite Captain's orders, we too, were throwing all manner of things down to the people. English coins mostly. Then English cigarettes, seasick pills and anything else we happened to have. That evening we were all pretty excited. We had been swamped with photographers and newsmen taking all kinds of pictures and asking all manner of questions.

The next morning we boarded the train for our final destination. I looked back at that proud old ship, and I treasure the souvenir card we all received, a reproduction of a water-colour painting and on the reverse side the message, "The Ship's Company of the *Aquitania* send you best wishes for your happiness and good fortune in your new life in the great Dominion, the country of your adoption—March, 1946.''

I found it a chore to keep my active youngster reasonably still on the train. He wanted to crawl one minute, then up to see the horses and cows through the window the next. The train was slow compared to our fast-moving English express trains, and I wondered when it was going to speed up a bit. It was Sunday, and I was due in Calgary Thursday morning, and I could not figure out how we'd ever make it.

After starving to death on the ship through sea-sickness, I made up for it on the train. Here again, I ran into the indigestion problem. Finally, the nurse sent me to the Medical Officer who rightfully thought I was a little bit mad to go on eating all the long unforseen goodies and suffering miseries as a result.

It was exciting when the train stopped at a town and we witnessed reunions between man and wife. Most of the girls rushed off to stores to buy items of clothing and candies. It was truly amazing how much they could pick up and pay for during a half-hour stop.

We came to Medicine Hat during the early hours of Thursday morning, and one of the girls due to get off there, had slept in unknown to us. Her husband, obviously wondering where she was, somehow managed to board the train and in his excitement ran down our aisle opening our curtains one by one shouting, ''Where is she?'' He finally found her and she left the train with his coat over her pyjamas, all her plans for meeting him looking real ''spiffy'' gone forever!

At last, here was Calgary, my stop. The Canadian Red Cross were there with a reception committee, and quite a few war brides from the first war. For a little while it all seemed strange and bewildering.

My husband had rented a room in a hotel for a few days before leaving for Elnora, my new home. I had very little in the line of clothing, so went on a wonderful shopping spree. It felt marvellous to be able to buy anything I wanted. The one thing that threw me was the size of the shoes. Two sizes larger here than in England, and I thought it sounded awful.

The grocery stores with their windows full of fruit fascinated me to the point where I went in and bought three oranges, three bananas, and four hot-house tomatoes. That night before I fell asleep, I ate the whole works. My husband was quite sure I would be sick, but I slept like a baby. What did bother me was the heat in the hotel room. I thought I would suffocate and kept flinging windows up to get some cold fresh air.

Everyone everywhere knew I was a war bride. The accent I suppose. People kept asking me how I liked Canada, before I'd had a chance to find out. Another problem I ran into was trying to figure out what everything cost in English currency. I didn't know whether $20.00 was expensive for a dress, or $5.95 too much for shoes. I could not get used to the expression "Holy Cow." It sounded so obscene. So many English words had a different meaning. For instance the word "homely." In England it meant a sweet homebody, a loveable person. I really made a "faux pas" when I told a newly-made friend what a homely person her mother was, only to receive a freezing stare and a cold shoulder. Oh dear!

When we reached the small town where I was to begin my new life, I felt ill at ease meeting my in-laws, even though we had exchanged many letters. David helped me over this bridge as he was the hit of the day, the new and only grandson and nephew. I met so many people, that I had an awful job putting names to faces. The way the teenagers called their elders by their first name, and the free and easy student-teacher relationship, amazed me.

Like all English girls, I did not know what a shower

was. And when on Saturday night I was told to put on my best dress because a neighbour was "putting on a shower" for me, I naturally thought the lucky lady must be blessed with running water, but darned if I knew why I had to dress up just to take a shower. Maybe, I thought, it was some kind of ritual, or initiation for new residents, and to say that I was somewhat puzzled, is putting it mildly. No one had thought to tell me that this would be a shower of gifts and not hot water. A shower was an understatement. It was more like a torrential thunderstorm! Ladies came from miles around—total strangers, each carrying a lovely and useful gift. All the faces around me were smiling, and I found that wretched baseball back in my throat and had difficulty trying to swallow it while stammering, "thank you."

The day arrived when we moved in to our own farm after spending many hours cleaning and painting the house. When I look back on it all, I marvel at myself. How could I, a city-born girl, expect to transfer myself to a Canadian farm with no running water, no electricity, and no central heating. I didn't even know the front end of a steer from the hind end, until I found that the hind end could kick! I innocently asked my husband which was a steer and which was a heifer. He told me that the little boy was the steer, and I'm sure he must have wondered whether this English critter would ever shape into a farmer's wife. I did, eventually. I even learned to roll my own cigarettes and wondered what my family would think if they could see me rolling a la John Wayne!

My weekly wash day was a real chore. Our pump water was too hard to make suds, so I used the rain water from the barrel. And if that wasn't enough, my husband hauled it from a slough, and we heated it on our coal stove. It took all day in the winter to melt enough for the next day's wash. My washing machine was a real antique. It was boat-shaped, stood on a stand with a handle in the middle, and a body had to rock the thing from side to side for twenty or more minutes per load. Washday was just that, a whole day's work.

Next day came the ironing with a big clumsy gas iron. The thing had a small tank attached to the back of the handle which was filled with high-test gas. I always said a prayer before I did the ironing just in case the thing blew it's top and I got to meet St. Peter sooner than anticipated.

I was absolutely fascinated with the radio programmes, especially the singing commercials. After our very, very serious BBC announcers at home, the Canadian ones were so breezy. I even got a "thing" about soap operas for a while. I listened to Laura's troubles, and Big Sister's horrible life until the novelty wore thin.

To be a half-decent farmer's wife, one had to know how to make one's own butter and bread. I was determined to do both. I bought a small churn and flung a couple of quarts of cream into it, churned away with the paddle, and lo and behold, I wound up with a nice mound of butter.

Making my own bread was a different matter. Nobody but nobody bought store bread in those days. All I knew about bread at that point was, it contained flour and yeast. As I reached for my trusty cook book, friend husband told me that I didn't need it as he knew how his mum made her bread. Trusting him implicitly, I followed his orders. Into a huge enamel bowl I poured about a gallon or more of water. Added a cake of yeast and some salt.

Following his instructions, I began to add flour, and add flour, until I had an awful sticky mass which I tried in vain, to knead. This horrible mass weighed at least a ton, and I wound up with the sticky goo up to my elbows. My husband kept telling me to add more flour, so on I struggled until I was forced to tell him that I was thoroughly exhausted and confronted with the beastly thought that the horror I had created would surely raise the roof clear off the house, if and when it began to double in bulk.

He finally admitted that he must have had his wires crossed about the amount of water necessary. We decided to get rid of "it" and try again. I couldn't lift the bowl off the table, so he hauled it off and took it into the bush and dumped it. It is still there—petrified—and offering a welcome seat by the wayside for trail hikers! The next day I popped over to my new and very good neighbour and learned how to make bread the easy way.

The great difference in temperature did not bother me too much. During my first winter here, I did not feel the cold, and would run out to the wood shed with just a thin dress on in thirty below zero weather. I coped much better with the cold than I did the sweltering heat of the prairie summer.

The only material thing I really and truly missed from my soft city life was the good old flush toilet. Oh! How I hated that trek out to the "biffy" in winter. It was hardly conducive to regularity and good kidney habits. It also had the elements of a horror story after dark when one would no sooner close the creaky door, than a pack of coyotes would start up their chorus. As harmless as they are to man, their racket never failed to curdle my blood and turn my legs to jelly.

Other things I missed in a minor way were the "patchwork quilt" fields of England; the bluebells; buttercups and daisies; the quaint friendly pubs; the little villages every two or three miles; and, to a greater degree, the sea. Having been brought up by it, I missed the thundering of the winter seas against the cliffs. Someone once suggested that if I missed it so much, why didn't I go out to the lake once in a while? Yes. . . . Quite!

I didn't find the change from English girl to Canadian gal too difficult. Perhaps it was due to the fact that I had made up my mind that since Canada was to be my future home, I had better start out by liking it. There was to be no crying for the hills of home. That would prove futile considering the long walk to get there. It worked for me anyway.

Sure, I got homesick quite often and the toughest thing to bear was when I lost a loved one. But these things are hard to take no matter where.

I still get the odd twinge of homesickness after all these years in Canada, but I have never regretted the move. This is a vast and beautiful country comparable with any other in the world. I grumble along with the rest about politics, city council, the weather, the cost of living and so on. But this country has been good to me, and I'm very glad I had the chance to make it my home.

****

Lena and Charles Jones
California

The Royal Montreal Regiment was stationed in Sutton, Surrey during the latter part of 1940 and all of 1941. Many local girls married soldiers from this regiment, and I was one.

I met Charles at a company dance in Sutton where he was introduced to me by a friend of my sister's. Our courtship was hilarious at times because Chas did some really wacky things. Once, we saw a guy with a barrow full of pansy plants. Chas bought a couple of dozen and

Transport Drivers of the Royal Montreal Regiment (M.G.) taken in
Aldershot, 1940

made the chap cut off all the flowers for a bouquet for me. Then, he gave him back all the roots!

Marriage to Charles was a second for me. I had a son from my first marriage and when Keith was nearly seven years old, we came to Canada on the *Mauretania* in January 1945. My most vivid recollection of this journey was the lights of Halifax harbour.

We were allowed on deck after dark, and as Keith and I stood at the rail looking across the sea, Keith, who had never seen a street light let alone harbour lights, said, "Look mum. It's like a great big Christmas tree."

The train ride was ghastly as there were no lights or any heat in the carriage. As it was January, everything was invisible through the window because of a snowstorm. Every few hours the train shunted onto a siding to let a fast freight through. Half of the girls were ready to return to England right there and then, especially the ones going out west. Of course I realized after, we were not travelling at the best time of year.

Charles was still overseas, so Keith and I made our home with his family in Montreal. I hated Montreal and found life in general difficult. My only outings were to go shopping.

During the first week, I lined up at Eaton's department store and bought two pairs of silk stockings. I shall always remember this because I had been wearing a pair of army issue that my sister had given me. I had bleached and redyed them and they were the only pair I had had for a long time. They were very precious. These brand new silk ones were like manna from heaven.

I also recall my first visit to a supermarket and my amazement at the variety of goods for sale, and my anger at two women who were grumbling at what they called "shortages."

When Chas came home, Keith and I were already living on our own. Later, we moved into a war-time housing unit in Longue Pointe, the eastern part of the city. Perhaps, I thought, now that we were altogether I would like the city better. I did not. I hated it, and still do. After several years we discussed moving, and California was our choice. Keith stayed in Montreal, for by this time he was working.

We lived on the California coast and the year round warm climate was heavenly after the damp cold and snowy winters. We both worked, and life was quite enjoyable. Two of my sisters had moved to Australia, and I was able to visit them one year. Living that much closer made it easier on my pocket book.

When Chas retires this year, we are moving back to Canada, near Toronto, which we like, to be near Keith and his family. We are very proud of him. His life has been most successful. We shall miss the California sunshine, but the cost of living there is far too high for those on a limited income.

Would I do it all again? I cannot answer that honestly. So much depends on the time and circumstances. It was no picnic living in a strange land, in a city one disliked, with no job and a young child to look after. But on the whole, I know I have fared better on this side of the Atlantic than I would have had I stayed in England.

****

Anonymous

The war was nearly over when I met my husband in Ireland. He swept me off my feet; enchanted me with wonderful stories of Canada; promised that after the first good crop, we would return to visit my Ireland home. Sad to say, that good crop never came. We married after knowing each other three months, if one can know a person in such a short time. He was anxious for us to

262

marry knowing that any day he would be sent back to Canada.

A year passed before I received my orders to sail and after an uneventful journey, arrived in a large Albertan city on my twenty-fourth birthday. My husband and most of his relatives met me. After one night with them, we left for our own house some miles out of town. When I saw the vast bareness of the countryside, and the shacks, I was so disappointed. It was nothing like I had imagined from the stories I had heard and I felt so homesick.

Arriving at our farmhouse, my husband carried me over the threshold for good luck. The house was large, no foundation, and barely livable. It was built on a treeless hill, and oh! how I remember the howling wind in the winter time that made it feel like sixty below zero. That first winter was too cold to forget. All I could see was miles and miles of snow-covered land, hear the wind and the cry of the coyote. It was so lonely that I cried myself to sleep night after night.

A few months after my arrival, around Christmas, my dear dad passed away, then soon after, my favourite sister. This made things worse because I wanted so badly to go home, and couldn't.

Our first child was born the following November . . . a boy. Eleven months later, we had a baby girl, so I didn't have any time after that to sit and cry.

There were no modern facilities in the house; no bathroom or running water; just an outhouse which I dreaded. And water was hauled into the house from a stream about half a mile away.

After our third child was born, I caught rheumatic fever and spent some time in hospital. We moved in with the in-laws while I was recuperating. I cannot say I enjoyed living there, for I was too timid to go against their wishes. I put up with the dominance and aggressiveness, always hoping things would get better.

My husband and his mother had a close relationship which excluded me and did not help as far as our marriage was concerned. I became pregnant again, and that alone kept my mind away from the unhappiness for a few months.

In all, we had twelve children—all healthy and good looking—six boys and six girls. They never went hungry for too long. The people on the next farm were very good to us and provided meat and eggs. We had no car and often I would stand outside our house and wait for someone to give me a lift into the nearest town where I bought supplies. We had to eat. Neighbours were wonderful, and I shall always have a soft spot in my heart for all they did to help me over some very rough times.

There were some joyous times. Bringing the new babies home from the hospital was one. They were nearly all born during the winter, and I would walk from the taxi, knee deep in snow to the house where the others waited anxiously to see their new baby brother or sister.

My husband and I argued, for he did not want to work except for himself. I always threatened to leave but knew I had to stay with the children . . . it was my duty. We had a few head of cattle, but the crops never amounted to anything.

Sometimes for Christmas, a relative in Ireland would send me a few dollars which I always spent on buying chicks or piglets at auction markets. I raised turkeys once, and enjoyed working with the animals and poultry. It was hard work plus the household chores as well as the looking after and raising of twelve children. My husband visited his mother a lot so the kids and I were alone quite often.

Tragedy struck in 1966 when our eldest daughter

drowned when she got caught in a deep hole in the river nearby. This was a hard blow. I wanted to pull all my hair out, but, thank God, I knew I had to be calm for the sake of the others. Never will I get over her death. The year after we lost her, we sold the farm for a small price and moved to another province. In spite of the cold and hardships we endured, we hated to leave.

Now, when they are all home for Christmas, the children joke and laugh about the different things that happened while they were growing up: the time when some of them had matches upstairs and started a fire—fortunately, I always kept a pail of water in the house, but oh! how my knees would shake going up those stairs; they also say that although I was very small, they were scared of me. We have some good memories which mean so much to all of us now.

My husband has been in and out of hospital for the last few years and had many operations. He lost one leg, and the circulation has affected the other.

I have been lucky that God gave me good health and the determination to keep going against all odds. No matter how many trials one goes through, one has to be strong-willed and courageous. This is most important. We have to take the bad times with the good and stay together within the family circle.

If I had the chance to live my life again, I would probably do it all again. Human nature is weak, and war-time did so much to us . . . and the idea of travel, seeing different places and people was exciting.

****

Mary and Frank Kasza
Ontario

Apart from being employed as a typist with a firm called "Platignum" who made fountain pens in peace time and parts for army uniforms and other articles during the war, I also worked part-time at the Air Raid Wardens Control office delivering and relaying messages to the area wardens.

Many a story could be told about what happened when the German bombers came over every night. A memorable one was the bombing of the London dock yards. The whole city was lit up from the hundreds of fires. I remember going to work and finding a few girls missing, then discovering they had been killed during the night. I also remember bombs dropping close to our house and wondering what we'd find when we emerged from our shelter in the morning. There were so many times we just missed being bombed by a split second. Then, there were the "doodle bugs." How terrifying it was listening to their engine cut off and praying it would not explode on top of us.

Frank and I met at a dance hall in Tottenham Court Road in London, late 1943. Leaving at 10 p.m. to catch the last bus home, he accompanied me to the underground station and would not let me go until I had given him my address—which I did, just to get rid of him. And that's how it all started.

We went out together for a long time before we were married in August 1945. Our honeymoon was spent in a boarding house at Southend-on-sea. The lady of the house, knowing we were honeymooners, served us our first breakfast in bed. When she brought it to us, we stared at the huge fish on Frank's plate. He nearly choked at the thought of eating this gruesome thing with the big bulgy eyes so early in the morning. I cannot remember what we did with it; I do know he did not touch it.

Frank left England for Italy, Holland, and finally Canada, and I followed at the end of June, 1946.

In the London hostel room, I wondered who would be

266

Mary and Frank Kasza

my room-mate, when two people entered and I was somewhat puzzled by their connection. The woman was elderly and the young girl with her looked about nineteen years old. In conversation the mystery was solved. The older lady had married a Canadian soldier, a second marriage, and the girl was her daughter. Looking back, I don't suppose the lady was that old as the girl was only sixteen.

We left for Southampton the next morning and boarded the *Queen Mary*. This ship was like a huge floating hotel with it's wide staircases and halls. Everything was so beautiful. The cabins had their own bathroom, and the lighting set into the walls gave them a shadowy effect. There was plenty of cupboard space, and the food, excellent.

There were such a lot of babies on board! Some lovely and some really scruffy. One girl had three little boys all under four years and was expecting another, yet she managed to keep them spic and span. The girl I made friends with, Bella, and I felt left out as nearly every girl had one or more children. Most girls we spoke to were determined to go home to England as soon as possible. I wonder how many did.

There was a ship concert one evening and we started it singing, "O Canada." As soon as we had finished, there was a rousing chorus of "There'll always be an England." It showed where our hearts were.

This ship was so huge that Bella and I were often lost and wandered round and round many times until we found what we were looking for. The funniest thing was, amid all the excitement of leaving home, staying at the hostel, boarding the *Queen* with all her luxury and meeting so many new people, Bella and I completely forgot about our husbands. I'm sure they would have been delighted to hear this!

We left the ship in groups to board the train. As I was in group twenty, and Bella in seventeen, we said a fond farewell thinking we would not see each other again. Before we started, we were told that tea and doughnuts could be had at a stall on the platform, and I was delighted to run into Bella again. We were situated at opposite ends of the train, but at least we could walk through it and visit.

There was some excitement when the officer in charge came into the carriage to tell us there had been some thefts on the train. Police inspectors searched our luggage and two cameras were found in someone's bag. We never found out who the guilty person was nor what happened to her. What kind of person was it to do such a thing? We were all in the same position—no one particularly well-off.

A lot of wives were being met in Toronto and at 5 a.m. the girls started sprucing up and putting on their best clothes—the children too. Poor kids! They kept getting screamed at and if I heard one mother say, "Don't you dare move. What will daddy say if he sees you all dirty?" I heard it from dozens. The kids didn't care and played as usual with lots of clouts from the distracted mums. By the time we were almost to Toronto, the kids had had more than enough. They were at the end of their tether, and were mostly cross and yelling their heads off. As for me, I never wanted to see another baby for a hell of a long time.

At last Windsor . . . and Frank. It wasn't he who got to me first, but his mother. She hugged and kissed me so much that Frank said, "Well. Where do I come in?" The house was full of people waiting to meet me and there was a huge iced cake with the words "Welcome home Mary" written on it. And the gifts! I couldn't utter a word for I was so choked with emotion.

We stayed with Frank's mum and dad, and I have often wondered if any other war bride faced the same situation as I. Frank is Hungarian in descent, and although I was in Canada, it could have been Hungary. All their friends were the same nationality and spoke in their native tongue which made it difficult for me. They all came to see this "English war bride" and discussed me back and forth making me feel a complete outsider. There was no harm meant, of course, and soon I made friends of my own.

Frank and I bought a farm which proved to be quite interesting for me, a city girl. Not knowing the first thing about country life, getting acquainted with the animals was a terrifying experience. I had an awful time

269

Mary Kasza on the farm

Mary and Frank Kasza

trying to help Frank harness a horse; and as for milking a cow. . . .

There was no indoor plumbing . . . an out-house half-way across a field and a pump outside the kitchen door.

After a few years on the farm, tragedy struck. Our house burned to the ground and we were left with nothing. Everything gone as well as all our beautiful wedding presents. The main thing was, we all got out safely. By this time we had three little boys, and it was far from easy starting all over again. But always a silver lining. We managed and I settled quite nicely into the Canadian way of life.

In later years, we gave up the farm and moved to the city. The boys are on their own now, and recently we moved to a smaller town.

The years have flown by, but I wouldn't change them for anything. I have a wonderful husband, and have been very happy in Canada and proud to call it home.

****

Ada and Bill Hicklin
Ontario

As a First World War bride, I would say that my experiences in a new country differed somewhat from the girls who came as brides of the Second World War. The times were certainly different but I imagine the events that led to my marriage were similar, for were not they all based on love and a sense of adventure?

My "soon-to-be-husband" had seen service in Salonica with the Canadian Army Medical Corps. Returning to England he was re-classified unfit for active duty, and along with twenty-four others was sent to Matlock, in Derbyshire, to staff a convalescent hospital for Canadian officers. This hospital was formerly a luxury hotel and hydropathic establishment operated by Germans and confiscated by the British government when war broke out. These Canadians and some Royal Air Force boys were the only troops in Matlock so a lot of people opened their homes to them, and that is how I met my husband.

Bill and I soon realized we were in love, and I shall never forget how romantic the incident was when he proposed to me. The Duke of Devonshire was Governor General of Canada at the time, and his residence, Chatsworth House, was about eight miles from Matlock. The Duke invited the Canadian boys to a picnic and tour of the house, and each was allowed to bring a girl. This was where Bill proposed to me, in Chatsworth Park while the band played, "My little gray home in the west."

We were married August 7, 1918. I was nineteen years old, and Bill twenty-three. After the armistice on November 11, arrangements were soon under-way to get wives of Canadian servicemen over to Canada with Colonel Oben-Smith in charge. We were told that we must take the first opportunity offered us otherwise it could be some months before another passage would be available.

I was booked on the old Allan liner *Tunisian* which sailed December 24, 1918 from Liverpool. As I was two months pregnant, we decided it was better for me to go to Bill's people rather than wait until the baby was born. Bill came with me to the ship, and the Colonel was at the gangplank as we went aboard. I remember him saying to Bill, "Take good care of her laddie." However, it was much later that Bill reached Canada.

The *Tunisian* was still being used as a troopship, and when I reached my cabin I saw, to my horror, rats scampering along the partitions. Not being consoled when told that rats always desert a sinking ship, I slept on a couch in one of the lounges for the whole trip.

Despite a calm sea, we didn't reach Halifax until

272

eleven days later. This meant that I had spent Christmas and New Year aboard—my first away from home and family. However, youth, good health and love overcame the nostalgia, and I joined in the planned entertainment on board. There was such an atmosphere of thanksgiving and joy that the war was over, and so happy were these men who were returning to their homes and loved ones, that one put their personal feelings aside.

We were given such a rousing welcome when we docked, and there were many volunteer workers ready to help such as myself that I had no problem passing through customs.

The train bound for Montreal was packed with troops and no berths were available. During the journey I sat entranced looking out over the vast expanse of snow with so little sign of habitation that I wondered what Montreal would be like.

The train pulled in at the old Grand Trunk station, and here again, hundreds of people gathered to meet the troops and brides. Such confusion! But I found Bill's family and stayed with them until he came home. They were a great help to me in adjusting to my new surroundings.

Looking back now, I realize that Canada was only fifty years old, and Montreal a bustling inland port metropolis so different from my hometown. I was intrigued by the many different nationalities; street after street of flats all heated by stoves with long lengths of stove pipes; and horse-drawn sleighs delivering bread, milk, and ice.

In 1925 there was an epidemic of typhoid attributed to contaminated milk. We were living on Montreal's south shore at the time and Bill commuted to his office in Montreal. He ate his lunch in a restaurant, and contacted the disease. I was allowed to keep him home and nurse him myself, and in view of our medical services today, I love to tell about the night the disease

273

reached it's crisis. The doctor came to the house and helped me pack the patient in ice-cold sheets. The ice was taken from the ice-box and placed in a bath of cold water. He stayed with me until he assured me that Bill was out of danger.

By the 1930's Bill was well established in the Civil Service and had been transferred to Ottawa. The Civil Servants were among the fortunate people who were affected very little by the depression. They took a ten per cent cut in salary, and all promotions were cancelled.

I became interested in missionary work with the United church and held the office of Supply secretary. Thus I was aware of people who were in need, especially the western provinces were the drought added to their troubles.

My committee packed endless supplies of clothing and utilities for shipment to congregations and Indian Reserves in the west. The Canadian National Railway shipped them free of charge. I wish I still had the many letters of grateful thanks. I recall one church had six hundred families on relief.

Bill retired in 1959, and we took a trip around the world in a freighter. Life is still full and rewarding, and we are still that young couple who were so happy in Chatsworth Park so very long ago.

****

Kay and Fred Garside
Saskatchewan

During the dance intermission, the fellow I was with took me to the pub across the street for a drink. He introduced me to Fred, a friend of his from the same regiment which was stationed in Dorking, Surrey, a short train ride from my home in Wimbledon.

Fred and I went together off and on for about a year. Nothing serious. Then he was sent away on a course and we lost touch. This was in 1942.

I very much wanted to join the Woman's Auxiliary Air Force but my work as a stenographer for a small company located near London Bridge that made plastic armour for naval guns, was considered a reserved occupation, so, I had to "stay put."

Christmas 1942 I received a card from Fred. He was back in Dorking and wanted to see me. From then on, things began to get serious, and we were married in January 1944.

Our wedding day was supposed to have been in November, but Fred was hospitalized with yellow jaundice. I always tease him that he got it on purpose to get out of the wedding. All arrangements had to be cancelled and re-done for January—quite a headache!

Ours was a small wedding—a few relatives and close friends with Fred's brother as best man. There was an air-raid in the early evening, of course, and I recall we all stood at the back door watching the planes. An aunt insisted on taking the bus all the way to her home in New Malden to get her accordian so we could have some music.

There was a pre-wedding catastrophe (as if the postponement wasn't enough). My mother made our wedding cake. The ingredients for this were begged, borrowed and practically stolen from friends and relatives. A girl who worked in the office with me offered to decorate it differently from the traditional kind. It was different all right! All the colours ran into each other making it obvious she had done something not quite right. I was hysterical. It was only a small cake, but I did want it to look nice.

My cousin came to the rescue and scraped all the messy icing off. Again, we went through the begging

Kay and Fred Garside

performance for icing sugar, and the night before the wedding, she re-iced it, and it did look lovely.

Our wedding took place at 3 p.m. and at noon hour I was sent to buy fish and chips for our dinner, although mother did not think it proper for the bride to do that. Then Fred came to the house to pick up some shirts and I was made to hide in case he saw me.

I blew all my clothing coupons on a much needed camel hair coat, so no white wedding. But I thought I looked pretty sharp in it with burgundy accessories and carrying the traditional silver horse-shoes for good luck. The girl who messed up the cake felt so terrible about it that she insisted on buying me a corsage of orchids to make up for her "boo-boo."

Contrary to reports that many Canadian servicemen were discouraged from marrying British girls, Fred did not encounter this problem. His Commanding Officer asked only if he were sure of his feelings, and neither of us have heard of anyone having any problem.

Fred was still overseas when the time came for me to leave for Canada. I shall never forget sitting inside the bus that was taking me and other brides to the centre where we stayed before going to Liverpool. I was an only child, and looking out the window seeing my mum and dad standing there so forlorn and lonely, made me realize at that moment, just what I was doing. Yet, it was too late to change things.

After that, things were a bit blurry. I do not remember boarding the boat, but I DO remember the horrible seven-day trip and being sick the whole time. Just one sniff of all the delicious food and I headed for the hills! Oranges were the only thing that kept me going. I was so happy to see dry land, and felt much better on the train and really "tucked in" to the good meals.

I enjoyed the train ride and sleeping on it, and was amazed that we got clean linen every night. With all the soot and dust, we needed it. I do not remember what Quebec looked like from the train, but Ontario seemed to be all lakes and forest.

We stopped for the whole day in Winnipeg and the Red Cross ladies took us on a tour of the city by street car. We went to a large park, a conservatory, had a fish

277

and chip luncheon at Eaton's and did some shopping where I recall buying a blue frilly maternity dress and some shoes.

One girl remains in my memory. She was a Scottish girl who spent the whole day in a beauty parlour getting her hair dyed a different colour. She made it back to the train just in time. I have often wondered if her husband recognized her when she got to wherever she was going.

Meeting me in Regina were Fred's family. I was very nervous and tried to make a good impression. Being a "dumb bunny" in those days, I didn't know just what kind of impression I was trying to give. They were very kind, and a friend of the family presented me with a lovely bouquet of flowers. We stayed overnight in Regina, and I was quite impressed with everything except the toilet which was a chemical one, and not flush. Little did I know that on my in-laws' farm where I was to live until Fred came home, the toilet was an outhouse.

Before we left Regina, we went to a restaurant where I was asked what I would like. I chose bananas and cream as this was a luxury I hadn't had in years. I was so disappointed when it came. I had imagined the cream as thick as our Devonshire cream—instead it was like milk.

On the way to the farm, I kept seeing grain elevators in the distance and would think, "Oh. Now we must be coming to the town." But time went on and on, and still we did not reach it. I thought we'd never get there and didn't know what to expect when we did. Not being smart enough to question my husband about a lot of things, I cannot say I was disappointed, but oh! it was so different from the suburb of London where I had lived, and London itself, where I had worked.

I was overwhelmed by the vastness of the prairies and still think the loneliest sound in the world is the wind blowing through a screen door of a prairie farm, and the second loneliest is the sound of a train whistle on a very cold calm winter's night.

A big event in the summer on the prairie is "Sports Day." I was quite indignant when I had to sit in the car eating very inferior ice-cream, while my husband sat in the local beer parlour where I was not allowed. After our friendly English pubs, I could not understand this and thought Canada definitely a man's country, and it really was in those days.

That first summer in Canada was so very hot. There was no shade anywhere. I sat on the shadiest side of the house, trying to knit—which I hated—with a dog for company. When I wrote and told my parents this, they did not believe me for they knew me as a girl who was always out dancing and going to movies night after night.

War brides in Weyburn, Saskatchewan, 1946, courtesy of Kay Garside

Fred and I had two children and eventually moved to a veteran's house in Regina. I worked to help out like a lot of other women. Both of us will retire soon and it is good to think that we can, hopefully, enjoy our retirement years.

Strangely enough, I never once thought of going back to England. Maybe it was because of what people would say after having departed in a cloud of romance and going "all the way to Canada" and then having to face all the questions as to "what happened?" Or perhaps it was pride in making my marriage work that kept me from leaving; I don't know. But I stayed, as did most of us, struggling through the hard times, tragedies and homesickness. I do know that no one else could possibly understand how hard it was, except another war bride.

War brides in Weyburn, Saskatchewan, 1946, courtesy of Kay Garside

****

Remember When . . .

Our table steward on the *Brittanic* was quite a character. He bet my two friends and I half a crown each that we'd be seasick. The food was so good that we decided we could not afford to miss a meal. We took on the bet and collected our winnings when we docked in Halifax, much to the chagrin of our steward.

During the first week I was in my new home, my husband invited another couple for dinner. I had no idea what to serve them, so prepared a pan full of "bubble and squeak" and cooked corn-on-the-cob. The corn was so tough we couldn't eat it. I didn't know there were more than one kind and apparently I cooked the wrong one.

Returning to Canada was a wonderful experience for me. You see, I was born in Alberta and moved with my parents to England prior to the war. The only difference between myself and other war brides was . . . I was already Canadian when I married.

I was looking forward to starting a new life on a rented farm near Red Deer, Alberta. The previous tenant had not harvested the crops, so when spring came the place was over-run with mice and gophers, to say nothing of the weeds that grew after these crops had been planted.

My husband was "batching" it until I arrived in the July and was so busy fixing up everything and looking after baby chicks, that he hadn't noticed the mice in the house or the gophers in the yard. I complained about them but he just laughed and said, "Oh! They just want to see what a war bride looks like."

That was all very well, until one day I was sitting in the "wee house" out back, and a gopher as bold as brass came in under the door and would have climbed up beside me had I not shouted and frightened him. I was so furious and vowed I would leave if something wasn't done . . . and soon! My husband claims this was the only time I threatened to go home to mother.

Walking down town with my husband one day, I was horrified when I noticed the words THE RAPIST painted in large gold lettering on a window of an office building.
"Is this the way Canadians advertise?" I asked him.
"Look again," he said.
A frame divided the window in two, and so was the word THERAPIST!

The language barrier was my worst problem. I was Dutch and spoke little English and found it difficult to learn.
Shopping was not easy, and I recall the day when I needed an egg. Thinking in vain, I just could not remember the English word "egg." I went to the people who owned the apartment building and stood at their door cackling like a hen and making an oval shape with my hands hoping they would understand what I wanted.
Finally, they did. I was so grateful, that I didn't stop to think how funny I must have looked and sounded. I bet they had a good laugh after I had departed with egg in hand.

Never have I been so embarrassed as I was the first morning at sea, Cardinal McQuigan was on board the *Aquitania* returning from Rome after being ordained. It was a Sunday morning, and he was conducting the Mass in the officers lounge at 6 a.m.
I was feeling fine when the service started, then suddenly I was sea-sick all down the back of a red plush chair. I was horrified and stumbled out to the railing

only to find all space taken with girls feeling the same way.

When the maternity doctor I visited soon after my arrival told me to bring a "sample" on my next visit, I was quite puzzled. Born and brought up in London's east end, a sampler was known as a piece of embroidery, and I thought this was what he meant. On the way home I stopped to visit and tell a friend.

"Don't go to that doctor," I told her. "If he think's I'm going to buy a yard of material to embroider, he's nuts!"

"Don't buy any. I'll give you a piece," she said. Next visit I took it with me and the doctor and his nurse roared with laughter as they explained the kind of "sample" they were expecting.

After a week in my new Canadian home, my in-laws went on vacation leaving me to run the house as I saw fit.

There was washing to be done so I thought I had better tackle it. I never had seen a washing machine before let alone know how to operate one. I was doing fine until a pair of my mother-in-law's best sheets became entwined somehow, around the wretched machine rollers.

A burning smell permeated the room as I desperately tried to untangle the sheets, then the machine conked out. I had burned the motor. The only way I knew to remove the sheets was to cut them off with a knife. I was scared stiff!

I didn't have a sheet to my name, and was in a panic wondering what to do. The next day a letter arrived from my aunt in Alberta saying she had mailed sheets and pillow cases for a wedding gift to me. What a relief that was!

It was interesting to observe the many different types on board. Some of the younger brides had had some really weird tales told to them by their husbands, I guess. One girl was proudly telling everyone she was going to Montreal where her husband's people owned all the sardines in the lakes around that city and had a large canning factory as well! It was amazing how gullible some girls were, and rather sad, too.

Another girl from the east end of London had named her son "Buzz Bomb" because he had been born during one of these raids. He had no other name. Poor kid!

In 1947 we bought our own farm north of Edmonton. We bought it through the Veteran's Land Act, and when everything was concluded, it was winter time so we could not look around the farm too much. The man we bought it from told us there was a good fresh-water spring on the place that would provide us with lots of water.

When springtime came, we hunted high and low for this darn spring, and failed to locate it. When we saw the previous owner, we asked him where it was. "Oh! It's in the well!" he said in broken English.

From a large industrial city near London, I came to a lonely farm in Alberta and lived in a converted chicken house—not too converted either. It was so lonely. But after war-time restrictions and the drabness of Britain, I revelled in the wide open spaces, the big blue sky of the west, and the fields of golden wheat.

I had never seen vegetables in their growing stage before, so my husband had to explain what was what. But the most surprising thing of all was the sheer weight of the work load that farm wives undertook as a matter of course.

They canned everything that moved or grew; carried heavy buckets of water for huge wash loads that, when hung on the line, were as white as snow; cooked enormous meals for the hired men as well as their own family; helped with outside chores, and did their own housework as well; I presumed then, in the middle of the night! They were fabulous cooks, whereas I could even louse up cornflakes!

I have never really been homesick, only a few pangs during what passes for spring in Alberta.

On the train from Halifax, I became friendly with a girl who was making her home in London, Ontario—not too far from where I was going. Feeling a bit bored after a few weeks, I decided to visit her.

I had no idea how long the train ride would take, so I settled back to enjoy the ride. After a while the train stopped. The few people on it got off, and the porter pushed the back of the seats to face the other way. I did likewise, and off we went again. This backward and forward business with the seats went on all afternoon, and I thought, "What a carry on."

Finally I asked the porter how long it would be before we reached London. He said, "You've been there and back a dozen times, lady." Well! I had had a good ride for fifty cents if nothing else. Never did get to visit that girl.

The Canadian Provost Corps were stationed on deck to make certain we were never without our life jackets. My friends and I often teased them unmercifully. Two of them said we had better "watch it" for they were really RCMPs. We didn't believe them and thought we'd have some more fun at their expense.

Looking over the railing into the wake of the ship, and in a voice loud enough for them to hear, my friend Eileen said, "I can't see them anywhere. I wonder if they drowned?"

The two supposed RCMPs hurriedly came over, and very excitedly said, "Did we hear you say someone had drowned?"

With a twinkle in her eyes, and a grin from ear to ear, Eileen very sweetly said, "We were looking for your horses. We thought they'd be swimming to Canada!"

At the end of the trip, I think they were ready to kill us.

My destination was a farm in southern Manitoba. How different it was from the coastal town in Cornwall that had been my home since birth.

After two weeks of insufferable prairie heat, I asked my husband during a Sunday morning breakfast if we could possibly spend the day at the sea-side.

"Sure," he replied. "Which one would you like to go to—Atlantic or Pacific? They're both about two thousand miles away."

Jack and I lived with his family for the first three months, and as they were all working, I undertook to keep house.

Knowing the many shortages of food in Britain, everyone contributed extra grocery money, and gave me full rein to buy them. I had a ball! I cooked and baked until pies and cakes were coming out of our ears, and for weeks we lived like kings. I would startle them with desserts like deep apple pie, peaches stewed and served with cream. (I had not seen many fresh peaches and did not realize they could be eaten in their natural state.)

I couldn't get enough sweet stuff, especially ice-cream. Jack tried to appease my appetite by taking me for a large sundae every evening. After a while, I had had enough, but I sure made up for the time I went without.

Our military wedding was performed in a church in

Topcliffe and untrue to form, the groom was late due to a last minute change of billets, while I was beginning to think he had had second thoughts. The only people there, apart from the minister, were two of Lee's friends, and two of mine . . . all in uniform.

After the short ceremony, we adjourned to the local pub where our friends toasted us many times. We "released" a metal horseshoe from the wall for good luck, before we left to go back to base after hitching a ride in the back of a lorry.

We rashly let our friends get our suitcases from our billets; then we got another "hitch" to Thirsk, again in a lorry where we laughed and giggled until our driver said, "You must be the two who got married today." He doubtless heard us!

When we were settled in our hotel room we opened our suitcases. They were packed full of confetti. It was all over the place and our clothes were full of it. I pitied

Daphne and Lee Arnott, North Bay

287

the poor cleaning lady next morning. But all she said was, "You've got a nice young man there." And I heartily agreed.

I was a bride who got "cold feet" when the time came for me to leave England. Stan, my husband, had already returned to Canada, and after numerous letters, phone calls, and telegrams, he landed back in England. We lived and worked there until 1956 when he persuaded me to try living in Canada. I agreed, and we boarded the *Scythia* one cold February morning.

CUNARD R.M.S. SCYTHIA   19,930 TONS.

Arriving in Halifax I said to Stan, "Are you sure this is Canada. It looks more like the North Pole to me." I had never seen so much snow.

We were going to Montreal and arrived during one of the worst blizzards of the winter. After two weeks of that, I had had enough. We moved to Toronto only to hit their worst winter blizzard. Seems I couldn't win. There was no more moving, so I had to put up with it.

We found rooms in a large comfortable old house. Stan found work, and after getting settled, I found a job as well. The landlord was very nice and on the evening before I started work, he was with Stan and I in our room. I asked him if he would kindly knock me up at seven in the morning. He thought this expression hilarious, and all evening he kept saying, "I wish it was seven o'clock so that I could knock Doris up!" I never used that expression again.

In England, if one does not feel well, a common saying is, "I do feel a bit queer." This is what I said on my first visit to a doctor who replied with, "Well. If you do, you don't need me then!"

I made plenty of silly mistakes, but I think the best of all was when I put coffee beans in the percolater with the hopes of showing Stan that I could make coffee as well as tea. How was I supposed to know one had to grind the beans first?

The only type of stove I had ever used was electric, and a coal and wood stove was what I had to use for cooking when I first came to Canada. I was young and inexperienced and not too sure about this peculiar-looking stove, nor had my husband thought to show me how to use it.

Well here goes, I thought, as I placed the roast in the oven for dinner, then pushed over a funny-looking lever at the back of the stove. Considering the oven "on" I went about my other household chores. When my husband came home, there was the meat still in it's raw state.

"You have to put wood in the stove to heat the oven

you know," said he, looking with distaste at the lump of red meat. "Well," said I. "Isn't that thing at the back the switch to turn it on?" That "thing" was the damper!

We came from different backgrounds . . . from all walks of life. On board the *Aquitania*, I remember a curly red-headed bride from London who spoke only of the film industry and of the stage and movie stars she had met; an orphan girl, pregnant, whose auntie Maudie had brought her up and had packed her trunk for the big trip; a clergyman's daughter, and a "barrow boy's" daughter . . . all with one thing in common . . . stars in their eyes, and hope and dreams in their heart.

The War Brides Today

Approximately ten percent of the fifty thousand or so war brides returned to their homeland within a year of their arrival in Canada. Those who remained, settled down after the first few years, raised families, and became Canadian housewives. In addition to household duties, many became business women and established successful careers.

Most will admit to preferring the Canadian way of life to that of the homeland, and yet, even in Canada the life-style of many war brides changed greatly. After years of marriage came traumatic changes resulting from divorce and widowhood, and again adjustments were not always easy. Many re-married and made new lives for themselves with their new partner and new families.

There are those who express a desire to return to their homeland to live out their remaining years. But with families here, these ties are stronger than the ties they left back home.

During the early years, war bride clubs were formed throughout the country. The Salvation Army and Red

Salvation Army War brides club, 1946

First Christmas party for children, Salvation Army Club, 1946

Christmas party for children, Salvation Army, 1946

Cross societies helped the brides adjust to the Canadian life with lessons in Canadian cooking, geographical studies and Canadian customs. To help them feel at home, these societies organized Christmas parties for them, their husbands and children.

Gradually the girls settled down, and the rearing of their children took priority. The clubs faded into the background as they found home-making more demanding. Although many friendships were fashioned through these clubs, and most have endured, the need to be with one's own kind was not quite so important, as they began to meet more and more people.

Today, their families grown and rearing children of their own, the need to recapture those long-ago days has returned. Reunions have been organized for the past few years in different parts of the country.

Alberta, B.C. and Saskatchewan have chartered associations, the latter held every year alternately in Regina and Saskatoon. Their committee, headed by Gloria Brock and Kay Garside, work hard to organize these gatherings as their membership continues to grow.

A few years ago, the province of Ontario commenced the re-uniting of war brides and each year they gather in a different town or city. Community parties also take place in the smaller towns and villages across the country.

These reunions provide the stimulus the war brides now feel is important. There is a common bond; the need to "get together," to reminisce; to renew old friendships; to enjoy a nostalgic weekend, not only for themselves, but for their husbands as well.

The members of the Saskatchewan Association would like to see the war brides from all provinces form their own organization. Unless they start now, there will be no time. For the years pass all too quickly, and time is essential if this is to be accomplished.

Movement Control and Transportation

The Embarkation Transit Unit Movement Control (ETU) in Halifax was one of the biggest movement centres, and probably the most composite organization to be found in Canada during World War II. It was comprised as follows: Ship's Army Conducting Staffs; Train Conducting Staffs; Railway Traffic Staffs; Military Forwarding Staffs; Wives Bureau Overseas; Auxiliary Officers; Canadian Woman's Army Corps; Red Cross; Civilian Personnel, doctors, nurses, and Movement Control in London, England.

These people, all experts in rail and ship traffic, gave the same precise care to a move whether it be the diminutive *Lady Rodney* or the giant *Queen Mary*.

Movement Control operated in conjunction with the Canadian Pacific and Canadian National railways in moving troops and vital freight. The train military staffs remained in tact for the war brides and their children. The railways were justifiably proud of their part in the war, for operations were entirely free of accidents.

At the outset of war, twenty liners were converted to troopships, and four to hospital ships. These were at the disposal of the unit, and each had an Army Conducting Staff to discipline the troops safely across and back on the Atlantic. By the end of the war there were as many as fifty-eight ships employed in the large-scale move of bringing the boys home, as well as their wives and children.

When a cable was received that a ship was on the way, the two hundred staff members galvanized into action, and Movement Control really moved, right down the line from Embarkation Commandant to the CWAC switchboard operator.

To complete such a move involved scores of people.

Colonel Sutherland, Prime Minister McKenzie King, Nursing Sisters and #1 Conducting Staff, June 1946

Days before the ship arrived, ETU held numerous meetings, and each group worked out their individual stages of operation. The landing programme, immigration schedule, train departures were finalized, and an information sheet prepared for each bride.

A lot of late night work was spent in compiling the disembarkation programme from repat bureaus all across Canada. The Red Cross worked in conjunction with the CPR and CNR railway officers in Moncton, Montreal, Winnipeg and Vancouver. After listing the final destination of each bride and child, it was teleprinted to the ETU in Halifax.

Days before and after a ship docked, the wires burned across the nation with the latest information on docking and departure of trains, so that the next of kin could be given the answer to those pet questions, "What train is he or she on?" and, "When does it get here?"

Over 180,000 troops arrived in Canada by the end of 1945. They were men with high points and husbands slated to precede their brides. Beginning in March 1946, the movement of war brides and children commenced at a fast rate of approximately six thousand per month.

When the brides boarded ship, the period before sailing was devoted to interviews, for it was the last opportunity for them to turn back or remain on board ship. Some were emotionally upset leaving parents and friends for a country they knew little about. They were shown maps and books describing their destination, and the majority were excited about settling in Canada.

Army Conducting Staffs plying the ocean back and forth, numbered over 250 personnel, composed of Royal Canadian Army Service Corps, doctors, nursing sisters and members of the Voluntary Aid Detachment (VADs). For the first few voyages, medical staff officers, their three or four nursing sisters and orderlies were overworked attending the brides and children. Sea-

War brides and children in hostel in London, England, before boarding ship

Brides on their way to their new homes, 1945, courtesy of C. Reavely

sickness was a problem; prepared formulae and the odour of diapers, washed and hung in cabins, permeated the decks. A call went out for Red Cross nurses, and they arranged for crates of disposable diapers to be loaded on board ships. During those years, the Red Cross performed many duties on hospital and bride ships, trains, and at the Wives Bureau in London.

The orderly room was generally located in a prominent area of the ship and was the heart of operations. Here, troops and brides came with their problems or for information. It was the area where Standing Orders were typed out in the nature of "Thou Shalt and Thou Shalt Not" which were posted on the bulletin board. The Sergeant-Major accountable for work turnout, had two sergeants to help with nominal rolls, correspondence, voyage reports, war diaries and arranging stop-overs for troops en route to destination.

Children were often "lost" and brought here where the orderly staff pacified them, dried their tears, wiped their noses, changed their bums and returned them to their frustrated mums. The men in the orderly rooms soon became known as the "Diaper Brigade."

Disembarkation in Halifax was always exciting for the brides. Eager faces of the women and children would peer over the side of the ship; they shouted and waved, threw pennies and shrieked with laughter when the waiting band played, "Here Comes the Bride."

Most of the ETU staff had their favourite "bride" story and one that was laughed about in particular was where the young bride rebuked her small son for eating with his mouth open. "Close your mouth, William. You remind me too much of your Canadian father!"

Then the one about the woman who couldn't find the ladder to get into her upper berth until the good lady down the car poked her head out and shouted, "You can borrow mine for a minute!"

Prime Minister W.L. McKenzie King, Red Cross officers #1 Conducting Staff

When the *Queen Mary* pulled in with two thousand or more brides, there were women of all shapes and sizes. They loved to talk, tell jokes, and wanted to know about clothes, what Canada was like and when did they get off the train . . . usually all said in one mouthful.

If staff members had not heard of their particular new hometown or their husband, they looked at them with that superb English look, which said, "Are all Canadians as stupid as you are?" Of course they were reminded that Canada was kind of large, and not everyone had visited their little town of Scragg Hollow out in the great west.

The men and women of the ETU had a difficult and responsible job. They guaranteed the bride safe passage from the old home to the new. Everything was done for them, and as one bride aptly stated, "We didn't even have to think for ourselves." Capable medical staffs on ships and trains looked after the health of the women and children. Port staffs made certain that brides, children and their luggage were all on the same train. It all sounds so easy. But mistakes did occur, and confusion reigned at times: the wife on the wrong train; a child with the wrong mother; the wrong wife sent to a husband in central Canada. But they were all straightened out and remembered with a chuckle.

The staff at ETU really enjoyed making things comfortable for the brides simply because they appreciated it. The boxes of candy and the magazines the Red Cross girls handed them, the willing port crews who handled their luggage and helped with the children from ship to train, made them think they had landed in paradise . . . after war-torn Britain and Europe, perhaps they had.

Contributed by SQMS J. Searle Crate attached to #1 and #2 Ship's Conducting Staff. Passages quoted from an article written by Captain R.T. Vaughan, Army Public

302

Relations Officer which were contributed by Lieutenant-Colonel W. Evan Sutherland, OBE, Officer in Charge of #1 and #5 Ship's Conducting Staff.

Many brides will recall with fond memory the particular ship they called "home" whether for four or fourteen days. Some were lucky to spend those days on converted ocean liners; other not so fortunate travelled on smaller ships and the voyages were rough and longer.

Lady Nelson and *Lady Rodney:* These were two of the smaller ships, but war brides will remember their accommodation and cuisine was as fine or better than most big liners.

Lady Rodney

Volendam: This small Dutch ship was reported to be the only troopship at sea when word came through via radio that Germany had accepted the terms of unconditional surrender on May 8, 1945. She was heading for Liverpool, England, and on her return trip to Halifax, she carried war brides for the first time.

Empress of Scotland: During the war years, the Empress travelled 600,000 miles sailing the Atlantic, Mediterranean, Aegean and Black Seas. She was damaged once in an air attack off Belfast in November 1944. But the closest she came to sinking was in August 1944. The ship was four and a half days at sea when the Captain sighted a light close to the water of port-side bow. The ship's instruments recorded undersea-craft

Volendam

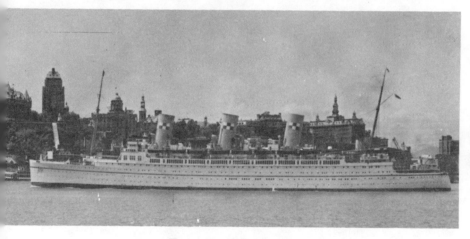

Empress of Scotland

soundings. There was a call to stand by for ramming, but the U-boat submerged in time.

Franconia: In February 1945 the Yalta Conference was held aboard this ship. The leaders of the chief Allied Nations—Prime Minister Winston Churchill of Great

Britain, President Franklin D. Roosevelt of the United States and Premier Josef Stalin of Soviet Russia—met to make decisions about how to end the war.

Aquitania: Her trooping service began in November 1939 when she brought over to Britain from Halifax the first contingent of Canadian troops. Another phase of her career was the bringing of settlers to Canada in 1948/49.

R.M.S. AQUITANIA with WAR-BRIDES at HALIFAX N.S. MARCH 2nd 1946

Ile de France: This prize of war was the third-largest troop-carrying liner on the Atlantic, exceeded only by the *Queens.* War brides will remember her beautiful first-class lounges.

ILE-DE-FRANCE at HALIFAX N.S. JANY 26TH 1946

Queen Mary and *Queen Elizabeth:* Huge, colossal and beautiful, these two gigantic liners carried more than one million fighting men, and travelled more than 950,000 miles between them. The *Queen Mary* ended her wartime career with a flourish bringing more than nine thousand war brides, and four thousand children to Canada. Her sister had war brides on board as early as 1944.

Many other ships played major roles in bringing troops and brides to Canada including: *Georgic, Nea Hellis, Niew Amsterdam, Letitia, Samaria, Andes, Brittanic, Monarch of Bermuda,* and the *Duchess of Richmond.*

Contributed by SQMS J. Searle Crate, attached to #1 and #2 Ship's Conducting Staff.

R.M.S. QUEEN MARY with WAR-BRIDES ARRIVING AT HALIFAX N.S. JULY 4th 1946

QUEEN·ELIZABETH

R.M.S. QUEEN ELIZABETH entering at HALIFAX. N.S. NOV 19th 1945

2

CUNARD WHITE STAR M.V. "GEORGIC."

Andes

I've been around the Empire;
I've felt the War-God's grip.
And I'll be there when it's over—
A tired, but wiser ship.

And in the steam-ship's graveyard
Where the bulks lie, pair by pair,
No doubt you'll see me with them;
I'll be there . . . yes, I'll be there.

At sea April 8, 1945

Author unknown

Appendix

The Canadian Wives Bureau in London, England, recorded the number of dependents in the United Kingdom and Europe as of August 1, 1946 as follows:

U.K.	Wives	Children	Total
Total dependents recorded	42,879	17,445	60,324
Sailed	29,925	13,672	43,597
Still in U.K.	12,954	3,773	16,727
Approved ready to sail	7,206	3,482	10,688

The balance were either in the hands of the emigration or unwilling to proceed.

Europe	Total
Applications received for wives and children	2,839
Sailed	517
Still in Europe	2,322

Contributed by Lieutenant-Colonel W. Evan Sutherland, OBE, Officer in Charge of #1 and #5 Ship's Conducting Staff.

Colonel Sutherland and Ships No. 1 Conducting Staff